Study Guide

AUDITING

An Integrated Approach

Sixth Edition

Dennis L. Kimmell
University of Akron

Study Guide

AUDITING

An Integrated Approach
Sixth Edition

Alvin A. Arens
Price Waterhouse
Auditing Professsor
Michigan State University

James K. Loebbecke
Kenneth A. Sorensen
Peat Marwick Professor of Accounting
University of Utah

Prentice Hall, Englewood Cliffs, New Jersey 07632

Project manager: Benjamin D. Smith
Acquisitions editor: Bill Webber
Production coordinator: Herb Klein

All multiple choice questions in this text, with the exceptions of questions numbered 5, 7, and 8 in Chapter 24, are AICPA reprinted (or adapted).

A Paramount Communications Company
Englewood Cliffs, New Jersey 07632

Printed in the United States of America

10 9 8 7 6 5 4 3 2 1

ISBN 0-13-289118-2

Prentice-Hall International (UK) Limited, *London*
Prentice-Hall of Australia Pty. Limited, *Sydney*
Prentice-Hall Canada Inc., *Toronto*
Prentice-Hall Hispanoamericana, S.A., *Mexico*
Prentice-Hall of India Private Limited, *New Delhi*
Prentice-Hall of Japan, Inc., *Tokyo*
Simon & Schuster Asia Pte. Ltd., *Singapore*
Editora Prentice-Hall do Brasil, Ltda., *Rio de Janeiro*

CONTENTS

TO THE STUDENT

The purpose of this *Study Guide* is to assist your study of *Auditing: An Integrated Approach* by Alvin A. Arens and James K. Loebbecke. It is not a substitute for becoming thoroughly familiar with the textbook, but it should help you organize and master the material.

For each textbook chapter there is a corresponding *Study Guide* chapter which discusses the chapter objectives and summarizes its content. In addition, each *Study Guide* chapter contains a series of True/False statements, completion statements, and multiple-choice questions to help you learn the subject matter. Solutions to these self-assessment items can be found in the appendix at the end of the *Study Guide*.

A recommended approach to using this guide is to read the chapter material from the text first, then read the Study Guide and complete the self-assessment section. Reviewing the guide should be an effective means of preparing for examinations.

Study hard and good luck.

Dennis L. Kimmell, DBA, CPA
The University of Akron

Study Guide

AUDITING

An Integrated Approach

Sixth Edition

1

AN OVERVIEW OF AUDITING

CHAPTER OBJECTIVE

The purpose of this chapter is to discuss the nature of auditing and the environment in which auditors work.

CHAPTER SUMMARY

OBJECTIVE 1:
DEFINE AND EXPLAIN AUDITING

1. **Definition**. Auditing is the accumulation and evaluation of evidence about quantifiable information of an economic entity to determine and report on the degree of correspondence between the information and established criteria. Auditing should be done by a competent independent person.
   a. The quantifiable information and established criteria depend on the objectives of the audit.
   b. The specific economic entity and designated time period define the boundaries of the audit.
   c. Evidence of acceptable quality is gathered in sufficient quantity to evaluate the correspondence of the evidence with the established criteria; e.g. GAAP or the Internal Revenue Code.
   d. In judging whether a high degree of correspondence has been achieved, a qualified, competent auditor must maintain an independent mental attitude.
   e. The auditor's report communicates the audit findings to users interested in the information.

OBJECTIVE 2:
DISTINGUISH BETWEEN AUDITING AND ACCOUNTING

2. An **accountant** accumulates and reports information to decision makers. In contrast, an **auditor** evaluates and reports whether the information prepared by the accountant corresponds to established accounting criteria; e.g. GAAP.

3. Auditors, therefore, must not only possess the expertise of an accountant but also that of gathering and evaluating audit evidence.

OBJECTIVE 3:
DESCRIBE THE THREE PRIMARY TYPES OF AUDITS

4. There are three primary types of audits: financial statement, operational, and compliance.
   a. A **financial statement audit** results in an evaluation of whether the financial statements are prepared in accordance with an established criteria such as GAAP.
   b. **Operational audits** evaluate the effectiveness and efficiency of operating procedures and methods.
   c. A **compliance audit** evaluates whether specific procedures, rules, or regulations established by a higher authority are followed.

OBJECTIVE 4:
DESCRIBE THE PRIMARY TYPES OF AUDITORS

5. There are four widely known types of auditors.
   a. **Certified Public Accountants** primarily perform financial statement audits on all publicly traded companies, most large companies, and many smaller companies and nonprofit organizations.
   b. **General Accounting Office Auditors** perform the audit function for Congress. They may perform compliance, operational, or financial audits.
   c. **Internal Revenue Agents** audit taxpayer returns for compliance with tax laws.
   d. An **internal auditor** is employed by a specific company to report the results of compliance, operational, or financial statement audits to top executives and/or the audit committee of the board of directors. Information users outside the entity would not regard the internal auditor as being independent.

OBJECTIVE 5:
DISCUSS WHY REDUCING INFORMATION RISK IS THE PRIME ECONOMIC REASON BEHIND THE DEMAND FOR AUDITS.

6. **Information risk** is the probability that information used in decision making is incorrect.

7. Auditing services are used extensively because they directly affect the level of information risk.

8. Factors influencing the degree of information risk include
   a. **remoteness of information**,
   b. **bias and motives of the information provider**,
   c. **voluminous data**, and
   d. **complexity of accounting transactions**.

9. Three approaches are available to manage information risk.

a. The user may verify the information. This is generally not practical when more than one user wants to do this.
b. The user may share the risk with management in that the user can sue management for losses sustained from having relied on inaccurate information provided by management. However, there may be no assets from which to receive compensation for losses.
c. The user may rely on audit reports provided by certified public accountants.
    1. It is cost efficient.
    2. Auditors have the expertise to perform the work.
    3. Auditors can be sued if the statements prove to be materially misstated.

10. Reliance on auditors is increasing. Federal and state regulations require many companies to be audited and many states require periodic audits of governmental units.

OBJECTIVE 6:
DESCRIBE THE REQUIREMENTS FOR BEING A CPA

11. Qualifications required for an individual to take the CPA exam and to obtain licensing are established by the individual states in three areas.
    a. Education requirements (usually an undergraduate degree in accounting with some states requiring 150 semester credit hours of collegiate education).
    b. Uniform CPA examination.
    c. Experience requirements.

OBJECTIVE 7:
DESCRIBE THE NATURE OF CPA FIRMS, WHAT THEY DO, AND THEIR STRUCTURE

12. **Certified Public Accounting Firms** are often classified into one of four types.
    a. **Big six firms** audit nearly all the largest companies in the United States and have offices in cities throughout the world.
    b. **National firms** compete directly with the big six firms, have offices in most major cities in the United States, and maintain an affiliation with accounting firms in other countries.
    c. **Large local and regional firms** usually do not compete for clients beyond a given radius such as within a state.
    d. **Small local firms** usually have fewer than 25 professionals operating within a single-office firm.

13. CPA firms may perform the following four activities.
    a. **Attestation services** result in the CPA expressing some form of assurance about the assertions made by another person.
        1. The CPA may **audit** historical financial statements to express an opinion on their conformity to GAAP.
        2. The CPA may **review** historical financial statements to express limited assurance about them.
        3. The CPA may perform other types of attestation services involving such things as prospective financial statements.
    b. **Tax services** involve tax planning and the preparation of the entire spectrum of tax returns, including corporate, individual, estate, gift, and payroll tax returns.

c. **Management advisory services** help clients manage their businesses more effectively. Consulting covers a broad range of topics including such things as developing cost accounting systems and completing computer feasibility studies.

d. **Accounting and bookkeeping services** (write-up work) are performed by CPA firms for clients who do not have personnel qualified to do the work.

14. CPA firms are organized as **proprietorships**, **partnerships**, **professional corporations, or regular corporations**. Regardless of the legal form of the firm, the organizational chart usually includes partners, managers, supervisors, seniors, and assistants. The normal time period in each grade while progressing from assistant to partner is from two to three years.

15. The CPA designation is required to become a partner. The national qualifying examination covering the fields of auditing, accounting practice, accounting theory, and business law is administered by the American Institute of Certified Public Accountants **(AICPA)** each May and November.

OBJECTIVE 8:
DESCRIBE THE KEY FUNCTIONS PERFORMED BY THE AICPA

16. The AICPA is the national professional organization for CPAs. Members of the AICPA must be CPAs, but a CPA is not required to be a member of the AICPA.

17. Activities of the AICPA fall into four broad areas: establishing standards and rules, conducting research and publishing, preparing and grading the CPA examination, and offering continuing education.

18. Standards and rules set by the AICPA must be followed by members and other practicing CPAs.
    a. **Auditing standards** in the form of Statements on Auditing Standards (SASs) are established by the **Auditing Standards Board**.
    b. **Compilation and review standards** in the form of Statements on Standards for Accounting and Review Services (SSARS) are established by the **Compilation and Review Standards Committee**.
    c. **Other attestation standards** for services such as prospective financial information are established by the AICPA.
    d. ***Code of Professional Conduct*** in the form of rules of conduct is established by the membership and is administered by the Committee on Professional Ethics.

OBJECTIVE 9:
IDENTIFY WAYS CPAs ARE ENCOURAGED TO PERFORM EFFECTIVELY

19. Many factors influence auditors to achieve high levels of audit quality and professional conduct.
    a. GAAS and interpretations.
    b. Continuing education requirements.
    c. Legal liability.
    d. Division of CPA firms.
    e. *Code of Professional Conduct*.
    f. SEC.
    g. Peer or quality review.

h. Quality control.
i. CPA examination.

OBJECTIVE 10:
USE GENERALLY ACCEPTED AUDITING STANDARDS AS A BASIS FOR FURTHER STUDY

20. The AICPA established ten generally accepted auditing standards **(GAAS)** to serve as guidelines for the professional qualities a CPA should strive to maintain in the conduct of his/her practice. SAS 1 lists the following (abridged) standards. The auditor should:
    a. **GENERAL STANDARDS**
        1. Be proficient and technically trained.
        2. Maintain an independent mental attitude.
        3. Exercise due professional care.
    b. **STANDARDS OF FIELD WORK**
        1. Adequately plan and supervise the work.
        2. Understand the client's internal control structure to plan the audit and the nature, timing, and extent of tests to be performed.
        3. Obtain sufficient competent evidential matter.
    c. **STANDARDS FOR REPORTING**
        1. State whether the financial statements follow GAAP.
        2. Identify circumstances where a lack of consistency has been observed.
        3. Report circumstances where disclosures are inadequate.
        4. Express an opinion regarding the financial statements. If an overall opinion cannot be expressed, state the reasons why. Clearly indicate the character of the audit and the degree of responsibility the auditor assumes.

21. Statements of Auditing Standards **(SASs)** are interpretations of GAAS. They may be classified by their SAS number which is based on the order in which other SASs have been issued or by their AU number which identifies their topical order in the AICPA codification of all SASs.

22. GAAS and the SASs qualify as **authoritative** literature through Rule of Conduct 202 of the *Code of Professional Conduct* and therefore must be followed by all members of the profession. They represent the minimum standard. Auditors who depart from them should be prepared to justify their decision.

23. This body of authoritative literature specifies only a few required audit procedures. Consequently, the conduct of an audit is not a mechanistic exercise but requires the exercise of professional judgement.

24. More specific guidance can be found in less authoritative sources; e.g. textbooks, journals, and trade publications.

OBJECTIVE 11:
IDENTIFY QUALITY CONTROL STANDARDS AND PRACTICES WITHIN THE ACCOUNTING PROFESSION

25. SAS 25 (AU 161) specifies the establishment of quality control standards for CPA firms.
    a. Engagement personnel should be independent.

b. Engagement personnel should be proficient and technically trained.
c. Procedures should ensure that auditors with technical problems seek guidance from qualified firm personnel.
d. Policies should assure proper supervision of work at all levels.
e. New personnel should be qualified to perform their work.
f. All personnel should receive sufficient professional development.
g. Policies should ensure that promoted personnel are qualified.
h. The integrity of potential/existing clients should be evaluated.
i. Policies should ensure that quality control standards are met.

26. In an effort to improve its self-regulation the AICPA established two divisions which CPA firms may join. Membership is not required but a firm may belong to either or both the **SEC Practice Section** or the **Private Companies Practice Section**. A CPA firm that audits a publicly traded company and has members who belong to the AICPA must belong to the SEC Practice Section.

27. Both sections require member firms to adhere to the quality control standards, to submit to a **peer review** every three years and to have members meet continuing education requirements (usually completing 120 hours of continuing professional education every 3 years). The SEC Practice Section also requires partner rotation, concurring partner review, proscription of certain services, reporting on disagreements with clients, and reporting on management advisory services performed.

28. Peer review results in an assessment of whether a CPA firm has complied with the quality control standards required by SAS 25. The review may be conducted by another CPA firm or an AICPA selected team of CPAs.

29. The **Public Oversight Board**, a special AICPA committee, is comprised of respected individuals from business and other professions. They establish policies and solutions to regulating the SEC Practice Section.

OBJECTIVE 12:
SUMMARIZE THE ROLE OF THE SECURITIES AND EXCHANGE COMMISSION IN ACCOUNTING AND AUDITING

30. The **Securities and Exchange Commission** (SEC) allows accounting principles and auditing standards to be set by the Accounting Profession but has established additional basic regulations such as **Regulation S-X**, **Accounting Series Releases, and Accounting and Auditing Enforcement Releases** which affect accounting/auditing issues.

31. The **Securities Act of 1933** and the **Securities Exchange Act of 1934** require audited financial statements of publicly traded companies. Other reports are required by the securities acts.
    a. Forms S-1 to S-16 relate to new securities offerings.
    b. Form 8-K reports an event of interest to public investors.
    c. Form 10-K must be filed annually within 90 days of year-end.
    d. Form 10-Q must be filed quarterly for all publicly held companies.

SELF-ASSESSMENT

TRUE-FALSE STATEMENTS

Indicate whether each of the following statements is true or false.

1. A CPA is not permitted to audit non-financial statement information.

2. If a CPA's audit fee is paid by the company being audited, the auditor is regarded as having lost his/her independence.

3. Auditing and accounting are not interchangeable terms.

4. Operational audits are performed to determine whether the entity has complied with government regulations concerning the recording of operating transactions.

5. Compliance audits are performed to determine whether the auditee has followed specific procedures or rules set down by some higher authority.

6. When an IRS agent audits a tax return, it is considered a financial statement audit of fair presentation in accordance with the Income Tax Basis of Accounting.

7. The audit function for the Congress of the United States is performed by the Internal Revenue Service.

8. GAO auditors complete financial, compliance, and operational audits.

9. Internal auditors, although employed by the auditee, serve as an extension of the external auditors by reporting all audit findings directly to them.

10. The license to practice as a CPA is issued by the state in which the CPA practices rather than by the American Institute of Certified Public Accountants (AICPA).

11. Because of the CPA exam's rigor, licensing of the CPA ordinarily does not also require qualifying experience.

12. If a CPA decides to change employment from public accounting to industry or government, he/she is not required to forfeit the CPA certificate.

13. The auditing profession is particularly important because of the effect it has on a client's business risk.

14. Information risk reflects the possibility that the information upon which a business decision is made is inaccurate.

15. If the factors causing information risk exist, it is generally more effective and economical for users of financial information to reduce their information risk by verifying information individually.

16. Because of their specialized training and the certification process, CPAs are only permitted to perform attestation services.

17. Management advisory services have been provided when the CPA and one of the members of management of the client discuss personal financial planning matters for that individual.

18. CPA firms may be organized as proprietorships, partnerships, professional corporations, or regular corporations.

19. The CPA exam is offered twice annually in May and November covering four broad subject areas: Business Law & Professional Responsibilities, Auditing, Accounting & Reporting (Taxation, Managerial, and Governmental and Not-for-profit organizations) and Financial Accounting & Reporting (Business Enterprises).

20. A CPA is not required to be a member of the AICPA in order to practice public accountancy.

21. The AICPA has four major functions: establishing standards and rules, conducting research and publication, offering continuing education, and preparing and grading the CPA examination.

22. The rules of conduct of the *Code of Professional Conduct* apply to all services performed by CPAs and subsume the technical standards.

23. The twelve generally accepted auditing standards were developed in the early 1900s to provide specific guidance on auditing related matters.

24. The *Generally Accepted Auditing Standards* (GAAS) may be classified into three groups: general standards, standards of field work, and standards of reporting.

25. Interpretations of GAAS take the form of Statements on Auditing Standards (SASs) and are successors to the statements on auditing procedures.

26. Quality control comprises the methods used by a CPA firm to make sure that its professional responsibilities to clients have been met.

27. SAS 25 (AU 161) on quality control sets specific procedures a CPA firm should follow to fulfill its responsibilities.

28. The AICPA is divided into three sections: the SEC Practice Section, the Private Companies Practice Section, and the General Practice Section.

29. Because of strict admittance standards, member firms of an AICPA section are not required to have their practice reviewed for adherence to quality control standards.

COMPLETION STATEMENTS

Complete each of the following statements by filling in the blank space with the appropriate word or words.

1. An audit is to be completed by a person or persons having adequate__________ training and___________ as an auditor.

2. In all matters relating to the engagement the auditor is to maintain an ___________ in mental attitude.

3. An auditor is expected to apply due ___________ care in performing the audit and __________ the report.

4. The audit should be adequately ___________ and assistants should be properly ____________.

5. The auditor should obtain an _____________ of the internal control structure to ______________ the audit and to determine the nature, time, and extent of tests to be performed.

6. Inspection, observation, inquiries, and confirmations should be performed to gather __________ ___________ evidential matter to afford a reasonable basis for an opinion regarding the financial statements under audit.

7. The auditor's report should state whether the financial statements are presented in ______________ with _____________ accepted accounting principles.

8. Circumstances in which Generally Accepted Accounting _____________ have not been ____________ observed in the current period in relation to the preceding period should be identified in the report.

9. Unless otherwise stated in the report informative ______________ in the financial statements are to be regarded as reasonably _____________.

10. The report should _____________ an opinion regarding the financial statements, taken as a whole, or state that an opinion cannot be expressed.

11. The Securities Act of 1933 requires that companies planning to issue new ____________ to the public submit a _______________ statement to the SEC for approval.

12. The SEC has taken the position that accounting and auditing standards should be set by the Accounting ______________.

13. The SEC requirements of greatest interest to CPAs are set forth in the commission's ______________, Accounting _______________ Releases, and Accounting and Auditing Enforcement Releases.

14. To do an audit, information must be in a verifiable form and there must be some established _____________ by which to evaluate it.

15. The scope of the auditor's responsibility involves defining the ____________entity and the ________________period.

16. The purpose of an operational audit is to evaluate the _____________ and _____________of the organization.

17. The purpose of an audit of financial statements is to determine whether the financial statements are stated in accordance with specified ______________.

18. Results of a compliance audit are generally reported to someone ___________the organizational unit being audited.

19. There are four widely known types of auditors. They are general accounting office auditors, certified public accountants, internal auditors, and ___________ __________ ____________.

20. The causes of information risk are remoteness of information, bias and motives of the _____________, voluminous data, and complex exchange _________.

21. CPA firms may be classified into one of four sizes: big ___________firms, other national firms, large local and ___________ firms, and small __________ firms.

22. Four broad categories of service are provided by CPA firms: attestation services, ____________ services, management advisory services, and __________ services.

23. The AICPA has authority to establish standards for auditing, ___________ and ____________standards, other attestation standards, and professional ethics.

MULTIPLE-CHOICE QUESTIONS

Choose the best answer to the following statements/questions.

1. The primary purpose of a management advisory services engagement is to help the client
   a. Become more profitable by relying upon the CPA's existing personal knowledge about the client's business.
   b. Improve the use of its capabilities and resources to achieve its objectives.
   c. Document and quantify its future plans without impairing the CPA's objectivity or allowing the CPA to assume the role of management.
   d. Obtain benefits that are guaranteed implicitly by the CPA.

2. As guidance for measuring the quality of the performance of an auditor, the auditor should refer to
   a. Statements of the Financial Accounting Standards Board.
   b. Generally Accepted Auditing Standards.
   c. Interpretations of the Statements on Auditing Standards.
   d. Statements on Quality Control Standards.

3. A basic objective of a CPA firm is to provide professional services that conform with professional standards. Reasonable assurance of achieving this basic objective is provided through
   a. A system of peer review.
   b. Continuing professional education.
   c. A system of quality control.
   d. Compliance with generally accepted reporting standards.

4. Which of the following is **not** required by the Generally Accepted Auditing Standard that states that due professional care is to be exercised in the performance of the audit?
   a. Observance of the standards of field work and reporting.
   b. Critical review of the audit work performed at every level of supervision.
   c. Degree of skill commonly possessed by others in the profession.
   d. Responsibility for losses because of errors of judgment.

5. In connection with the element of professional development, a CPA firm's system of quality control should ordinarily provide that all personnel
   a. Have the knowledge required to enable them to fulfill responsibilities assigned.
   b. Possess judgment, motivation, and adequate experience.
   c. Seek assistance from persons having appropriate levels of knowledge, judgment, and authority.
   d. Demonstrate compliance with peer review directives.

6. Which of the following best describes what is meant by Generally Accepted Auditing Standards?
   a. Pronouncements issued by the Auditing Standards Board.
   b. Procedures to be used to gather evidence to support financial statements.
   c. Rules acknowledged by the accounting profession because of their universal compliance.
   d. Measures of the quality of the auditor's performance.

7. Each of the following might, by itself, form a valid basis for an auditor to decide to omit a test except for the
   a. Difficulty and expense involved in testing a particular item.
   b. Degree of reliance on the relevant internal controls.
   c. Relative risk involved.
   d. Relationship between the cost of obtaining evidence and its usefulness.

8. The exercise of due professional care requires that an auditor
   a. Use error-free judgement.
   b. Consider internal control, including tests of controls (compliance tests).
   c. Critically review the work done at every level of supervision.
   d. Examine all corroborating evidence available.

2

AUDIT REPORTS

CHAPTER OBJECTIVE

Professional standards require an auditor to issue some type of report whenever an association exists between the CPA and the client's financial statements. This chapter discusses the four basic types of auditor's reports on basic financial statements and the circumstances under which the CPA would elect to issue each.

CHAPTER SUMMARY

OBJECTIVE 1:
DESCRIBE THE NATURE OF AND NEED FOR THE AUDITOR'S REPORT

1. This chapter discusses the first of the following four categories of attestation reports issued by CPAs.
   a. Audit reports on GAAP based historical financial statements.
   b. Special audit reports on financial statements based on another comprehensive basis of accounting, agreed upon audit procedures, or specific accounts.
   c. Attestation reports based on performing an attestation engagement.
   d. Review reports based on performing a review engagement.

2. Uniformity in reporting reduces confusion and interpretation problems for users. The requirements of the four GAAS for reporting and the example reports found in the SASs help achieve it.

OBJECTIVE 2:
SPECIFY THE CONDITIONS THAT JUSTIFY ISSUING THE STANDARD UNQUALIFIED AUDIT REPORT, AND DESCRIBE THE REPORT.

3. There are four types of audit reports.

a. The unqualified opinion audit report (standard and modified versions).
b. The qualified opinion audit report.
c. The adverse opinion audit report.
d. The disclaimer of opinion audit report.

4. Issuing a standard unqualified audit report is appropriate when the auditor has adhered to the ten Generally Accepted Auditing Standards and additional explanations or wording by the auditor is not required.

5. There are seven parts to the **standard unqualified audit report**.
   a. A report title which contains the word **independent**.
   b. The name and address of the recipients of the report (e.g. The Stockholders, XYZ Company).
   c. An **introductory paragraph** stating that an audit has been performed, identifying the financial statements audited, and stating that the statements are management's responsibility while the opinion about them is the auditor's responsibility.
   d. A **scope paragraph** briefly describing what an audit is (**reasonable assurance** on a **test basis**) and that GAAS were followed.
   e. An **opinion paragraph** stating that the financial statements are presented **fairly** in accordance with GAAP.
   f. An audit report date indicating the end of the period through which the auditor searched for significant subsequent events.
   g. The name of the accounting firm issuing the report.

OBJECTIVE 3: LIST THE THREE CONDITIONS REQUIRING A DEPARTURE FROM AN UNQUALIFIED AUDIT REPORT

6. Any of three conditions, if material, would require the auditor's report to depart from an unqualified opinion.
   a. A scope restriction may be imposed by the client or by circumstances beyond the auditor's or client's control.
   b. The financial statements may have been prepared under accounting principles which are not generally accepted.
   c. The auditor is not independent.

OBJECTIVE 4: IDENTIFY THE THREE TYPES OF AUDIT REPORTS THAT CAN BE ISSUED WHEN AN UNQUALIFIED OPINION IS NOT JUSTIFIED

7. A departure from an unqualified report may be one of three types.
   a. An **adverse** opinion is issued when the auditor believes that the financial statements, overall, are so materially misstated that they are NOT presented fairly in accordance with GAAP.
   b. A **disclaimer** of opinion is given when the auditor is NOT independent and/or lacks knowledge about the financial statements because available procedures did not produce sufficient, competent evidence upon which to base an opinion.
   c. A **qualified** opinion is issued when there is or may be a material misstatement in the financial statements but overall they are fairly presented in accordance with GAAP. If the scope of the audit was restricted, both the scope and opinion

paragraphs of the report would be qualified with an "except for," and if GAAP was not followed the opinion paragraph would be qualified with an "except for."

OBJECTIVE 5:
EXPLAIN HOW MATERIALITY AFFECTS AUDIT REPORTING DECISIONS

8. A misstatement in the financial statements falls into one of three size categories.
   a. Immaterial - the auditor's opinion is not changed because user's decisions are unlikely to be affected.
   b. Material without overshadowing the financial statements - the auditor's opinion would be qualified with "except for" on the premise that a user's decision would be affected by knowledge of the misstatement.
   c. Highly material or pervasive so that overall fair presentation is affected - The auditor would give a disclaimer for a potential misstatement or an adverse opinion for a known misstatement on the premise that a user's decision would be significantly affected by knowledge of the potential or known misstatement.

9. Materiality decisions required for non-GAAP conditions involve known misstatements while materiality decisions required for scope limitation conditions involve potential misstatements. In either case the auditor considers the dollar amounts compared with a base, measurability, and the nature of the item.

OBJECTIVE 6:
DRAFT APPROPRIATELY MODIFIED AUDIT REPORTS UNDER A VARIETY OF CIRCUMSTANCES

10. A client may restrict the scope of the audit for legitimate reasons (e.g., to save audit fees or to minimize disputes with customers), but the purpose might also be to hide misstated information from the auditor. The AICPA encourages auditors to consider issuing a disclaimer of opinion whenever the client has imposed scope restrictions.

11. If circumstances prevent the application of normal procedures (e.g., being engaged after year-end so that observing the client count inventory is precluded) but alternative procedures provide enough appropriate evidence, an unqualified opinion may be issued.

12. When circumstances restrict the scope of the audit and alternative procedures are inappropriate or do not provide the required evidence, the standard report is modified as follows:
   a. The scope paragraph states that an audit was performed except as noted in a qualifying paragraph.
   b. A qualifying paragraph discusses the scope restriction.
   c. The opinion paragraph states that the financial statements are fairly presented in accordance with GAAP except for the effects of any adjustments which might have been required had the restriction not occurred.

13. If the auditor **qualifies** the report because the client followed **non-GAAP accounting principles**, the standard introductory and scope paragraphs are presented, a qualifying paragraph is added to explain the departure from GAAP and the effects of the departure on the financial statements, and the opinion paragraph states that except for the effects of the departure the financial statements are fairly presented in accordance with GAAP.

14. If the auditor issues an **adverse opinion** report because of **non-GAAP accounting principles**, the standard introductory and scope paragraphs are presented, a qualifying paragraph is added to explain the departure from GAAP and the effects of the departure on the financial statements, and the opinion paragraph states that because of the effects of the departure the financial statements are NOT fairly presented in accordance with GAAP.

15. If the auditor believes the client's financial statements do not adequately disclose information necessary for fair presentation, the auditor's report would contain the standard introductory and scope paragraphs, a paragraph which discusses the item that should have been disclosed, and the opinion paragraph which would be qualified by an exception for the omission discussed in the preceding paragraph. If the item omitted is a statement of cash flows, the qualifying third paragraph would explain that the statement of cash flows is required for fair presentation, but it would not actually present the omitted financial statement.

16. When the auditor is not independent, a single paragraph report is issued stating that the auditor is not independent and as a result no opinion is expressed on the financial statements.

OBJECTIVE 7:
DESCRIBE THE SIX CIRCUMSTANCES WHEN AN UNQUALIFIED REPORT WITH AN EXPLANATORY PARAGRAPH OR MODIFIED WORDING IS APPROPRIATE

17. An unqualified opinion report with an explanatory paragraph may be used by the auditor to provide additional information which he/she believes is important to readers when any of the following five circumstances are encountered.
    a. Lack of consistent application of GAAP.
    b. Material uncertainties.
    c. Substantial doubt about going concern.
    d. A departure from promulgated accounting principles with which the auditor concurs.
    e. Emphasis of a matter.

18. A modified unqualified opinion report is used when the primary auditor wants to indicated that responsibility for the audit is shared with another CPA firm.

19. When the auditor concurs with a client's change in accounting principle, he/she adds a fourth, explanatory paragraph directing the statement readers' attention to a financial statement footnote which discusses the inconsistency caused by the change in accounting principle. If the auditor does not concur with the change a qualified opinion is given.

20. Even if the client has adequately disclosed an existing FASB 5 type uncertainty and/or a going concern uncertainty, the auditor must discuss it in a fourth, explanatory paragraph.

21. When significant recurring operating losses, working capital deficiencies, or other indications raise serious doubt about the client's ability to continue operations or to meet obligations an explanatory paragraph similar to that used for uncertainties is added to the auditor's report.

22. In very rare circumstances a client may, to achieve fair presentation, follow an accounting principle which departs from one promulgated by appropriate authority. If the auditor concurs, a fourth, explanatory paragraph would describe the departure, the dollar effects of following the alternative principle (if determinable), and the reasons why the generally accepted principle would have been misleading.

23. When a principal auditor elects to share reporting responsibility with a second auditor, each of the three paragraphs in a standard report are modified as follows.
    a. Introductory paragraph - the portion of the company audited by others is identified by name and by the absolute dollar amount of total assets and total revenues of that part of the company.
    b. Scope paragraph - the primary auditor refers to the report of the other auditors as providing a reasonable basis in addition to his/her own audit for the opinion expressed.
    c. Opinion paragraph - the auditor states that his/her opinion is based on his/her own audit and the report of the other auditors.

24. The principle auditor may issue a qualified or disclaimer of opinion when the second auditor's report is qualified or when the principal auditor is unwilling to assume any responsibility for the other auditor's work.

25. All conditions requiring a departure from the standard report must be discussed unless one "neutralizes" the effect of the others. In the following examples of multiple conditions, all items would be included in the report.
    a. Lack of independence and knowledge that GAAP was not followed.
    b. Scope limitation and knowledge of a material litigation contingency.
    c. Going-concern question and inadequate disclosure of the related causes.

26. The following table shows which paragraphs are used with each type of auditor's report. An "S" indicates standard wording and a "C" indicates wording appropriate to the specific circumstance.

	INTRODUCTORY PARAGRAPH	SCOPE PARAGRAPH	QUALIFYING PARAGRAPH	OPINION PARAGRAPH	EXPLANATORY PARAGRAPH
Standard Unqualified	S	S		S	
Modified Unqualified					
General	S	S		S	C
Other CPAs	C	C		C	
Qualified					
Scope	S	C	C	C	
GAAP	S	S	C	C	
Adverse	S	S	C	C	
Disclaimer					
Scope	C		C	C	
Independence				C	

27. "Negative assurances" (wording such as "nothing came to our attention. . . . ") are prohibited in audit reports because readers might be confused about the work done and the responsibility assumed by the auditor.

OBJECTIVE 8: DESCRIBE THE PROCESS FOR DECIDING THE APPROPRIATE AUDIT REPORT

28. A four step process is completed by auditors to determine the appropriate audit report to issue.
    a. Determine whether any condition exists requiring a departure from a standard unqualified report.
    b. Decide the materiality for each condition.
    c. Decide the appropriate type of report for the condition, given the materiality level.
    d. Write the audit report.

SELF-ASSESSMENT

TRUE-FALSE STATEMENTS

Indicate whether each of the following statements is true or false.

__ 1. As a general rule, the only part of the audit effort third parties see is the audit report.

__ 2. The content of the auditor's report is influenced strongly by the five Generally Accepted Auditing Standards for reporting.

__ 3. The opinion given in the audit report must clearly indicate the degree of responsibility the auditor has assumed.

__ 4. Auditors are expected to exhibit a great deal of personal discretion in wording the auditor's report.

__ 5. Because of the complexity of accounting transactions and information risk, a low percentage of audit reports are classified as standard unqualified audit reports.

__ 6. The main paragraphs of a standard unqualified audit report are the scope paragraph and the opinion paragraph.

__ 7. The audit report's title must contain the word independent.

__ 8. It is customary to address the report to the stockholders to further emphasize the auditor's independence.

__ 9. The introductory paragraph of the auditor's report explains who the audit firm is and identifies the principal partner responsible for the engagement.

___ 10. The scope paragraph indicates that an audit can be expected to provide reasonable assurance that the financial statements are not misstated by a material amount.

___ 11. Auditors certify in the opinion paragraph of the audit report as to the precision of the financial statements.

___ 12. The report date is understood to mark the last day for which the auditor is responsible for discovering significant events that occurred in the new period which have a bearing on the period being audited.

___ 13. Material uncertainties such as litigation which cannot be reasonably estimated at the balance sheet date result in the issue of a qualified opinion.

___ 14. Any of the following conditions, if material, would require the auditor to issue a modified unqualified opinion: inconsistent application of GAAP, reports involving other auditors, or a departure from promulgated accounting principles with which the auditor agrees.

___ 15. When a second auditor examines a component of a client, the principal auditor is required by professional standards to make reference in the report to the fact that other auditors were involved.

___ 16. The scope of the auditor may be restricted by the client or by circumstances beyond the control of the client or the auditor.

___ 17. When an auditor is not independent a qualified report must be issued.

___ 18. If the financial statements have not been prepared in accordance with GAAP, the materiality of the departure(s) governs whether the opinion is unqualified, qualified, or adverse.

___ 19. A disclaimer of opinion is issued when the auditor has been unable to obtain sufficient, competent evidence to support an opinion.

___ 20. A common base for establishing materiality is net income.

___ 21. The difference between immaterial, material, and highly material misstatements is clearly defined in the accounting literature.

___ 22. When conditions restrict the scope of the audit but the auditor is able to gather satisfactory evidence with the use of alternative procedures an unqualified opinion can be given.

___ 23. If the client has imposed scope restrictions, the auditor is encouraged by professional standards to give a disclaimer.

___ 24. If a disclaimer is given because of scope limitations, the scope paragraph of the auditor's report is omitted entirely.

_ 25. When multiple conditions exist which individually would require a departure from an unqualified opinion the auditor's report discusses only the one which in the auditor's professional judgment is the most important.

_ 26. A negative assurance is a statement to the effect that nothing came to the attention of the auditor which would lead him/her to believe that the financial statements are not stated fairly.

_ 27. When an auditor gives a disclaimer of opinion, the use of a negative assurance helps the reader clarify the nature of the auditor and the degree of responsibility being assumed in the report.

COMPLETION STATEMENTS

Complete each of the following statements by filling in the blank space(s) with the appropriate word(s).

1. Professional standards require that a report be issued whenever a CPA is __________ with financial statements.

2. A standard unqualified audit report would be issued when (a) all the financial statements are included, (b) Generally Accepted Auditing Standards have been followed, and (c) a fourth, ______________paragraph is not required.

3. The introductory and scope paragraphs contain a series of ____________ statements while the opinion paragraph expresses a _____________.

4. The standard introductory paragraph states that an audit was done, lists the financial statements audited, and states that _____________ for the financial statements rests with management while the ___________is responsible for an opinion about the fair presentation of the financial statements.

5. The scope paragraph states that the auditor followed ___________and that the audit provides a ___________ basis for an opinion.

6. The opinion paragraph is not a statement of absolute fact or a ___________.

7. When the principal auditor shares responsibility in the report with a second auditor, __________ (one, two, or three) standard paragraphs are modified and a fourth, explanatory paragraph __________ (is, is not) added.

8. If changes such as a change in accounting estimate affect comparability, they _________ (are, are not) required to be discussed in the audit report.

9. An auditor may emphasize specific matters such as the existence of significant ____________ party transactions in a fourth, explanatory paragraph.

10. When the principal auditor is unwilling to assume any responsibility for the work of a second auditor, the opinion paragraph would either be a ____________ or ____________opinion.

11. A misstatement is regarded as immaterial if it is ___________ to affect the decisions of _________ users.

12. When an exception or misstatement affects so many different parts of the financial statements that they are not fairly stated the misstatement is said to be ___________.

13. When an auditor lacks independence a ___________ opinion must be given under the ____________ of the *Code of Professional Conduct*.

14. Materiality decisions involve GAAP, a dollar comparison with a base, measurability, and the ___________ of the item.

15. Qualified, adverse, and disclaimers of opinion other than for lack of independence require the use of a third, ___________ paragraph inserted between the ___________ and opinion paragraphs.

16. Common scope restrictions imposed by clients include prohibiting ___________ of physical inventories and ___________ of accounts receivable.

17. Professional standards encourage auditors to disclaim an opinion when a client has imposed scope limitations because the motivation of the restriction may be to ___________ discovery of ___________ information.

18. Frequently, clients impose scope limitations on the auditor in order to reduce audit ___________.

19. All conditions requiring a departure from the standard report must be discussed unless one ___________ the effect of the others.

MULTIPLE-CHOICE QUESTIONS

Indicate the best answer to the following statements/questions.

1. A limitation on the scope of the auditor sufficient to preclude an unqualified opinion will always result when management
   a. Prevents the auditor from reviewing the working papers of the predecessor auditor.
   b. Engages the auditor after the year-end physical inventory count is completed.
   c. Fails to correct a material weakness in the internal control structure that had been identified during the prior year's audit.
   d. Refuses to furnish a management representation letter to the auditor.

2. If the financial statements, including accompanying notes, fail to disclose information that is required by Generally Accepted Accounting Principles, the auditor should express either a (an)
   a. "Except for" qualified opinion or an adverse opinion.
   b. Adverse opinion or a "subject to" qualified opinion.
   c. "Subject to" qualified opinion or an unqualified opinion with a separate explanatory paragraph.
   d. Unqualified opinion with a separate explanatory paragraph or an "except for" qualified opinion.

3. When an auditor qualifies an opinion because of a scope limitation, which paragraph(s) of the auditor's report should indicate that the qualification pertains to the possible effects on the financial statements and **not** to the scope limitation itself?
   a. The scope paragraph and the separate qualifying paragraph.
   b. The introductory paragraph.
   c. The scope paragraph only.
   d. The opinion paragraph only.

4. The management of a client company believes that the statement of cash flows is not a useful document and refuses to include one in the annual report to stockholders. As a result of this circumstance, the auditor's opinion should be
   a. Adverse.
   b. Unqualified.
   c. Qualified due to inadequate disclosure.
   d. Qualified due to a scope limitation.

5. The principal auditor is satisfied with the independence and professional reputation of the other auditor who has audited a subsidiary but wants to indicate the division of responsibility. The principal auditor should
   a. Modify only the introductory paragraph.
   b. Modify only the scope paragraph.
   c. Modify the introductory, scope and opinion paragraphs.
   d. Modify only the opinion paragraph.

6. The auditor would most likely issue a disclaimer of opinion because of
   a. The client's failure to present supplementary information required by the FASB.
   b. Inadequate disclosure of material information.
   c. A client imposed scope limitation.
   d. The qualification of an opinion by the other auditor of a subsidiary where there is a division of responsibility.

7. When there is a significant change in accounting principle, an auditor's report should refer to the inconsistent application of Generally Accepted Accounting Principles in
   a. The scope paragraph.
   b. An explanatory paragraph between the second paragraph and the opinion paragraph.
   c. The opinion paragraph.
   d. An explanatory paragraph following the opinion paragraph.

8. How are management's responsibility and the auditor's responsibility represented in the standard auditor's report?

	MANAGEMENT'S RESPONSIBILITY	AUDITOR'S RESPONSIBILITY
a.	Explicitly	Explicitly
b.	Implicitly	Implicitly
c.	Implicitly	Explicitly
d.	Explicitly	Implicitly

9. Grant Company's financial statements adequately disclose uncertainties that concern future events, the outcome of which are not susceptible of reasonable estimation. The auditor's report should include a(an)
   a. Unqualified opinion.

b. "Subject to" qualified opinion.
c. "Except for" qualified opinion.
d. Adverse opinion.

10. An auditor should disclose the substantive reasons for expressing an adverse opinion in an explanatory paragraph
    a. Preceding the scope paragraph.
    b. Preceding the opinion paragraph.
    c. Following the opinion paragraph.
    d. Within the notes to the financial statements.

3

PROFESSIONAL ETHICS

CHAPTER OBJECTIVE

This chapter defines ethics in a general sense, presents a method of resolving ethical dilemmas, and explains the rules of ethical conduct required by the AICPA *Code of Professional Conduct*.

CHAPTER SUMMARY

OBJECTIVE 1: DISTINGUISH ETHICAL FROM UNETHICAL BEHAVIOR IN PERSONAL, PROFESSIONAL, AND BUSINESS CONTEXTS

1. Ethics, broadly defined, is a set of moral principles or values. The Josephson Institute for the Advancement of Ethics prescribed ten ethical principles (abridged).
   a. Honesty
   b. Integrity
   c. Promise-Keeping
   d. Loyalty (fidelity)
   e. Fairness
   f. Caring for others
   g. Respect for others
   h. Responsible citizenship
   i. Pursuit of excellence
   j. Accountability

2. People disagree about what constitutes ethical behavior and the relative importance of principles accepted as ethical because life experiences are so diverse.

3. Ethical behavior helps society function in an orderly manner.

4. Unethical behavior, behaving in an inappropriate manner for the circumstances, usually happens for two reasons.
   a. The person's ethical standards differ from those of society at large.
   b. The person chooses to act selfishly.

5. Widespread publicity generated by unethical business practices have potentially detrimental effects on business and society.
   a. The impression may be created that unethical business practices are normal behavior.
   b. Observers may conclude that ethical business practices hinder financial success.
   c. Society's sensitivity to these practices may diminish so that only extreme circumstances are regarded as unethical.

6. Many corporations have developed a formal code of ethical conduct. Rotary International's Four Way Test is used extensively by millions of business people.
   a. Is it the truth?
   b. Is it fair to all concerned?
   c. Will it build goodwill and better friendships?
   d. Will it be beneficial to all concerned?

OBJECTIVE 2:
IDENTIFY ETHICAL DILEMMAS AND DESCRIBE HOW THEY CAN BE ADDRESSED

7. Unethical behavior is often justified through the process of rationalization.
   a. Everybody does it.
   b. If it's legal, it's ethical.
   c. The likelihood of discovery is small and/or the consequences of being discovered are not formidable.

8. Ethical dilemmas can be resolved with a six step approach.
   a. Obtain the relevant facts.
   b. Identify the ethical issues from the facts.
   c. Determine who is affected by the outcome of the dilemma and how each person or group is affected.
   d. Identify the alternatives available to the person who must resolve the dilemma.
   e. Identify the likely consequence of each alternative.
   f. Decide the appropriate action.

OBJECTIVE 3:
DESCRIBE THE ETHICAL CONCERNS SPECIFIC TO THE ACCOUNTING PROFESSION

9. Users of services provided by a professional (e.g., CPAs, attorneys, doctors) generally cannot evaluate the quality of the professional's performance because of its complexity. The profession's ability to serve is greatly enhanced when the public confidence has been raised by high levels of professional conduct.

10. Many factors influence the ethical conduct of individual practitioners.
   a. *Code of Professional Conduct.*
   b. Peer review or quality review.
   c. Division of CPA firms.
   d. Legal liability.
   e. Continuing education requirements.
   f. GAAS and interpretations.
   g. CPA examinations.

h. Quality control.
i. SEC.

OBJECTIVE 4:
EXPLAIN THE PURPOSE AND CONTENT OF THE AICPA *CODE OF PROFESSIONAL CONDUCT*

11. Advantages and disadvantages of expressing a code of conduct as general statements of ideal conduct and as specific rules of defining unacceptable behavior are:

	general statement	specific rule
advantage	emphasis on positive activities encouraging high performance	enforceability of minimum standards of behavior and performance
disadvantage	difficulty of enforcement	tendency for rules to become maximum standards.

12. The AICPA *Code of Professional Conduct* has four parts.
    a. Principles (not enforceable).
    b. Rules of conduct (enforceable).
    c. Interpretations (not enforceable but departure must be justified).
    d. Ethical rulings (not enforceable but departure must be justified).

13. There are six Principles of Professional Conduct.
    a. Responsibilities (exercise sensitive professional and moral judgments).
    b. The Public Interest (demonstrate commitment to professionalism by serving the public interest and honoring the public trust).
    c. Integrity (maintain the highest sense of integrity).
    d. Objectivity and Independence (remain free of conflicts of interest and when providing attestation services be independent in fact and in appearance).
    e. Due Care (observe standards and continually strive to improve quality of services and discharge of responsibilities).
    f. Scope and Nature of Services (observe *Code of Professional Conduct* in determining the scope and nature of services to be provided).

14. The first five Principles apply to all AICPA members, but the last Principle applies only to members that are in public practice.

15. Ethics Interpretations express the consensus of a committee comprised largely of practicing CPAs. Key people in the profession may comment on proposed interpretations.

16. The executive committee of the professional ethics division explains acceptable behavior for specific factual circumstances in the ethical rulings.

17. The rules of conduct are enforceable. They apply to all members of the AICPA except for those few specific statements which identify requirements applicable only to members in public practice. Individual states have rules of conduct required for licensing by the state. A member may not permit another to commit

an act for the member which is prohibited by the rules of conduct. Members are jointly responsible for rule violations committed by employees, partners, or shareholders.

OBJECTIVE 5:
DISCUSS INDEPENDENCE AS IT APPLIES TO THE AICPA CODE

18. Rule 101-Independence (possession of an unbiased viewpoint) should be maintained in appearance (i.e., how others perceive the auditor) and in fact (i.e., the auditor's true mental state) as required by standards promulgated by bodies designated by Council (i.e., when performing attestation services). Independence may be compromised if the auditor has one or more of the specified types of financial interest in the client, serves in a decision-making capacity with the client, and/or is involved in litigation with the client.

19. The rule on independence applies to all partners or shareholders of the CPA firm such that if one partner has a financial interest in a client the CPA firm's independence has been compromised even though that partner may not be assigned to the engagement and/or may not work in the office which performs the audit. Nonpartners or nonshareholders are affected by the independence rule only when they are involved in the engagement or when the engagement is being performed by staff who are employed in the same office as they.

20. A variety of financial arrangements may compromise independence.
    a. A direct financial interest or a material indirect financial interest in the client.
    b. A material joint business investment with a client or any of its principals (an interpretation defines materiality in this instance to be the more restrictive of either 5% of the audit client's total assets or operating income before taxes).
    c. A loan to or from the client or any of its principals except for those loans from financial institutions which are made under normal lending procedures such as the following:
        1. Loans not material to the borrower's net worth.
        2. A home mortgage.
        3. Secured loans if not secured by the member's firm.
        4. Automobile loans.
        5. Loans fully collateralized by cash deposits at the same financial institution.
        6. Unpaid credit card balances not exceeding $5,000.

21. A direct financial interest occurs when the auditor or any member of his/her immediate family owns an equity interest in the client. An indirect interest exists when a close but not direct member of the auditor's family (e.g., a grandparent) owns an equity interest in the client or when the auditor owns securities in the same entity as the mutual fund he/she is auditing. Infrequent contact or geographical separation may mitigate the significance of a close relationship.

22. The Materiality of an indirect financial interest is judged in relation to the member's wealth and income.

23. If a retired partner owns a material interest in a client and is active or held out to be associated with the CPA firm, the independence rule is considered to have been violated.

24. It is presumed that if an auditor also served the client in a decision making capacity during the period of the audit, the auditor could not be unbiased (objective) in conducting the examination. Arrangements which would be considered violations include being an officer, director, employee, underwriter, promoter, or voting trustee of the client or a trustee of a pension or profit-sharing plan of the client.

25. Although the SEC regards the performance of bookkeeping services and auditing by the same auditor to be a violation of independence, the AICPA permits this arrangement if three conditions are met.
   a. The client accepts full responsibility for the financial statements.
   b. The CPA has not acted in the capacity of a manager or employee of the client by authorizing transactions, maintaining custody of assets, or preparing source documents.
   c. The CPA performs an audit in accordance with GAAS.

26. Several factors encourage CPAs to be independent and influence the public to perceive them as being independent.
   a. Legal liability.
   b. Rule 101, interpretations and rulings.
   c. GAAS.
   d. AICPA quality control standards.
   e. Division of firms.
   f. Audit committees.
   g. Communications with predecessor auditors.
   h. SAS 50's requirements for providing written or oral opinions on the application of GAAP.
   i. Increasing number of companies requiring stockholder approval of the CPA firm.

OBJECTIVE 6:
DISCUSS INTEGRITY AND OBJECTIVITY AS THEY APPLY TO THE AICPA CODE

27. Rule 102-Integrity and Objectivity requires the CPA to have no conflicts of interest, to maintain objectivity and integrity, to not knowingly misrepresent the facts, and to not subordinate his/her judgment to others in all aspects of his/her work.

OBJECTIVE 7:
DISCUSS THE AICPA CODE RULE ON TECHNICAL STANDARDS

28. Rule 201-General Standards requires the CPA to comply with four general standards of conduct:
   a. Agree to perform professional services only when the CPA believes that the engagement can be completed with professional competence.
   b. Exercise due professional care in performing professional services.
   c. Adequately plan and supervise the performance of professional services.

d. Base conclusions or recommendations on reasonably sufficient relevant data.

29. Rule 202-Compliance with Standards requires a member to perform professional services (audit, review, compilation, management advisory, tax or other) according to standards established by bodies designated by Council to do so.

30. Rule 203-Accounting Principles requires that if an auditor opines that financial statements are presented in accordance with GAAP or states that he or she is unaware of any material changes that should be made to the Financial Statements to make them conform to GAAP, they must follow principles promulgated by the body designated by the AICPA to establish such principles unless unusual circumstances warrant a departure. The CPA's reporting requirements increase when conditions warrant a departure.
a. The report must describe the departure.
b. The report must describe the effects of the departure.
c. The report must discuss the reasons why adhering to the promulgated principle would have been misleading.

OBJECTIVE 8:
DISCUSS THE AICPA CODE RULES ON THE CPA's RESPONSIBILITIES TO CLIENTS REGARDING CONFIDENTIALITY AND CONTINGENT FEES

31. Rule 301-Confidential Client Information prohibits a member from disclosing such information unless one of five conditions applies.
a. Rule 202 and/or Rule 203 requires the disclosure.
b. The CPA is responding to a valid subpoena or summons or complying with applicable laws and government regulations.
c. The CPA is submitting to a peer review under AICPA, State CPA Society, or State Board of Accountancy authorization.
d. The CPA is initiating or responding to an inquiry from a recognized investigative or disciplinary body (e.g., the AICPA Ethics Division Trial Board).
e. The member has obtained written permission from the client.

32. Rule 302-Contingent Fees permits a CPA's fees to vary with the complexity of the service provided, to be based on the outcome of a judicial proceeding or a finding of a governmental agency for tax matters, or to be fixed by a court or other public authority. The fee for tax return preparation and attestation services (i.e., an audit, a review, a compilation which a third party is likely to use, and an examination of prospective financial information) may not be determined on a contingent basis. The fee for nonattestation professional services may be dependent on the findings or results of the CPA's work if the CPA does not also perform attestation services for the same client.

OBJECTIVE 9:
EXPLAIN THE AICPA CODE RULE ON DISCREDITABLE ACTS

33. Rule 501-Acts Discreditable prohibits a member from committing an act discreditable to the profession. Examples of acts considered discreditable to the profession such as the following can be found in the interpretations.

a. Refusing to return a client's records when requested.
b. Discriminating on the basis of age, race, sex, religion, color, or national origin.

34. The AICPA bylaws require termination of a CPA's membership if he/she is convicted of any of four crimes.
   a. A crime punishable by imprisonment for more than one year.
   b. Failing to file any income tax return as an individual taxpayer.
   c. Filing a false or fraudulent income tax return.
   d. Willfully aiding in the preparation and presentation of a false or fraudulent income tax return of a client.

OBJECTIVE 10:
EXPLAIN THE AICPA CODE RULES ON ADVERTISING, SOLICITATION, COMMISSIONS, AND REFERRAL FEES AND DISCUSS THEIR IMPACT ON COMPETITION AMONG CPAs

35. Rule 502-Advertising and Other Forms of Solicitation prohibits false, misleading, or deceptive advertising and the use of coercion, overreaching, or harassing conduct to obtain clients.

36. Rule 503-Commissions prohibits a CPA firm from paying a commission to obtain a client or receiving a commission for referring a client to the product or service of another when performing attestation services for that same client.
   a. Retirement benefits and payments to purchase an accounting practice are exempt.
   b. Commissions and referral fees paid or received by a CPA when attestation services are not involved must be disclosed to affected parties.

OBJECTIVE 11:
EXPLAIN THE ACCEPTABLE FORMS OF PRACTICE OF CPA FIRMS AND THE REQUIREMENTS OF EACH FORM

37. Rule 505-Form of Practice and Name requires that the CPA firm be organized in a form permitted by state law or regulation. In addition to the proprietorship, partnership, or professional corporation format, some states permit CPA firms to organize as regular corporations. Using a misleading name or implying an incorrect form of business is prohibited. All partners and shareholders must belong to the AICPA for the firm to be designated as a member of the AICPA.

OBJECTIVE 12:
DESCRIBE THE ENFORCEMENT MECHANISMS FOR THE AICPA AND STATE BOARD OF ACCOUNTANCY RULES OF CONDUCT

38. Enforcement by the Institute may result in remedial or corrective action for less serious offenses or in suspension or expulsion from membership in the AICPA for serious offenses.

39. Most state boards of accountancy have adopted the AICPA's rules of conduct or more restrictive codes. Violations of these rules can result in the state board

of accountancy revoking the CPA's certificate and license to practice public accounting.

SELF-ASSESSMENT

TRUE-FALSE STATEMENTS

Indicate whether each of the following statements is true of false.

___ 1. One of the major reasons a profession adopts a code of ethics is to create public confidence in the service provided by that profession.

___ 2. *The Code of Professional Conduct* is one of several ways the accounting profession encourages CPAs to maintain their practice of accounting at a high level.

___ 3. One disadvantage of having a set of specific rules defining the behavior of members is that the rules are not as easy to enforce as are general statements of ideal conduct.

___ 4. Interpretations of the rules of conduct by the AICPA Division of Professional Ethics are enforceable.

___ 5. Ethical rulings in response to questions about the rules of conduct submitted by parties interested in ethical requirements are not enforceable.

___ 6. The principles of professional ethics are divided into six categories of ethical principles.

___ 7. The rules of conduct are enforceable rules which must be followed by every CPA who practices public accounting.

___ 8. Interpretations of the rules of conduct are prepared by a committee of the Division of Professional Ethics with consideration given to comments received from a large number of key people in the profession.

___ 9. Ethical rulings are structured in the form of a question about a factual circumstance and an answer by the ethics executive committee explaining the expected ethical behavior for that situation.

___ 10. All members of the AICPA whether practicing public accounting or not are required to adhere to all the Rules of Conduct.

___ 11. The rules of conduct do not apply when some other person violates one of the rules on behalf of a member but only when the member, personally, has actually committed the transgression.

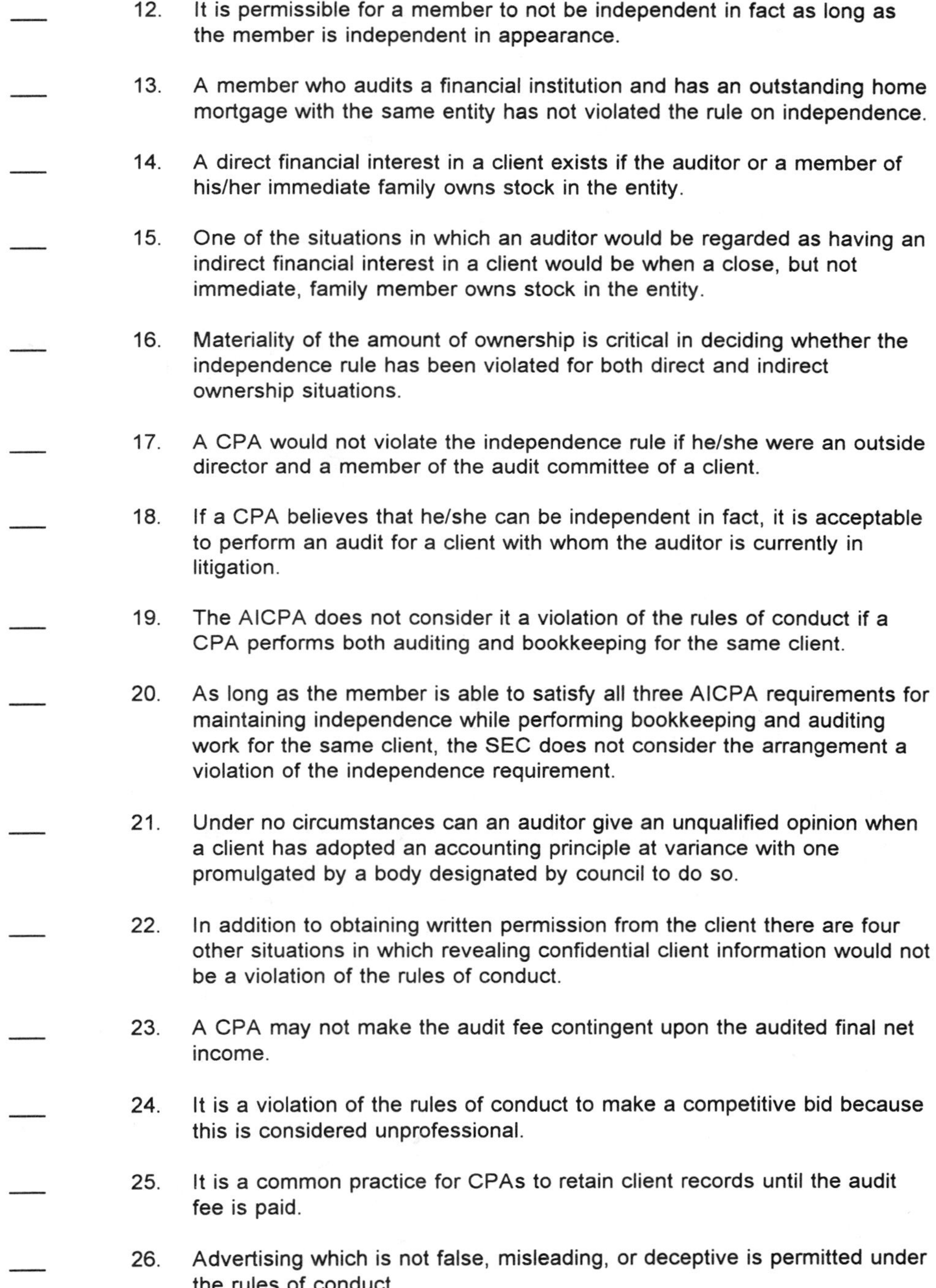

___ 12. It is permissible for a member to not be independent in fact as long as the member is independent in appearance.

___ 13. A member who audits a financial institution and has an outstanding home mortgage with the same entity has not violated the rule on independence.

___ 14. A direct financial interest in a client exists if the auditor or a member of his/her immediate family owns stock in the entity.

___ 15. One of the situations in which an auditor would be regarded as having an indirect financial interest in a client would be when a close, but not immediate, family member owns stock in the entity.

___ 16. Materiality of the amount of ownership is critical in deciding whether the independence rule has been violated for both direct and indirect ownership situations.

___ 17. A CPA would not violate the independence rule if he/she were an outside director and a member of the audit committee of a client.

___ 18. If a CPA believes that he/she can be independent in fact, it is acceptable to perform an audit for a client with whom the auditor is currently in litigation.

___ 19. The AICPA does not consider it a violation of the rules of conduct if a CPA performs both auditing and bookkeeping for the same client.

___ 20. As long as the member is able to satisfy all three AICPA requirements for maintaining independence while performing bookkeeping and auditing work for the same client, the SEC does not consider the arrangement a violation of the independence requirement.

___ 21. Under no circumstances can an auditor give an unqualified opinion when a client has adopted an accounting principle at variance with one promulgated by a body designated by council to do so.

___ 22. In addition to obtaining written permission from the client there are four other situations in which revealing confidential client information would not be a violation of the rules of conduct.

___ 23. A CPA may not make the audit fee contingent upon the audited final net income.

___ 24. It is a violation of the rules of conduct to make a competitive bid because this is considered unprofessional.

___ 25. It is a common practice for CPAs to retain client records until the audit fee is paid.

___ 26. Advertising which is not false, misleading, or deceptive is permitted under the rules of conduct.

COMPLETION STATEMENTS

Complete each of the following statements by filling in the blank space(s) with the appropriate word(s).

1. The most severe sanction which the AICPA can impose on a member who violates the rules of conduct is ____________.

2. The two primary levels of disciplinary action occur at the _________ or corrective action level and the ___________ trial board level.

3. The right to practice public accountancy is granted by each state's _______ of accountancy.

4. A member's firm may be structured as a proprietorship, a partnership, a regular corporation, or as a _______________ corporation.

5. One aid to maintaining independence is communicating with the predecessor ___________.

6. Prohibiting a member who performs attestation services for a client from receiving a ___________ fee is designed to help assure the CPA firm's independence and to prevent the CPA from charging for something other than for professional _________ performed.

7. __________ CPA firms are more likely to benefit from being permitted to advertise than _________ ones.

8. Until 1978, advertising was __________, but now advertising which is not false, misleading, or __________ is acceptable.

9. Three of the four violations of the AICPA bylaws which would result in termination of membership without a hearing are convictions in matters dealing with ________ ________ returns.

10. In late 1990, the AICPA and the Federal Trade Commission reached an agreement which eliminated restrictions on contingent fees for ____________ services unless the CPA firm also performed attestation services for the same client.

11. Professional fees dependent upon the decisions of a court or other recognized authority are not regarded as ____________ fees.

12. If a peer review is ___________ by the AICPA, examination of workpapers containing confidential client information by the review team does not require ________ from the client in order to conform to rule 301.

13. When a retiring CPA sells his/her professional practice to a second CPA, ____________ must be received from the client in order for the retiring CPA to turn over the workpapers to the second CPA.

14. The effect of rule 201 is to make a violation of auditing standards automatically a ____________ of the rules of ___________.

15. A member can give an ___________ opinion on financial statements prepared under a principle which contains a departure from a promulgated GAAP if ____________ circumstances would otherwise have made the financial statements misleading.

16. Accepting an audit engagement with a new client whose principal business was in a specialized industry would not be a violation of the rules of conduct providing the auditor possessed the _________ ________ to complete the assignment.

17. An auditor must maintain independence in ______ and _________.

18. The prohibition against having a financial interest in one of the firm's clients applies to _______ partners and shareholders and to nonpartners and nonshareholders when they are __________ in the engagement or when it is performed by staff of the office in which they work.

19. An independent auditor should maintain an __________ viewpoint in the conduct of the audit.

20. The four parts to the *Code of Professional Conduct* are __________, rules of conduct, ______________, and ethical rulings.

MULTIPLE-CHOICE QUESTIONS

Indicate the best answer to the following statements/questions.

1. The AICPA *Code of Professional Conduct* contains both general ethical principles that are aspirational in character and also a
   a. List of violations that would cause the automatic suspension of the CPA's license.
   b. Set of specific, mandatory rules describing minimum levels of conduct the CPA must maintain.
   c. Description of the CPA's procedures for responding to an inquiry from a trial board.
   d. List of specific crimes that would be considered as acts discreditable to the profession.

2. A violation of the profession's ethical standards would most likely have occurred when a CPA
   a. Made arrangements with a bank to collect notes issued by a client in payment of fees due.
   b. Joined an accounting firm made up of three non-CPA practitioners.
   c. Issued an unqualified opinion on the 1985 financial statements when fees for the 1984 audit were unpaid.
   d. Purchased a bookkeeping firm's practice of monthly write-ups for a percentage of fees received over a three-year period.

3. Prior to beginning the field work on a new audit engagement in which a CPA does not possess expertise in the industry in which the client operates, the CPA should
   a. Reduce audit risk by lowering the preliminary levels of materiality.
   b. Design special substantive tests to compensate for the lack of industry expertise.
   c. Engage financial experts familiar with the nature of the industry.
   d. Obtain a knowledge of matters that relate to the nature of the entity's business.

4. The concept of materiality would be least important to an auditor when considering the
   a. Decision whether to use positive or negative confirmations of accounts receivable.
   b. Adequacy of disclosure of a client's illegal act.
   c. Discovery of weaknesses in a client's internal control structure.
   d. Effects of a direct financial interest in the client upon the CPA's independence.

4

LEGAL LIABILITY

CHAPTER OBJECTIVE

The purpose of this chapter is to discuss the legal environment in which CPAs work. Sources of potential liability and the nature of lawsuits against CPAs are presented.

CHAPTER SUMMARY

OBJECTIVE 1:
APPRECIATE THE LITIGIOUS ENVIRONMENT IN WHICH CPAs PRACTICE

1. In 1991, the six largest CPA firms incurred legal settlement and defense costs of $477 million. Major sources of legal liability for auditors include the following.

CASES UNDER COMMON LAW

CLAIMANT	Basis of Claim
Client	Breach of Contract
Client	Tort-Negligence, Gross Negligence, Fraud
Third Party Beneficiary (may include foreseen or foreseeable third parties)	Tort-Negligence, Gross Negligence, Fraud
Other Third Party	Tort-Gross Negligence, Fraud

CASES UNDER FEDERAL STATUTORY LAW

CLAIMANT	Basis of Claim
Third Party - Civil	Securities Act of 1933
Third Party - Civil	Securities and Exchange Act of 1934
Government - Criminal	Various

2. Several factors have increased CPAs' potential legal liability.
   a. Users are more knowledgeable of the CPA's responsibility.
   b. The SEC is making a greater effort to protect investors' interests.

c. The technical environment in which audits are conducted is more complex because of factors such as globalization and increased size.
d. The doctrine of joint and several liability often results in judgements against those able to pay regardless of the extent to which they are at fault; i.e., the "deep-pocket" concept of liability.
e. Large judgements have been awarded in a few contingent-fee basis cases.
f. CPAs are often willing to settle out of court (avoid fees and publicity).
g. Courts often have difficulty understanding technical accounting and auditing matters.

OBJECTIVE 2:
EXPLAIN WHY THE FAILURE OF FINANCIAL STATEMENT USERS TO DIFFERENTIATE AMONG BUSINESS FAILURE, AUDIT FAILURE, AND AUDIT RISK HAS RESULTED IN LAWSUITS

3. **Business failure** occurs when poor management decisions, extreme economic conditions, or unexpected competition prevent investor's or creditor's expectations for investment recovery from being realized. **Bankruptcy** is the extreme case of business failure.

4. An **audit failure** occurs when the auditor's opinion is incorrect because the auditor did not perform the examination in accordance with GAAS.

5. **Audit risk** is the potential that a material misstatement in the financial statements will go undetected because the audit process is based on sampling. If audit risk happens, the auditor's opinion is incorrect.

6. When the auditor's opinion is wrong, the courts generally have the complex task of deciding whether audit risk was experienced or whether audit failure occurred through auditor negligence.

7. When there has been a business failure the auditor must often defend his\her opinion against claims of audit failure because users are encouraged by the notion of the "deep-pocket" approach to seeking restitution and because users often do not understand what the auditor's responsibility really is.

OBJECTIVE 3:
DEFINE THE PRIMARY LEGAL CONCEPTS AND TERMS CONCERNING ACCOUNTANT's LIABILITY

8. The CPA is legally responsible for his/her professional work whether it is auditing, taxes, management advisory services, or write-up work and may extend to any or all of the following areas:
   a. Liability to clients.
   b. Civil liability to third parties under common and statutory law.
   c. Criminal liability.

9. Three important legal concepts apply to the work auditors perform.
   a. To be considered neither negligent nor to have performed in bad faith or dishonestly, the prudent man concept requires auditors to exercise reasonable care and diligence commonly followed by others in the profession.

b. Liability for acts of others holds partners or shareholders jointly liable for the work of other partners, employees, and other CPA firms or specialists engaged to do part of the work.
c. Lack of privileged communication denies CPAs the right to withhold written or oral information or communications with a client from the court's investigation.

10. Several legal terms relate to a CPA's potential legal liability.
    a. Ordinary Negligence - absence of reasonable care (not a prudent man).
    b. Gross negligence - lack of even slight care, tantamount to reckless behavior.
    c. Constructive fraud - extreme or unusual negligence without intent to deceive or harm.
    d. Tort action for negligence - failure to fulfill a social or professional obligation, contractual or otherwise.
    e. Fraud - knowingly misstating facts with the intent to deceive.
    f. Breach of contract - failure to fulfill contract requirements.
    g. Third-party beneficiary - a third party without privity of contract known to and intended by the contracting parties to have certain rights under the contract.
    h. Common law - precedent law developed through the court system.
    i. Statutory law - codified law passed by congress and the states.
    j. Joint and several liability - holding a defendant fully responsible for losses regardless of the extent to which the losses were caused by another.
    k. Separate and proportionate liability - holding a defendant responsible only for that portion of a loss caused by the defendant's negligence.

OBJECTIVE 4:
DESCRIBE ACCOUNTANT's LIABILITY TO CLIENTS, THE RELATED DEFENSES, AND SOME SIGNIFICANT LEGAL CASES

11. Under common law clients may sue for breach of contract or for negligence under a tort action. Clients are likely to receive larger awards under tort actions than breach of contract actions.

12. The auditor would raise one or a combination of defenses against the client.
    a. Lack of duty (the CPA was not engaged to perform the service described in the claimant's assertions).
    b. Nonnegligent performance (the audit was performed according to GAAS).
    c. Contributory negligence (the client's actions contributed to the misstatement).
    d. Absence of causal connection (the damage sustained was caused by some factor other than the auditor's performance).

13. *Cenco Incorporated* v. *Seidman & Seidman* and the *1136 Tenants* v. *Max Rothenberg and Company* are two important cases involving clients.
    a. In *Cenco*, the CPA firm was not held responsible for not discovering fraud because of management's efforts to prevent the discovery.
    b. In *1136 Tenants*, the CPA firm was held responsible for losses resulting from management embezzlement because of negligence for not resolving the issue of "missing invoices."

OBJECTIVE 5:
DESCRIBE ACCOUNTANT's LIABILITY TO THIRD PARTIES UNDER COMMON LAW, RELATED DEFENSES, AND SEVERAL SIGNIFICANT LEGAL CASES

14. Lawsuits brought under common law by third parties are tort actions. In suing for negligence under common law, clients, third-party beneficiaries, and in some jurisdictions foreseen and foreseeable users (all third parties as an extreme) would attempt to show four conditions.
    a. A loss had been incurred.
    b. The financial statements were materially misleading.
    c. Reliance on the misleading financial statement caused the loss.
    d. The auditor was negligent in conducting the audit by not discovering that the financial statements were materially misleading.

15. The auditor would raise one or a combination of defenses against the client.
    a. Lack of duty (the CPA was not engaged to perform the service described in the claimant's assertions).
    b. Nonnegligent performance (the audit was performed according to GAAS).
    c. Absence of causal connection (the damage sustained was caused by some factor other than the auditor's performance).
    d. Lack of privity of contract (there is no contract which establishes a relationship between parties).

16. In suing under common law all other third parties (those not included in 14 above) would attempt to show the same four conditions except that they would attempt to show gross negligence or fraud. Judicial jurisdiction bears heavily on the success of the lack of privity defense.

17. Several significant cases involve the relationship between the CPA and third parties.
    a. In *Ultramares* the auditors were not held responsible to third parties for ordinary negligence.
    b. In *Rusch Factors* the auditors were held responsible for ordinary negligence to an actually foreseen and limited class of persons.
    c. In *Rosenblum* the auditors were held responsible for ordinary negligence to all persons who the auditor could reasonably foresee as recipients and users of the financial statements.

OBJECTIVE 6:
DESCRIBE ACCOUNTANT's CIVIL LIABILITY UNDER THE FEDERAL SECURITIES LAWS, RELATED DEFENSES, AND SEVERAL SIGNIFICANT LEGAL CASES

18. Plaintiffs suing under Section 11 of the Securities Act of 1933 would attempt to show three conditions.
    a. The third party purchased securities described in a registration statement with which the auditor is associated.
    b. A loss was sustained (the original purchase price less the value of the securities at the time of the suit).
    c. The financial statements included in the registration statement were materially misleading.

19. In reply to a suit under Section 11 of the Securities Act of 1933 the auditor would advance one or more defenses.
    a. The financial statements were not materially misleading up to the effective date of the registration statement.
    b. The loss was caused by some other factor (e.g., downturn in the economy).

c. The auditor exercised due diligence.

20. Under Rule 10b-5 of the Securities Exchange Act of 1934, a plaintiff would attempt to show four conditions.
    a. A loss had been sustained.
    b. The financial statements were materially misleading.
    c. Reliance on the misleading financial statement caused the loss.
    d. The auditor was grossly negligent, reckless, or fraudulent in conducting the audit thereby not discovering the materially misleading financial statements.

21. The auditor may bring one or more defenses to bear under the Securities Exchange Act of 1934.
    a. The audit was conducted with due diligence (nonnegligent performance).
    b. The auditor did not have a duty to third parties to conduct the audit free of ordinary negligence.
    c. There is an absence of a causal connection.

22. In addition to judgements against them from the courts, CPAs may also receive sanctions from the SEC in the form of mandatory participation in continuing-education programs and in either temporary or permanent suspension from doing audits of SEC clients or accepting new SEC clients. These decisions are based on one of two findings.
    a. The CPA was not qualified to perform the service.
    b. The CPA lacked character and/or integrity and conducted professional activities improperly or unethically.

23. *Escott et. al.* v. *Bar Chris Construction Corporation* and *Hochfelder* v. *Ernst & Erns*t are two important cases under statutory law.
    a. In *Bar Chris*, under the Securities Act of 1933, the auditors were held responsible to third parties for not performing with due diligence.
    b. In *Hochfelder*, under the 1934 Securities and Exchange Act, the auditors were not held responsible for losses suffered by investors because the auditors did not have knowledge of the fraudulent scheme or an intent to deceive.

OBJECTIVE 7:
DISCUSS THE IMPACT OF THE RACKETEER INFLUENCED AND CORRUPT ORGANIZATION ACT AND THE FOREIGN CORRUPT PRACTICES ACT ON ACCOUNTANT's LIABILITY

24. Under the Racketeer Influenced and Corrupt Organization (RICO) Act triple damages and recovery of legal fees can be awarded to an injured party who demonstrates that the defendant was engaged in a "pattern of racketeering activity."
    a. A pattern of activity is established when two acts are committed within a ten-year period.
    b. The Supreme Court has ruled that outside professionals such as auditors who don't help run a corrupt business aren't liable under the provisions of RICO.

25. The Foreign Corrupt Practices Act of 1977 prohibits bribing an official of a foreign country to influence, obtain, or retain business, and requires all SEC registrants under the 1934 Act to maintain an internal control structure to meet specified objectives. The impact of this law on CPAs is not yet known.

OBJECTIVE 8:
SPECIFY WHAT CONSTITUTES CRIMINAL LIABILITY FOR ACCOUNTANTS, AND DESCRIBE SEVERAL SIGNIFICANT LEGAL CASES.

26. CPAs may be found criminally liable under both state and federal laws when they have knowingly been involved with false financial statements. Furthermore, Generally Accepted Accounting Principles cannot be relied upon exclusively in deciding whether financial statements are fairly presented. In *United States* v. *Simon* the Supreme Court found auditors criminally liable for knowingly certifying financial statements that were misstated.

OBJECTIVE 9:
DESCRIBE WHAT THE PROFESSION AND THE INDIVIDUAL CPA CAN DO AND WHAT IS BEING DONE TO REDUCE THE THREAT OF LITIGATION

27. There are several steps the AICPA and the profession can take to reduce the legal liability of CPAs.
    a. Continue conducting research in auditing.
    b. Continue to make standards and rule setting responsive to the changing needs of society.
    c. Continue setting procedural requirements to upgrade the quality of professional practice.
    d. Expand peer review requirements.
    e. Continue to oppose unwarranted lawsuits.
    f. Educate users about the auditor's work, responsibilities, and reporting requirements.
    g. Continue to sanction members for improper conduct and performance.
    h. Lobby for changes in the law.
        1. Replace joint and several liability laws with proportionate liability.
        2. Require plaintiffs to pay defendant's legal fees in cases found to be without merit.
        3. Allow auditors to conduct business as limited liability organizations.

28. Individual practitioners can also take steps to reduce their legal liability.
    a. Deal only with clients possessing integrity.
    b. Hire qualified personnel and train and supervise them properly.
    c. Follow the standards of the profession.
    d. Maintain independence.
    e. Understand the client's business.
    f. Perform quality audits.
    g. Document the work properly.
    h. Obtain an engagement letter and a representation letter.
    i. Maintain confidential relations.
    j. Carry adequate insurance.
    k. Seek legal counsel when needed.

29. Several changes in professional practice were brought about by cases cited in the chapter.
    a. *1136 Tenants* v. *Max Rothenberg and Company.*
        1. Auditors are expected to use engagement letters for unaudited financial statement engagements.

2. Statements on Standards for Accounting and Review Services set forth guidelines for unaudited engagements of nonpublic companies.

b. *Escott Et Al.* v. *Bar Chris Construction Corporation.*
   1. SAS 1 (AU 560) requires greater emphasis on reviewing subsequent events.
   2. Most auditing firms now place greater importance on having the audit staff understand the nature of the client's business and industry.

c. *United States* v. *Simon* and other criminal proceedings.
   1. SAS 7 (AU 315) guides auditors in their investigation of the integrity of management as part of the information required for deciding on the acceptability of a client.
   2. SAS 1 (AU 220) requires CPA firms to implement policies to assure independence in fact and in appearance.
   3. SAS 6 (AU 335) gives guidance in auditing related party transactions.
   4. In auditing a consolidated group of companies, the primary auditor may elect to audit all the component companies, even if one or more have already been audited by another CPA, in order to maintain desirable professional standards.
   5. Fair presentation of the financial statements may not be decided entirely by GAAP. Auditors must consider the substance of the statements and all related facts in rendering an opinion.
   6. Criminal liability can extend to partners and staff.
   7. Good documentation may be as important in defending criminal charges as civil ones.
   8. It is unlikely that the potential benefits to an auditor of knowingly committing a wrongful act could ever justify the potential consequences.

SELF-ASSESSMENT

TRUE-FALSE STATEMENTS

Indicate whether each of the following statements is true or false.

____ 1. Traditionally, the exercise of due care has been owed to third-party nonclients only in limited circumstances under common law unless that party is a known and intended beneficiary of the auditor's work.

____ 2. Over recent years several factors have contributed to a broadening of the court's definition of a known and intended beneficiary.

____ 3. Audit risk is the possibility that the auditor will be unable to complete the engagement at the agreed-upon due date.

____ 4. An audit failure occurs when the audit is completed after the agreed-upon date.

____ 5. Determining when an auditor has exercised due care is relatively easy because of Generally Accepted Auditing Standards and the SASs.

____ 6. It is common for a business failure to occur without there being a related audit failure.

____ 7. The prudent man concept obligates the auditor to the client for losses resulting from the auditor's negligence, bad faith, or dishonesty but not for errors in judgment.

____ 8. Under the concept of liability for acts of others, an auditor is responsible for the work of employees, specialists, and other accounting firms employed to do part of the work and jointly responsible for civil actions against a partner.

____ 9. Only a few states do not adhere to the concept of lack of privileged communication between auditor and auditee.

____ 10. Common law is codified law written by an empowered panel of federal judges selected for the task because of many years of experience.

____ 11. Statutory law is law passed by the U. S. Congress and other governmental units.

____ 12. Claims by clients against auditors for breach of contract or for a tort action for negligence often occur because the auditor failed to detect a defalcation.

____ 13. The special status held by clients allowing them to sue the auditor for breach of contract usually results in larger awards from the court than if the client had sued under a tort action.

____ 14. An auditor involved in litigation against a client would normally argue in his/her defense that the auditor did not have a duty to perform the service in question, that the audit was performed with due professional care, and/or that the client contributed to the negligence.

____ 15. In recent years, the concept of foreseeable user has broadened the auditor's responsibility for due care to include those the auditor should have been able to anticipate would rely on the financial statements.

____ 16. A claimant under the Securities Act of 1933 bringing suit against the auditor of the registration statement offering securities which the claimant purchased and upon which a loss has been sustained would attempt to show that the financial statements in the registration statement were materially misleading.

____ 17. An action under the Securities Exchange Act of 1934 requires the claimant to demonstrate that the required conditions under the 1933 Act were met and that the purchaser relied on the financial statements.

____ 18. Because the SEC is not a duly empowered court it can not impose sanctions on auditors.

____ 19. The Foreign Corrupt Practices Act requires all U. S. domestic firms to maintain an internal control structure which will achieve objectives specified in the Act.

____ 20. When an auditor is knowingly involved with materially false financial statements there is potential for being found guilty of criminal action under both state and federal statutes.

____ 21. *The Fund of Funds Limited* v. *Arthur Andersen & Co.* case demonstrates that it is possible for an auditor to be sued and lose the case for not having divulged confidential information of another client.

____ 22. The SEC can impose a sanction on individual CPAs and their firms such as requiring them to complete a stipulated number of continuing professional education hours, not accepting new SEC clients for a period of time, and suspending them from completing audits for any SEC clients for a given period.

____ 23. The "deep-pocket" concept of liability requires an auditor to file a statement with the state board of accountancy vouching that adequate insurance is maintained or that assets are held to protect the interests of investors and creditors of clients.

COMPLETION STATEMENTS

Complete each of the following statements by filling in the blank space(s) with the appropriate word(s).

1. An auditor can reduce the potential for audit risk by accepting a new client or continuing with a client that possesses ____________.

2. The best evidence concerning the nature of the engagement agreed to by the client and the auditor is an __________ letter.

3. When faced with serious concerns over the legal ramification of a particular problem, an auditor should seek ____________ __________.

4. In the criminal case of the *United States* v. *Simon* the auditors were __________ involved in issuance of misleading financial statements.

5. The current consensus is that auditors are not required to examine a client's internal control _________ to the extent necessary to determine whether the internal control __________ of the Foreign Corrupt Practices Act are being met.

6. In deciding whether financial statements are presented fairly, the courts may look beyond the requirements of Generally Accepted Accounting Principles to the ___________ of the statements considering all relevant __________.

7. In the case of *Hochfelder* v. *Ernst & Ernst* the U. S. Supreme Court held that some _________ and _________ to deceive must exist for a CPA to be held liable under Rule 10b-5.

8. In bringing an action under the Securities Act of 1933 a plaintiff does not have to show ____________ on the materially misstated financial statements.

9. Defenses that an auditor might offer against an action under the Securities Act of 1933 are that the financial statements are not materially misleading, that an ____________ audit was performed, or that the losses sustained by the plaintiff did not ___________ because of the misleading financial statements.

10. Under common law actions against an auditor by a third party the auditor would offer the defense that the audit was performed without __________ or that the claimant does not have the right of _______ of contract.

11. Under a common law tort action, a client would attempt to show that a loss was sustained as a result of ___________ on materially misleading financial statements which the auditor failed to detect because of ________ in the performance of the audit.

12. In cases where a client has brought suit because the auditor has failed to detect fraud which caused the financial statements to be materially misleading the auditor might claim _______________ negligence on the part of the client.

MULTIPLE-CHOICE QUESTIONS

Indicate the best answer to the following statements/questions.

1. Which of the following is a provision of the Foreign Corrupt Practices Act?
   a. It is a criminal offense for an auditor to fail to detect and report a bribe paid by an American business entity to a foreign official for the purpose of obtaining business.
   b. The auditor's detection of illegal acts committed by officials of the auditor's publicly held client in conjunction with foreign officials should be reported to the Enforcement Division of the Securities and Exchange Commission.
   c. If the auditor of a publicly held company concludes that the effects on the financial statements of a bribe given to a foreign official are not susceptible of reasonable estimation, the auditor's report should be modified.
   d. Every publicly held company must devise, document, and maintain an internal control structure sufficient to provide reasonable assurances that internal control objectives are met.

2. Lark, CPA, entered into a signed contract with Bale Corp. to perform management advisory services for Bale. If Lark repudiates the contract prior to the date performance is due to begin, which of the following is not correct?
   a. Bale could successfully maintain an action for breach of contract prior to the date performance is due to begin.
   b. Bale can obtain a judgment for the monetary damages it incurred as a result of the repudiation.
   c. Bale could successfully maintain an action for breach of contract after the date performance was due to begin.
   d. Bale can obtain a judgment ordering Lark to perform.

3. Which of the following statements is correct with respect to the registration requirements of the Securities Exchange Act of 1934?
   a. They require issuers of non-exempt securities traded on a national securities exchange to register with the SEC.

b. They permit issuers who comply with the Securities Act of 1933 to avoid the registration requirements of the Securities Exchange Act of 1934.
c. They permit issuers who comply with those requirements to avoid state registration requirements.
d. They permit issuers who comply with those requirements to avoid the registration requirements of the Securities Act of 1933.

Starr Corp. approved a plan of merger with Silo Corp. One of the determining factors in approving the merger was the strong financial statements of Silo which were audited by Cox & Co., CPAs. Starr had engaged Cox to audit Silo's financial statements. While performing the audit, Cox failed to discover certain irregularities which have subsequently caused Starr to suffer substantial losses. In order for Cox to be liable under common law, Starr at a minimum must prove that Cox
a. Acted recklessly or with a lack of reasonable grounds for belief.
b. Knew of the irregularities.
c. Failed to exercise due care.
d. Was grossly negligent.

If a stockholder sues a CPA for common law fraud based on false statements contained in the financial statements audited by the CPA, which of the following, if present, would be the CPA's best defense?
a. The stockholder lacks privity to sue.
b. The false statements were immaterial.
c. The CPA did not financially benefit from the alleged fraud.
d. There was contributory negligence on the part of the client.

Which one of the following, if present, would support a finding of constructive fraud on the part of a CPA?
a. Privity of contract.
b. Intent to deceive.
c. Reckless disregard.
d. Ordinary negligence.

Burt, CPA, issued an unqualified opinion on the financial statement of Midwest Corp. These financial statements were included in Midwest's annual report and Form 10-K filed with the SEC. As a result of Burt's reckless disregard for GAAS, material misstatements in the financial statements were not detected. Subsequently, Davis purchased stock in Midwest in the secondary market without ever seeing Midwest's annual report or Form 10-K. Shortly thereafter, Midwest became insolvent and the price of the stock declined drastically. Davis sued Burt for damages based on Section 10(b) and Rule 10b-5 of the Securities Exchange Act of 1934. Burt's best defense is that
a. There has been no subsequent sale for which a loss can be computed.
b. Davis did not purchase the stock as part of an initial offering.
c. Davis did not rely on the financial statements or Form 10-K.
d. Davis was not in privity with Burt.

Gold, CPA, rendered an unqualified opinion on the 19x7 financial statements of Eastern Power Co. Egan purchased Eastern bonds in a public offering subject to the Securities Act of 1933. The registration statement filed with the SEC included the financial statements. Gold is being sued by Egan under Section 11 of the Securities

Act of 1933 for the misstatements contained in the financial statements. To prevail Egan must prove

	Scienter	Reliance
a.	No	No
b.	No	Yes
c.	Yes	No
d.	Yes	Yes

5

AUDIT RESPONSIBILITIES AND OBJECTIVES

CHAPTER OBJECTIVE

The purpose of this chapter is to discuss the objectives of an audit and the process of evidence accumulation.

CHAPTER SUMMARY

OBJECTIVE 1:
KNOW THE OBJECTIVE OF CONDUCTING AN AUDIT OF FINANCIAL STATEMENTS

1. Ordinarily, the objective of an audit is to enable the auditor to express an opinion whether the financial statements of an entity present fairly, in all material respects, its financial position, results of operations, and cash flows in accordance with GAAP. The auditor's opinion is based on evidence accumulated for that purpose.

2. An opinion that fair presentation has been achieved is based on the auditor's belief that a prudent user of the financial statements would not be mislead by the information reported. An alternative opinion would be expressed if the auditor believed otherwise or could not reach a conclusion.

OBJECTIVE 2:
DESCRIBE MANAGEMENT's RESPONSIBILITIES IN PREPARING FINANCIAL STATEMENTS

3. **Management is responsible** for the financial statements. Acknowledgment of this responsibility is often presented by management in the **Report of Management's Responsibility** which appears in the annual report. The report typically includes three elements.

a. Acknowledgement of responsibility for fair presentation of the financial statements.
b. A statement concerning the importance of the internal control structure.
c. A statement concerning the role of the audit committee.

OBJECTIVE 3: DESCRIBE THE AUDITOR's RESPONSIBILITIES TO VERIFY FINANCIAL STATEMENTS AND DISCOVER MATERIAL ERRORS, IRREGULARITIES, AND ILLEGAL ACTS

4. The **auditor is responsible** for designing and completing an audit with an attitude of professional skepticism in order to provide reasonable assurance of detecting material misstatements in the financial statements.

5. GAAS requires only that sample evidence be obtained. As a result, the concept of reasonable assurance indicates that the auditor cannot guarantee or insure that management's representations are absolutely correct. To do so would make audits not economically feasible.

6. An **irregularity** is a misappropriation of assets or an intentional misstatement of the financial statements. An **error** is an unintentional misstatement of the financial statements.

7. Irregularities may be the result of either **employee fraud** (theft of assets or defalcations), or **management fraud** (fraudulent financial reporting).

8. Professional standards state that the auditor is less responsible for detecting management and employee fraud than for detecting errors. The likelihood of material management and employee fraud should be evaluated as part of understanding the internal control structure. Audit procedures should be expanded if material errors or irregularities could result because controls appeared to be inadequate or procedures were not being followed.

9. The potential for **management fraud** is increased when management lacks integrity (shows evidence of dishonesty or recklessness) or faces undue pressures (lack of working capital, recurring losses, absence of internal audit staff, or unusual number of financial failures in the client's industry). Audit scope should be expanded if management fraud is suspected.

10. **Illegal acts** are violations of laws or government regulations other than irregularities.
    a. A **direct effect illegal act** such as violating a federal tax law has a direct financial effect on specific account balances in the financial statements.
    b. An **indirect effect illegal act** such as violating an Occupational Health and Safety Administration regulation affects the financial statements only if there is a fine or other financial sanction.

11. There are three levels of responsibility for finding and reporting illegal acts.
    a. When there is no reason to believe indirect effect illegal acts exist normal evidence gathering procedures are followed and the auditor remains alert to the possibility that an illegal act might exist.

b. When there is reason to believe that direct or indirect effect illegal acts may exist the auditor should inquire of the next level of management, consult with the client's legal counsel, and consider accumulating additional evidence.
c. When the auditor knows an illegal act has been committed the auditor should consider the effects on the financial statements, the effect of the act on his relationship with management, and communicate the finding to the client's audit committee.

12. The extent to which auditors would search for errors and irregularities is governed by the likelihood of material misstatement in the financial statements.

OBJECTIVE 4: DESCRIBE THE FINANCIAL-STATEMENT-CYCLES APPROACH TO SEGMENTING THE AUDIT

13. Audits are **segmented** into components to make them more manageable and to achieve a division of labor.

14. The **cycle approach** to segmenting the audit results in closely related types of transactions (classes of transactions) and account balances being grouped together. This is more efficient than grouping accounts by the order in which they appear in the trial balance or by financial statement category.

15. The cycle approach combines related transactions recorded in different journals with the general ledger accounts that result from those transactions. For example, sales (the sales journal), sales returns and allowances (the general journal), and cash receipts and sales discounts (the cash receipts journal) are combined with accounts receivable and the allowance for doubtful accounts to comprise the sales and collection cycle.

16. The cycles used by this book and their related journals are:

CYCLE	JOURNAL
a. Sales and collection	Sales journal
	Cash receipts journal
	General journal
b. Acquisition and payments	Purchases journal
	Cash disbursements journal
	General journal
c. Payroll and personnel	Payroll journal
	General journal
d. Inventory and warehousing	Purchases journal
	Sales journal
	General journal
e. Capital acquisition and	Purchases journal
repayment	Cash disbursements journal
	General journal

17. Capital acquisitions and repayments are treated separately from other acquisitions and repayments for two reasons.
    a. The transactions are related to financing rather than operations.
    b. The transactions, although few in number, are material and should be audited thoroughly.

18. The inventory and warehousing cycle is closely related to all other cycles.

OBJECTIVE 5: DESCRIBE WHY THE AUDITOR OBTAINS ASSURANCE BY AUDITING CLASSES OF TRANSACTIONS AND ENDING BALANCES IN ACCOUNTS

19. Because it is impractical for auditors to obtain complete assurance about the correctness of a class of transactions processed during the accounting period, auditors are unable to have complete assurance about the ending account balances created by the class of transactions by only auditing those transactions.

20. By combining the assurance gained by auditing transactions for the period which create an account balance and the assurance gained by performing audit tests of the ending account balances themselves, auditors are able to reach the level of assurance necessary to give an opinion.

21. Thus, some audit objectives are transaction-related audit objectives and other audit objectives are balance-related audit objectives.

OBJECTIVE 6: IDENTIFY THE FIVE CATEGORIES OF MANAGEMENT ASSERTIONS ABOUT FINANCIAL INFORMATION

22. **Management's assertions** result in general audit objectives which in turn produce specific objectives for the audit of a given cycle. There are five broad categories of assertions which apply both to classes of transactions and account balances.
    a. Assertions about **existence or occurrence**. Management asserts that the asset exists or the transaction actually occurred. In other words, items or events are not fictitious.
    b. Assertions about **completeness**. Management asserts that all transactions that should be recorded are included in determining an account balance. In other words, items or events have not been omitted.
    c. Assertions about **rights and obligations**. Management asserts that it owns or has the right to use assets and the liabilities shown are obligations of the company.
    d. Assertions about **valuation and allocation**. Management asserts that accounts are recorded on the basis required by GAAP; e.g., historical cost for depreciable property or net realizable value for trade accounts receivable.
    e. Assertions about **presentation and disclosure**. Management asserts that the classification, description, and disclosure of accounts and related information is in accordance with GAAP.

OBJECTIVE 7: IDENTIFY THE FIVE GENERAL TRANSACTION-RELATED AUDIT OBJECTIVES, EXPLAIN THEIR PURPOSE, AND RELATE THEM TO MANAGEMENT ASSERTIONS

23. **General transaction-related audit objectives** resulting from management's assertions provide a framework for accumulating sufficient competent evidence about those transactions.
    a. **Existence** - recorded transactions exist.

b. **Completeness** - existing transactions are recorded.
c. **Accuracy** - recorded transactions are stated at the correct amount.
d. **Classification** - transactions included in the client's journals are properly classified.
e. **Timing** - transactions are recorded on the correct dates.
f. **Posting and summarization** - recorded transactions are included in the masterfiles and are correctly summarized.

OBJECTIVE 8:
IDENTIFY THE NINE GENERAL BALANCE-RELATED AUDIT OBJECTIVES, EXPLAIN THEIR PURPOSE, AND RELATE THEM TO MANAGEMENT ASSERTIONS

24. **General balance-related audit objectives** resulting from management's assertions provide a framework for accumulating sufficient competent evidence about ending balances.
    a. **Existence** - amounts included actually exist.
    b. **Completeness** - existing amounts are included.
    c. **Rights and Obligations** - amounts included are owned or owed.
    d. **Accuracy** - amounts included are stated at the correct amounts.
    e. **Classification** - amounts included in the client's listing are properly classified.
    f. **Cutoff** - transactions near the balance sheet date are recorded in the proper period.
    g. **Detail tie-in** - details in the account balance agree with related master file amounts, foot to the total in the account balance, and agree with the total in the general ledger.
    h. **Realizable Value** - assets are included at the amounts estimated to be realized.
    i. **Presentation and Disclosure** - account balances and related disclosure requirements are properly presented on the financial statements.

OBJECTIVE 9:
DESCRIBE THE PROCESS BY WHICH AUDIT OBJECTIVES ARE MET, AND USE IT AS A BASIS FOR FURTHER STUDY

25. In order to meet these objectives the auditor accumulates sufficient competent evidence following a four step process.
    a. **Plan and design an audit approach** to obtain the required evidence at a minimum cost. This requires an understanding of the client's business and the industry in which it functions. In addition, the auditor must obtain an understanding of the internal control structure to determine whether an audit is possible and to assess control risk that errors and irregularities would not be prevented or detected.
    b. **Test controls and transactions** for those controls for which the auditor has assessed a reduced level of control risk.
    c. **Complete analytical procedures and tests of details of balances** by accumulating evidence to meet specific audit objectives for each account. When through understanding the internal control system, assessing control risk, testing controls, and performing analytical procedures the auditor obtains reasonable assurance that the financial statements are fairly presented, tests of details of balances necessary to validate financial statement information can be reduced.

d. **Complete the audit and issue an audit report** based on an overall conclusion about the fair presentation of the financial statements.

SELF-ASSESSMENT

TRUE-FALSE STATEMENTS

Indicate whether each of the following statements is true or false.

_ 1. The purpose of accumulating audit evidence is to form an opinion about the fair presentation of the financial statements.

_ 2. The auditor has a great deal of responsibility for notifying all types of users of the financial statements and the auditor's report when the statements are not fairly presented.

_ 3. The auditor is responsible for making the client adopt sound accounting policies and implementing an adequate internal control structure.

_ 4. Management is responsible for all representations made in the financial statements even if the auditor has drafted the report or offered suggestions to management to use in its preparation.

_ 5. Publicly traded companies are required to include a **Report of Management's Responsibility** in their annual reports.

_ 6. Auditors are required to give an opinion on the Report of Management's Responsibility.

_ 7. An audit must be designed to provide absolute assurance that material misstatements in the financial statements will be detected.

_ 8. When during the course of the engagement the auditor considers the possibility that management might be dishonest the auditor has exercised an attitude of professional skepticism.

_ 9. To change the scope of the audit from providing reasonable assurance that material errors and irregularities will be detected to one for which the auditor guarantees detection would require little incremental cost.

_ 10. Irregularities are unintentional misstatements of the financial statements.

_ 11. Because of the intended deception associated with irregularities it is considered more difficult for auditors to detect them than to detect errors.

_ 12. **Management fraud** is also known as fraudulent financial reporting while **employee fraud** is also known as theft of assets or defalcation.

__ 13. Collusion by several employees does not affect the likelihood that an auditor will detect a material employee fraud.

__ 14. Obtaining an understanding of the internal control structure and the resulting assessment of control risk ordinarily would not be used as a basis for expanding procedures to detect material irregularities.

__ 15. An illegal act is a violation of law or government regulation.

__ 16. Direct effect illegal acts and indirect effect illegal acts are not equally as serious from an audit viewpoint.

__ 17. Because auditors lack legal expertise the auditing profession provides no assurance that indirect effect illegal acts will be detected.

__ 18. Auditors have three levels of responsibility for detecting and reporting illegal acts.

__ 19. When the auditor believes a direct or indirect effect illegal act may exist he/she should withdraw from the engagement.

__ 20. When the auditor knows that a client has committed an illegal act a report should be filed with the Securities and Exchange Commission.

__ 21. Greater efficiency is obtained if the audit is divided into segments based on the major transaction cycles.

__ 22. The assertions made by management about financial statement balances are directly related to Generally Accepted Accounting Principles.

__ 23. Management's assertion about existence means that all recorded transactions actually occurred.

__ 24. Management's assertion about completeness means that both the debit and credit side of transactions were recorded.

__ 25. Accumulating evidence that transaction-related audit objectives for a specific transaction cycle were achieved during the audit period provides complete assurance that the ending balance of the related balance sheet account is fairly stated.

COMPLETION STATEMENTS

Complete each of the following statements by filling in the blank space(s) with the appropriate word(s).

1. In a court of law an auditor demonstrates that the audit was conducted in a _________ manner and the conclusions were ___________ by presenting sufficient competent evidence to support that position.

2. The auditor notifies users of financial statements about unfair presentation through the __________ _______________.

3. Professional literature clearly indicates that management is ____________ for using correct accounting principles, maintaining an adequate internal control _________, and making adequate disclosure in the financial statements.

4. Management of many companies report on the activities enumerated in the immediately preceding statement (completion statement number 3) in the Report of ___________ ____________.

5. An audit should be designed to provide _____________ _____________ of detecting material misstatements in the financial statements.

6. If auditors were insurers or guarantors that financial statements did not contain any material misstatements, audits would not be ____________ ______________.

7. Misstatements may be classified as either ___________ or ____________.

8. Irregularities may be classified as either ____________ fraud or ___________fraud.

9. Theft of assets or defalcation is also known as ___________ ____________.

10. Fraudulent financial reporting is also known as ___________ ___________.

11. Irregularities are more difficult to discover than similar sized errors because of the ___________ __________.

12. When factors indicate that the likelihood of management fraud is high, audit procedures should be ____________ to search for it.

13. If early in the audit when obtaining an understanding of the internal control structure and assessing control risk the auditor finds controls to prevent and detect employee fraud inadequate, the amount of other audit evidence should be ___________.

14. An illegal act is a ___________ of ___________ or government regulations, other than irregularities.

15. The auditor has ____________ levels of responsibility for detecting and reporting illegal acts.

16. Auditing standards clearly indicate that the auditor __________ (does, does not) provide any _____________ that indirect effect illegal acts will be detected.

MULTIPLE-CHOICE QUESTIONS

Indicate the best answer to the following statements/questions.

1. When unable to obtain sufficient competent evidential matter to determine whether certain client acts are illegal, the auditor would most likely issue
   a. An unqualified opinion with a separate explanatory paragraph.
   b. Either a qualified opinion or an adverse opinion.
   c. Either a disclaimer of opinion or a qualified opinion.
   d. Either an adverse opinion or a disclaimer of opinion.

2. Which of the following statements best describes the auditor's responsibility regarding the detection of material errors and irregularities?
   a. The auditor is responsible for the failure to detect material errors and irregularities only when such failure results from the nonapplication of Generally Accepted Accounting Principles.
   b. Based on the assessed risk that a material error or irregularity may cause the financial statements to contain a material misstatement, the audit should be designed to provide reasonable assurance that material errors and irregularities are detected.
   c. The auditor is responsible for the failure to detect material errors and irregularities only when the auditor fails to confirm receivables or observe inventories.
   d. Extended auditing procedures are required to detect unrecorded transactions even if there is **no** evidence that material errors and irregularities may exist.

3. Which of the following factors most likely affects the auditor's judgment about the quantity, type, and content of working papers?
   a. The assessed control risk.
   b. The content of the client's representation letter.
   c. The timing of substantive tests completed prior to the balance sheet date.
   d. The usefulness of the working papers as a reference source for the client.

4. During the annual audit of BCD Corp., a publicly held company, Smith, CPA, a continuing auditor, determined that illegal political contributions had been made during each of the past seven years, including the year under audit. Smith notified the board of directors of BCD Corp. of the illegal contributions, but they refused to take any action because the amounts involved were immaterial to the financial statements. Smith should reconsider the intended degree of reliance to place on the
   a. Management representation letter.
   b. Preliminary judgment about materiality levels.
   c. Letter of audit inquiry to the client's attorney.
   d. Prior years' audit programs.

6

AUDIT EVIDENCE

CHAPTER OBJECTIVE

This chapter expands on the concept of sufficient competent evidence by discussing the four major decisions related to gathering evidence and the seven types of evidence available to accumulate with particular emphasis on analytical procedures.

CHAPTER SUMMARY

OBJECTIVE 1:
EXPLAIN THE NATURE OF AUDIT EVIDENCE

1. Table 6-1 (page 166) in *Auditing: An Integrated Approach* differentiates the characteristics of evidence used for scientific, legal, and audit opinion purposes. Auditors accumulate enough relevant corroborative evidence of varying degrees of persuasiveness to render an opinion about the fairness of the financial statements with a high degree of confidence.

OBJECTIVE 2:
DESCRIBE THE FOUR AUDIT EVIDENCE DECISIONS THAT THE AUDITOR MUST MAKE TO CREATE AN AUDIT PROGRAM

2. In gathering evidence to satisfy a specific audit objective the auditor must make four decisions.
   a. What audit procedures should be used.
   b. What sample size is required.
   c. Which particular items should be selected from the population.
   d. When the procedures should be performed.

3. An **audit procedure** is a detailed instruction or step the auditor must complete. For example, the auditor might be required to foot the purchases journal for a selected period and trace all totals to their postings in the general ledger.

4. The **sample size** required for an audit may vary from one to the entire population. Deciding how many items to audit involves a consideration of various risk factors to be discussed in a later chapter.

5. The decision as to which **particular items to select** calls for the exercise of judgement. If the auditor wants to use the scientific method (statistical sampling), random selection is required. Otherwise, any method might be chosen; e.g., select every 100th item and all items over a certain dollar amount or only those items which the auditor believes are likely to have an error.

6. Deciding **when to perform audit procedures** depends on several factors among which are the audit objective(s) being satisfied, personnel limitations, and the desired completion date.

7. An **audit program** is a listing of audit procedures chosen by the auditor to perform. Usually, how large a sample size to select, which particular items to select, and when the procedures should be performed are also specified.

OBJECTIVE 3:
EXPLAIN THE THIRD STANDARD OF FIELD WORK AND DISCUSS ITS RELATIONSHIP TO THE FOUR DETERMINANTS OF THE PERSUASIVENESS OF EVIDENCE

8. The third standard of field work requires the auditor to accumulate sufficient competent evidence to support the opinion issued.

9. Time and cost constraints necessitate the use of sampling rather than a 100% audit. As a result, auditors are **persuaded** that their opinions are correct beyond a reasonable doubt but are never completely convinced that the opinion is correct. To be persuasive, evidence must be relevant, competent, sufficient, and timely (timely data which is not competent would not be persuasive, etc.).
    a. **Relevance** - The evidence must relate to the objective being tested (tracing recorded purchase invoices to receiving reports would not be relevant to testing whether all purchases made had been recorded).
    b. **Competence** refers to the degree to which evidence can be considered believable or worthy of trust and is effected by five characteristics.
        1. **Independence of provider** - External evidence is more reliable than internal evidence (a bank confirmation received directly from a bank would be considered more reliable than a workingpaper prepared by the client's controller).
        2. **Effectiveness of client's internal control structure** - Evidence from a strong internal control structure is more reliable than evidence from a weak one.
        3. **Auditor's direct knowledge** - The results of procedures which the auditor has completed (physical examination, observation, and computation) are more reliable than those obtained from some other person.
        4. **Qualifications of individuals providing the information** - Information from qualified individuals is more reliable than from those who are not (e.g.,

confirmations from business persons compared to confirmations received from the public at large).

5. **Degree of objectivity** - Objective evidence is more reliable than subjective evidence (e.g., results of a cash count vs. attorney's opinion regarding pending lawsuits).

c. The **sufficiency** of audit evidence is a quantity decision. A larger sample is more sufficient than a smaller one. A sample which is not representative of the population would be insufficient.

d. **Timeliness** relates both to the point in time at which the evidence is obtained and to the time period covered by the financial statements. The closer evidence on balance sheet accounts is accumulated to the balance sheet date the more relevant it is. Evidence on purchase invoices for the entire year is more relevant for drawing conclusions about transaction processing for the entire year than evidence on purchase invoices covering transactions for the first six months of the year.

10. The relationships between evidence decisions and persuasiveness are

EVIDENCE DECISIONS	PERSUASIVENESS QUALITIES
Audit procedures	Relevance
	Competence
Sample size and items selected	Sufficiency
Timing	Timeliness

OBJECTIVE 4:
IDENTIFY AND DESCRIBE THE SEVEN TYPES OF EVIDENCE USED IN AUDITING

11. Auditing standards, types of evidence, and audit procedures range from broad, general guidelines to specific instructions for gathering evidence. Textbook figure 6-1 (page 172) shows these relationships

12. There are seven **types of audit evidence:** physical examination, confirmation, documentation, observation, inquiries of the client, reperformance, and analytical procedures.

13. **Physical examination** occurs when the auditor has inspected or counted a tangible asset, an item with inherent value. This procedure can provide evidence concerning existence, quantity, description, and condition or quality but not ownership or proper valuation.

14. **Confirmation** occurs when an independent third party provides verification (usually written) of requested information directly to the auditor. Auditing standards require that accounts receivable be confirmed whenever it is practicable and reasonable. Reliability of confirmations depends upon the auditor maintaining control over their preparation, mailing, receipt, and follow-up.

15. **Documentation** occurs when the auditor examines the client's documents and records to verify client assertions. This is a widely used, generally low-cost form of evidence. Using documentation to support recorded amounts or transactions is also known as **vouching**.

    a. **Internal documents** originate and remain within the client's organization.

b. **External documents** may originate with the client or a third party, have at one time been under the control of the third party, and are currently under the control of the client.

16. **Observation** occurs when the auditor witnesses conditions or activities of interest. For example, the auditor might observe that the receptionist opens the daily mail and prepares a list of cash received therein.

17. **Inquiries of the client** may be oral or written and in most cases must be substantiated with additional evidence.

18. **Reperformance** involves rechecking or recalculating client computations (such as recalculating extension and footings on purchase invoices) and tracing the transfer of information within the books and records (such as comparing the month's total cash receipts amount to the related debit in the cash account).

19. **Analytical procedures** are required for all audits. They are performed by using comparisons and relationships to assess whether an account balance is reasonably stated. This procedure can be used in several situations.
    a. In some cases it is the only evidence needed.
    b. In some cases it is used in conjunction with other evidence, the amount of which has been reduced by the apparent reliability of the analytical procedure.
    c. In some cases it is a means of identifying those areas which need further investigation.

20. Textbook table 6-4 (page 177) shows the relationship between each type of evidence and objectivity (reliability) of this type of evidence.
    1. There is a direct relationship between reliability and the internal control structure.
    2. If the internal control structure is effective, physical examination and reperformance evidence are likely to be highly reliable.
    3. A specific type of evidence is seldom sufficient by itself to provide competent evidence to satisfy an audit objective.

21. Since several types of evidence can be used to satisfy an audit objective, evidence is selected to satisfy the specified audit objective at minimum cost.
    a. Usually the two most expensive types of evidence are physical examination and confirmation.
    b. Usually the three least expensive types of evidence are observation, inquiries of clients, and reperformance.
    c. Documentation and analytical procedures are moderately costly.

22. Textbook table 6-5 (page 178) demonstrates the exercise of the four evidence decisions (procedure, sample size, specific item, timing) for three different types of evidence which are used to satisfy a particular audit objective.

OBJECTIVE 5: DEFINE TERMS COMMONLY USED IN AUDIT PROCEDURES

23. A comparison of audit terms and types of evidence follows:

TERM	TYPE OF EVIDENCE
Examine - detailed study of a	Documentation

Procedure	Type of evidence
document or a record	
Scan - less detailed review of a document for unusual condition	Analytical procedures
Read - examination of written information	Documentation
Compute - calculation by auditor	Analytical procedures
Recompute - auditor verification of prior client calculation	Reperformance
Foot - addition of a column	Reperformance
Trace - verifying the transfer of information from one place to another	Documentation and/or reperformance
Compare - comparison of information in two different locations (unit prices to approved list of prices)	Documentation
Count - determine the number of physical items on hand	Physical examination
Observe - witness an activity	Observation
Inquire - oral or written evidence usually obtained from the client	Inquiries

OBJECTIVE 6:
DISCUSS THE PURPOSES OF ANALYTICAL PROCEDURES

24. In using analytical procedures an auditor evaluates financial information by comparing recorded amounts with expected amounts that are based on credible relationships between financial and other financial or nonfinancial data. An auditor is required to use these procedures both in the planning and the overall review stages of an audit.

25. Analytical procedures can be used for several purposes.
    a. To gain an understanding of the client's business by identifying important trends or events (performed during the planning phase).
    b. To assess the client's ability to continue as a going concern (performed during the planning and completion phases).
    c. To determine the presence of possible material misstatements in the financial statements by **directing attention** to those cases where unusual fluctuations or differences occur when they were not expected or vice versa (performed during the planning, testing, and completion phases).
    d. To reduce or eliminate certain detailed audit tests when the analytical procedures provide the required amount and quality of evidence at a lower cost (performed during planning and testing phases).

26. Analytical procedures may be used at three different stages of the audit.
    a. **Planning stage** - to help identify items needing special attention during the audit which affect the nature, timing, and extent of work to be performed.
    b. **Testing phase** - when possible, to reduce the less cost effective tests of balances through substitution (i.e., items c and d in statement 25, immediately above).
    c. **Overall review stage** - to take one final objective look and review for material misstatement (i.e., items b and c in statement 25, immediately above).

OBJECTIVE 7:
SELECT THE MOST APPROPRIATE ANALYTICAL PROCEDURE FROM AMONG THE FIVE MAJOR TYPES

27. There are five major types of analytical procedures.
    a. Client data may be compared to industry data. These comparisons enhance the auditor's understanding of the client's business and assist in assessing the likelihood of financial failure. Care should be exercised because the comparisons could be meaningless as a result of different accounting methods and inherent differences between the nature of the client's business and the industry.
    b. Current client data may be compared with similar data from prior periods.
        1. Current year balances may be compared with those of prior years.
        2. The detail entries of an account may be compared with similar detail from prior years.
        3. Current ratios and percentages may be compared with prior years.
    c. Client data may be compared with client determined expected results; e.g., client determined budgets (after determining that the budgets are realistic and that current financial information was not changed to conform to the budget).
    d. Client data may be compared to auditor determined expected results; e.g., a projection based on historical trends.
    e. Client data may be compared with expected results utilizing nonfinancial data; e.g., the auditor may estimate expected hotel revenues based on nonfinancial occupancy data after obtaining assurance that the nonfinancial data are accurate.

OBJECTIVE 8:
EXPLAIN THE BENEFITS OF USING STATISTICAL TECHNIQUES AND COMPUTER SOFTWARE FOR ANALYTICAL PROCEDURES

28. Efficiency and relevancy of analytical procedures can be enhanced by modern methods.
    a. Statistical techniques permit more sophisticated analysis and enhance objectivity.
    b. Computer software allows extensive, inexpensive computerized calculations and manipulation of trial balances and adjusting entries and expedites updating calculations after giving affect to adjusting entries.

COMMON FINANCIAL RATIOS

29. Common financial ratios which the auditor might use include the following:
    a. **Short-term debt-paying ability**.
        1. Current ratio.
        2. Quick ratio.
        3. Cash ratio.
    b. **Short-term liquidity**.
        1. Average accounts receivable turnover.
        2. Average days to collect accounts receivable.
        3. Average inventory turnover.
        4. Average days to sell inventory.
        5. Average days to convert inventory to cash.
    c. **Ability to meet long-term debt obligations and preferred dividends**.

1. Debt to equity ratio.
2. Tangible net assets to equity ratio.
3. Times interest earned.
4. Times interest and preferred dividends earned.

d. **Operating and performance ratios**.
   1. Efficiency ratio.
   2. Profit margin ratio.
   3. Profitability ratio.
   4. Return on total assets ratio.
   5. Return on common equity ratio.
   6. Leverage ratios for each source of capital except common stock.
   7. Book value per common share.

SELF-ASSESSMENT

TRUE-FALSE STATEMENTS

Indicate whether each of the following statements is true or false.

__ 1. There are four major decisions regarding evidence accumulation.

__ 2. An audit procedure is a detailed instruction for the collection of specific audit evidence.

__ 3. The number of items examined (the sample size) may vary between 20% and 80% of the population depending upon the auditor's judgment and the use of statistical sampling.

__ 4. Selection of specific items to examine (sample selection) can be based on judgment or on statistical techniques.

__ 5. The timing of audit procedures is restricted to the period from year-end through completion of the audit.

__ 6. The audit program lists the results of the four evidence decisions; i.e., what procedure to perform, how many items to examine, which items to examine, and when to perform the tests.

__ 7. Evidence is persuasive if there is enough of it.

__ 8. Relevance of audit evidence is determined by considering whether it satisfies a specific audit objective.

__ 9. Evidence obtained from external sources is not as competent as internal evidence because the integrity of the external party has not been investigated.

__ 10. For a very large population, evidence from a sample of 50 items is as sufficient as evidence from a sample of 200 items.

_ 11. Once the internal control structure has been evaluated and control risk assessed for the year being audited, representative cash disbursements transactions may be selected from either the last two or three months of the year or from throughout the year with equal persuasiveness.

_ 12. How persuasive evidence is depends upon its relevance, competence, sufficiency, and timeliness.

_ 13. There are four broad categories of audit evidence.

_ 14. Physical examination is the verification of the existence of an asset through inspection or count.

_ 15. An auditor would typically perform a physical examination of sales invoices at selected points during the audit.

_ 16. A confirmation involves the direct receipt by the auditor of a written statement from a third party verifying the accuracy of information.

_ 17. Professional standards indicate that the decision to confirm accounts receivable is strictly an evidence judgment decision to be exercised by the individual auditor.

_ 18. Documentation involves the examination of client documents and records to support information contained in the financial statements.

_ 19. The observation of an activity or condition would ordinarily be corroborated by other kinds of evidence.

_ 20. A written or oral response to an inquiry made of the client is generally regarded as fairly conclusive audit evidence, especially if the respondent is part of management.

_ 21. Rechecking the transfer of monthly totals in the cash receipts journal to applicable general ledger accounts is an example of reperformance evidence.

_ 22. Analytical procedures involve the use of comparisons and relationships to determine whether the balance of an account appears to be reasonably stated.

_ 23. Analytical procedures involve the comparison of recorded financial information with expected financial data which are based on plausible relationships between that data and other financial and/or nonfinancial data.

_ 24. Although in general use, analytical procedures are not required by professional standards.

_ 25. Analytical procedures are used early in an engagement because they help direct the auditor's attention to audit areas where material misstatements might exist.

_ 26. The most common statistical technique used in analytical procedures is regression analysis.

__ 27. What makes the use of analytical procedures effective is the follow-up work performed when unusual fluctuations are found.

COMPLETION STATEMENTS

Complete each of the following statements by filling in the blank space(s) with the appropriate word(s).

1. The four major audit evidence decisions are what audit ___________ to use, what sample size to select, what ____________ items to select, and when to perform the procedures.

2. Sample selection can be based on statistics or on ______________.

3. Clients normally want the audit to be completed within ____________ to ____________ months of year-end.

4. Audit evidence is ____________ if it is relevant, competent, _____________, and timely.

5. Most audit evidence is _____________ to more than one, but not all audit objectives.

6. Audit evidence must convince the auditor that the opinion given is correct beyond a _____________ _____________.

7. Evidence from ____________ providers is more reliable than evidence obtained __________.

8. The ___________ of evidence gathered is sufficient when the auditor believes that it is representative of the population from which it was taken.

9. For balance sheet accounts, evidence obtained near year-end is more ___________ to verifying ending balances than evidence gathered throughout the year while evidence obtained over the _____________ year is usually more persuasive for income statement accounts than evidence for transactions occurring near year-end.

10. Evidence that the receptionist opens the mail daily and lists the cash received would be evidence ordinarily obtained by _________________.

11. The seven broad categories of audit evidence are physical ______________, confirmation, _____________, observation, inquiries, reperformance, and ____________ procedures.

12. Analytical procedures are required for both audit and _____________ service engagements.

MULTIPLE-CHOICE QUESTIONS

Indicate the best answer to the following statements/questions.

1. Audit evidence can come in different forms with different degrees of persuasiveness. Which of the following is the least persuasive type of evidence?

a. Bank statement obtained from the client.
b. Computations made by the client.
c. Prenumbered client sales invoice.
d. Vendor's invoice.

2. Which of the following audit procedures would provide the least reliable evidence that the client has legal title to inventories?
   a. Confirmation of inventories at locations outside the client's facilities.
   b. Analytical procedures comparing inventory balances to purchasing and sales activities.
   c. Observation of physical inventory counts.
   d. Examination of paid vendors' invoices.

3. Which of the following statements is generally correct about the competence of evidential matter?
   a. The auditor's direct personal knowledge, obtained through observation and inspection, is more persuasive than information obtained indirectly from independent outside sources.
   b. To be competent, evidential matter must be either valid or relevant, but need <u>not</u> be both.
   c. Accounting data alone may be considered sufficient competent evidential matter to issue an unqualified opinion on financial statements.
   d. Competence of evidential matter refers to the amount of corroborative evidence to be obtained.

4. An abnormal fluctuation in gross profit that might suggest the need for extended audit procedures for sales and inventories would most likely be identified in the planning phase of the audit by the use of
   a. Tests of transactions and balances.
   b. Procedures to obtain an understanding of the internal control structure.
   c. Specialized audit programs.
   d. Analytical procedures.

5. An example of an analytical procedure is the comparison of
   a. Financial information with similar information regarding the industry in which the entity operates.
   b. Recorded amounts of major disbursements with appropriate invoices.
   c. Results of a statistical sample with the expected characteristics of the actual population.
   d. EDP generated data with similar data generated by a manual accounting system.

6. To help plan the nature, timing, and extent of substantive auditing procedures, preliminary analytical procedures should focus on
   a. Enhancing the auditor's understanding of the client's business and events that have occurred since the last audit date.
   b. Developing plausible relationships that corroborate anticipated results with a measurable amount of precision.
   c. Applying ratio analysis to externally generated data such as published industry statistics or price indices.
   d. Comparing recorded financial information to the results of other tests of transactions and balances.

7

AUDIT PLANNING AND DOCUMENTATION

CHAPTER OBJECTIVE

This chapter focuses on procedures auditors can use to satisfy the portion of the first Generally Accepted Auditing Standard of field work that requires the work to be adequately planned. Using working papers to document procedures completed and conclusions reached is also discussed.

CHAPTER SUMMARY

OBJECTIVE 1:
DISCUSS WHY ADEQUATE AUDIT PLANNING IS ESSENTIAL

1. Audit engagements should be properly planned in order to control audit costs, avoid misunderstandings with the client, and gather sufficient competent evidence to support the opinion given.

2. There are seven steps to planning an audit. Textbook figure 7-3 (page 215) summarizes steps a, b, c, and d. Steps e, f, and g are discussed in chapters 8, 9, and 10 respectively):
   a. Preplan the audit.
   b. Obtain background information about the client.
   c. Obtain information about the client's legal obligations.
   d. Perform preliminary analytical procedures.
   e. Set materiality and assess acceptable audit risk and inherent risk.
   f. Gain an understanding of the internal control structure and assess control risk.
   g. Develop an overall audit plan and audit program.

3. Much of early audit planning involves gathering information to assess audit risk and inherent risk.

a. Audit risk is the potential that a material misstatement in the financial statements will not be detected by audit procedures, resulting in the auditor issuing an unqualified opinion. Acceptable audit risk is the probability the auditor is willing to take that audit risk occurs.
b. Inherent risk is the likelihood, without considering the internal control structure, that a material misstatement will enter the accounting records thereby affecting the financial statements.

4. Auditors can take steps to reduce audit risk and mitigate inherent risks.
   a. Accumulate more evidence to increase audit assurance.
   b. Assign more experienced staff to portions of the audit.
   c. Conduct workpaper reviews more carefully and completely.

OBJECTIVE 2:
APPLY THE STEPS INVOLVED IN PREPLANNING THE AUDIT

5. Auditors should preplan the audit.
   a. Decide whether to establish or maintain an audit relationship with a new or continuing client.
   b. Identify the client's reasons for the audit.
   c. Obtain an engagement letter [review textbook figure 7-2 (page 209)].
   d. Select staff.

6. Sources of information about a prospective client's standing in the business community and its financial stability include local attorneys, bankers, and community business leaders.

7. Relations between the prospective client and the **predecessor CPA** should be evaluated. Communication between the successor CPA and the predecessor CPA which is required by *SAS 7 (AU 315)* may reveal disputes over accounting principles, audit procedures, and/or fees. Information about the prospective client's integrity may also be obtained. Permission from the potential client is required to initiate the contact as well as for the predecessor to respond to the inquiry.

8. The AICPA *Code of Professional Conduct* would prevent a return engagement for an auditor if there were a lawsuit by the client against the CPA or vice versa. Other factors an auditor might consider in deciding not to accept a return engagement are previous conflicts over audit scope, the type of opinion issued, fees, and knowledge that the client lacks basic integrity.

9. Identifying the client's **reasons for the audit** helps the auditor assess potential legal liability which could result from giving an erroneous opinion. Exposure is greater when clients are publicly traded, have extensive debt, or will be sold in the near future.

10. GAAS requires the auditor to have **adequate technical training** and to complete the work **proficiently**. Several factors must be considered in assigning staff to meet these objectives.
    a. Assign people familiar with the client's industry.
    b. Maintain some continuity of personnel.
    c. Provide for experts where needed in areas such as computer auditing and statistical sampling.

11. The purpose of an **engagement letter** is to minimize misunderstandings between the client and the CPA. It is a contract between the client and the CPA.
    a. It determines the nature of the engagement (e.g., audit vs. review, etc.).
    b. It influences the nature and timing of the tests (types of procedures and when they are to be performed as a result of client imposed restrictions and deadlines).
    c. It influences the total amount of time required (whether the client is to assist in obtaining documents and records and in the preparation of schedules).
    d. It enumerates the other services to be provided by the CPA.
    e. It stipulates how the fee is to be determined.

OBJECTIVE 3:
KNOW APPROPRIATE BACKGROUND INFORMATION TO OBTAIN ABOUT AN AUDIT CLIENT

12. Knowledge about the industry in which a client does business is required by *SAS 22 (AU 311)* and can be obtained in several ways.
    a. Discussions with the auditor of prior years.
    b. Conferring with client personnel.
    c. Reading AICPA industry audit guides, textbooks, and technical magazines.
    d. Participating in industry associations and training programs.

13. Knowledge about the client's business can be obtained in several ways.
    a. Gathering information about the organization structure, marketing and distribution practices, inventory valuation methods, etc.
    b. Touring the client's facilities.
    c. Reviewing the company's policies.
    d. Identifying related parties (required by *SAS 6 (AU 335)*.
    e. Perform preliminary analytical procedures.

14. *SAS 11 (AU 336)* provides guidance to the auditor who requires the services of a specialist (e.g., actuary, appraiser, or a geologist).

OBJECTIVE 4:
KNOW APPROPRIATE INFORMATION TO OBTAIN ABOUT AN AUDIT CLIENT's LEGAL OBLIGATIONS

15. Information about the client's legal obligations can be obtained by reading the corporate charter and bylaws, minutes to meetings of the board of directors and stockholders, and contracts. Performing this task early in the audit permits better interpretation of evidence gathered throughout the audit and determination of required disclosure in the financial statements.

OBJECTIVE 5:
DISCUSS THE NATURE AND PURPOSES OF PRELIMINARY ANALYTICAL PROCEDURES

16. Preliminary analytical procedures help the auditor to understand the client's business, assess whether the client is a going concern, identify possible misstatements, and reduce detailed tests of balances.

OBJECTIVE 6: EXPLAIN THE PURPOSES OF AUDIT WORKING PAPERS

17. Audit **working papers** are the auditor's evidence that the work was performed in accordance with GAAS and that the opinion was appropriate. The working papers serve other useful purposes.
    a. They serve as a **basis for planning the next audit** because they contain documentation of the understanding of the internal control structure, the time budget for each audit area, the audit program, and the results of the current year's audit.
    b. They are a **record of the evidence accumulated and the results of the tests.**
    c. They provide the **data for determining the proper type of audit report.**
    d. They provide a **basis for review by supervisors and partners** in evaluating whether sufficient competent evidence has been accumulated and as a basis for the preparation of tax returns and other reports.

OBJECTIVE 7: DISCUSS AND APPLY THE CONCEPTS BEHIND THE PREPARATION AND ORGANIZATION OF AUDIT WORKING PAPERS

18. Working papers are usually divided into two types: permanent files and current files.

19. The **permanent files** contain historical information and data which is of continuing interest from year to year.
    a. Copies of long-term contracts, obligations, articles of incorporation, and bylaws.
    b. Analyses of accounts with continuing importance such as long-term asset and liability accounts.
    c. Information supporting the understanding of the internal control structure such as flowcharts.
    d. Results of analytical procedures from previous audits.

20. The **current files** contain all the other working papers relating to the year being audited.
    a. The **audit program** lists the audit procedures to be performed, and shows the initials of the auditor completing the task and the date the work was done.
    b. **General information** includes audit planning memos, notes on discussions with the client, reviewer comments and copies or abstracts of minutes of board of directors' meetings, and contracts and/or agreements not in the permanent file.
    c. **Lead schedules** group detailed accounts from the general ledger. Each detailed account is supported by appropriate evidence appearing on audit schedules.
    d. The **working trial balance** is a listing of the summary accounts and their balances appearing on the various lead schedules. It is in the same format as the financial statements.
    e. **Adjusting and reclassifying entries** which individually or collectively have a material effect on the financial statements are presented to the client for approval.
    f. Several types of **Supporting schedules** comprise the largest portion of the working papers.
        1. An **analysis** shows the activity in an account from beginning balance to ending balance.
        2. A **trial balance** provides the details comprising a control account such as the accounts receivable trial balance.

3. A **reconciliation of amounts** explains the differences between two sources of the same information such as a bank reconciliation.
4. A **test of reasonableness** provides a gauge as to whether an account appears to be properly stated.
5. A **summary of procedures** is a memo prepared by the auditor which explains and summarizes the procedures performed.
6. An **examination of supporting documents** shows detailed tests performed such as cut-off tests or the examination of documents.
7. **Informational data** include such items as time budgets and information for special reports such as tax returns. These are not audit evidence.
8. **Outside evidence** from confirmations and other sources are filed and indexed to support data on other schedules.

21. Working papers have common characteristics.
    a. **Proper identification** includes the client's name, period covered, contents, preparer, date prepared, and index code.
    b. **Indexing and cross-referencing** not only aids in organization and filing but it also facilitates supervisor review efforts and audit coordination.
    c. **Indication of work performed** is done three ways: (1) written memorandum, (2) by initialing the audit program for each step completed, and (3) notations made directly on the schedules.
    d. **Sufficient information** should be contained on each working paper to allow it to fulfill its objective.
    e. **Conclusions reached** about segments of the audit should be plainly expressed.

22. The audit working papers are **owned** by the CPA and are retained for future reference.

23. Access to audit working papers should be carefully controlled because of sensitive information contained therein and to adhere to the rule of conduct regarding confidentiality of client information.

SELF-ASSESSMENT

TRUE-FALSE STATEMENTS

Indicate whether each of the following statements is true or false.

__ 1. Planning the audit facilitates obtaining appropriate audit evidence and managing audit costs, but it does not reduce misunderstandings with the client.

__ 2. In planning the type and amount of evidence to gather the auditor must balance the pressure to minimize legal liability with the pressure to minimize audit costs.

__ 3. Because of legal and professional responsibilities most accounting firms investigate prospective clients for financial stability, reputation in the community, and relations with the prior CPA.

_ 4. Communication with a prospective client's predecessor auditor is an optional procedure.

_ 5. The potential successor auditor is required to obtain permission to contact the predecessor auditor but the predecessor auditor is exempt by professional standards from being required to obtain permission to reply to the successor auditor's inquiries.

_ 6. If the prospective client denies permission for the proposed contact between the predecessor and potential successor auditor, the potential successor auditor should seriously consider not accepting the engagement.

_ 7. Consideration of a continuing client's integrity is unnecessary because the stringent standards required of the client to establish the first engagement provides reasonable assurance that the client's integrity remains acceptable.

_ 8. The client's reason(s) for having an audit are of no concern to the auditor because they have no effect on the required evidence decisions made throughout the audit.

_ 9. Maintaining some continuity of the personnel assigned to an engagement provides no real benefit to the firm.

_ 10. The purpose of the engagement letter is to minimize misunderstandings between the client and the auditor.

_ 11. The legal responsibility of the auditor to the client is affected by the engagement letter because it establishes what service is to be performed.

_ 12. It is not a common practice for the engagement letter to actually discuss the audit fee in terms of an estimated amount because the auditor cannot estimate the length of time required to complete the engagement.

_ 13. Although possessing a reasonable understanding of the client's industry is advisable it is not required by professional standards for an auditor to have this knowledge.

_ 14. One source of information about selected special industries is the series of industry audit guides published by the AICPA.

_ 15. If a member of management hires a relative to work for the company this qualifies as a related party situation which the auditor should identify early in the engagement.

_ 16. An auditor should read the minutes of directors' meetings early in the engagement because they may contain information which will help the auditor interpret evidence gathered throughout the engagement.

_ 17. Working papers may be classified as either permanent files or temporary files.

_ 18. Although the working papers contain information about the client the auditor owns the papers.

__ 19. It is not necessary for the preparer of working papers to affix his/her name to them unless there is more than one CPA firm involved.

__ 20. The term foot means to place the working paper in question at the bottom of the file of working papers.

__ 21. Tracing provides documentary and/or reperformance evidence.

__ 22. An auditor indicates the work performed in three ways: written memorandum, signing the audit program, and by notations made directly on the pertinent working papers.

__ 23. An abstract of the board minutes would be filed in the current files as part of informational data.

COMPLETION STATEMENTS

Complete each of the following statements by filling in the blank space(s) with the appropriate word(s).

1. Proper planning of an audit helps the auditor to meet evidence requirements, keep __________ reasonable, and avoid __________ with the client.

2. Before accepting a new client the auditor should determine the prospective client's __________ in the business community, financial __________ , and relations with its previous auditor.

3. If an auditor and a continuing client are involved in a __________ , the CPA cannot do the audit because independence would be impaired.

4. Generally, other things being equal, an auditor would accumulate more evidence for a client that was ___________held, had extensive ________, or was going to be sold.

5. In the interest of maintaining good interpersonal relations with the client, the assignment manager should try to achieve some __________ when selecting personnel to staff the engagement.

6. All personnel assigned to the engagement should have adequate __________ training and ________ for the level of audit responsibility to which they are assigned.

7. An engagement letter describes, among other things, the __________ of engagement, other __________ to be provided, and restrictions imposed by the client.

8. Engagement letter details regarding deadlines, the client's commitment to providing assistance in obtaining documents and preparing schedules, and the nature of the engagement help the auditor in __________ the tests and estimating the total __________ required to complete the work.

9. A related-party transaction is any transaction between the client and a __________ __________ such as a subsidiary, an officer of the company, or another company under common ownership.

10. Related parties may be identified by __________ of management, reviewing SEC __________, and identifying principal stockholders.

11. Touring the client's office and plant provides an opportunity to learn the physical __________ and to meet people who might be in a position to provide __________ to questions arising during the audit.

12. The corporate charter and bylaws, __________ to meetings, and contracts can provide useful information about a client's __________ obligations.

MULTIPLE-CHOICE QUESTIONS

Indicate the best answer to the following statements/questions.

1. After discovering that a related party transaction exists, the auditor should be aware that the
   a. Substance of the transaction could be significantly different from its form.
   b. Adequacy of disclosure of the transaction is secondary to its legal form.
   c. Transaction is assumed to be outside the ordinary course of business.
   d. Financial statements should recognize the legal form of the transaction rather than its substance.

2. Which of the following statements concerning the auditor's use of the work of a specialist is correct?
   a. If the specialist is related to the client, the auditor is not permitted to use the specialist's findings as corroborative evidence.
   b. The specialist may be identified in the auditor's report only when the auditor issues a qualified opinion.
   c. The specialist should have an understanding of the auditor's corroborative use of the specialist's findings.
   d. If the auditor believes that the determinations made by the specialist are unreasonable, only an adverse opinion may be issued.

3. A written understanding between the auditor and the client concerning the auditor's responsibility for the discovery of illegal acts is usually set forth in a(an)
   a. Client representation letter.
   b. Letter of audit inquiry.
   c. Management letter.
   d. Engagement letter.

4. A CPA firm's quality control procedures pertaining to the acceptance of a prospective audit client would most likely include
   a. Inquiry of management as to whether disagreements between the predecessor auditor and the prospective client were resolved satisfactorily.
   b. Consideration of whether sufficient competent evidential matter may be obtained to afford a reasonable basis for an opinion.

c. Inquiry of third parties, such as the prospective client's bankers and attorneys, about information regarding the prospective client and its management.
d. Consideration of whether the internal control structure is sufficiently effective to permit a reduction in the extent of required substantive tests.

5. An auditor is planning an audit engagement for a new client in a business that is unfamiliar to the auditor. Which of the following would be the most useful source of information for the auditor during the preliminary planning stage, when the auditor is trying to obtain a general understanding of audit problems that might be encountered?
   a. Client manuals of accounts and charts of accounts.
   b. AICPA Audit and Accounting Guides.
   c. Prior year working papers of the predecessor auditor.
   d. Latest annual and interim financial statements issued by the client.

6. Working papers that record the procedures used by the auditor to gather evidence should be
   a. Considered the primary support for the financial statements being examined.
   b. Viewed as the connecting link between the books of account and the financial statements.
   c. Designed to meet the circumstances of the particular engagement.
   d. Destroyed when the audited entity ceases to be a client.

7. The permanent file section of the working papers that is kept for each audit client most likely contains
   a. Review notes pertaining to questions and comments regarding the audit work performed.
   b. A schedule of time spent on the engagement by each individual auditor.
   c. Correspondence with the client's legal counsel concerning pending litigation.
   d. Narrative description of the client's internal control structure.

8. In general, which of the following statements is correct with respect to ownership, possession, or access to workpapers prepared by a CPA firm in connection with an audit?
   a. The workpapers may be obtained by third parties where they appear to be relevant to issues raised in litigation.
   b. The workpapers are subject to the privileged communication rule which, in a majority of jurisdictions, prevents third-party access to the workpapers.
   c. The workpapers are the property of the client after the client pays the fee.
   d. The workpapers must be retained by the CPA firm for a period of ten years.

8

MATERIALITY AND RISK

CHAPTER OBJECTIVE

This chapter discusses the assessment of materiality and various elements of risk and how these factors are incorporated into planning the audit.

CHAPTER SUMMARY

OBJECTIVE 1: APPLY THE CONCEPT OF MATERIALITY TO THE AUDIT

1. Although the auditor's report may express an unqualified opinion, the report also warns the reader that there is some risk that the financial statements may not be fairly stated by using the phrase "in our opinion" and by stating that an audit provides reasonable assurance.

2. By using the phrases "free of material misstatement" and "in all material respects" the report further states in both the scope and opinion paragraphs that only information of a material size was considered in deciding that the financial statements **present fairly**.

3. A **material item** is considered to be one which is large enough to possibly influence the judgement of a reasonable person who might use it. Thus, in order to know what a material amount is, the auditor must know who the financial statement users are likely to be.

4. If the client refuses to correct a material misstatement discovered by the auditor, the opinion given will be either qualified or adverse.

5. There are five steps to incorporating materiality into the audit plan.
   a. Set a preliminary judgment about materiality.
   b. Allocate the preliminary judgment about materiality to segments.

c. Estimate total error in a segment.
d. Estimate the combined error.
e. Compare the combined estimated error to the preliminary or revised judgment about materiality.

OBJECTIVE 2: MAKE A PRELIMINARY JUDGMENT ABOUT WHAT AMOUNTS TO CONSIDER MATERIAL

6. The **preliminary judgement about materiality** inversely affects the amount of evidence the auditor plans to accumulate. The larger the amount considered material, the less evidence the auditor must accumulate and vice versa. During the course of the audit, revisions of what constitutes a material amount may be required because one or more factors used to determine the preliminary judgement may change.

7. Several factors are considered in setting the preliminary judgement about materiality.
   a. **Materiality is a relative rather than an absolute concept**; e.g., a $1 million misstatement could be material to one company's financial statements but not to another's.
   b. **Bases are needed for evaluating materiality** and the amount appropriate for each must be determined; e.g., a misstatement of $100,000 may be material for items affecting net income before taxes but $250,000 might be considered material for items affecting current assets.
   c. **Qualitative factors also affect materiality**.
      1. Amounts involving irregularities are usually more important than unintentional errors of the same size.
      2. Misstatements which otherwise would be minor may become material if they affect a contractual obligation.
      3. Misstatements which otherwise would be minor may be judged material if they affect a trend.

8. Quantitative guidelines have not been established for materiality by the FASB and the AICPA because it is important for auditors to consider all of the complex factors which determine what a material amount is.

9. Materiality guidelines for combined total misstatements established by one CPA firm can be depicted pictorially. These ranges are applied to all bases except total assets where the judgement range is 3% to 6%.

0%error	< ——— >	5%error	< ——————— >	10%error
	Not material		exercise professional judgement	material

OBJECTIVE 3: ALLOCATE PRELIMINARY MATERIALITY TO SEGMENTS OF THE AUDIT DURING PLANNING

10. The audit effort is divided into segments and in order to know how much evidence to accumulate for each segment the auditor must **allocate the preliminary judgement about materiality to each segment.**

11. Most auditors allocate materiality to balance sheet segments rather than income statement segments for several reasons.

a. Misstatements in income statement accounts usually affect balance sheet accounts.
b. There are fewer balance sheet accounts than income statement accounts.
c. Most audit procedures are directed toward balance sheet accounts.

12. The amount of materiality allocated to a segment is referred to as **tolerable misstatement**

13. There are three difficulties encountered in performing the allocation.
    a. Certain accounts are expected to have more errors than others.
    b. Consideration must be given to both overstatements and understatements.
    c. The relative cost of audit procedures may affect the allocation and should be minimized.

14. Tolerable misstatement allocated to any one account should be less than total tolerable misstatement and the sum of the tolerable misstatement amounts allocated to all accounts may exceed total tolerable misstatement because all accounts are unlikely to be misstated by the full amount of tolerable misstatement and the net misstatement (overstatements less understatements) is likely to be less than overall materiality.

15. There are various rationales for allocating different sizes of tolerable misstatement to different accounts.
    a. A zero or small tolerable misstatement may be allocated because the account can be completely audited at low cost and no misstatements are expected.
    b. A large tolerable misstatement may be allocated because the account is large and requires extensive sampling to audit it.
    c. A large tolerable misstatement may be allocated because analytical procedures can be used to verify the account at extremely low cost.
    d. A small tolerable misstatement may be allocated because the account does not need to be audited (it has not changed from the prior year).
    e. A moderately large tolerable misstatement may be allocated because a relatively large number of errors are expected.

16. Because of the difficulties involved, many CPA firms have developed rigorous guidelines and sophisticated statistical methods for making the allocation.
    a. Predicting which accounts are likely to be in error is difficult.
    b. Predicting whether misstatements are likely to be overstatements or understatements is difficult.
    c. Estimating the relative cost of audit procedures to be applied is difficult.

OBJECTIVE 4:
USE MATERIALITY TO EVALUATE AUDIT FINDINGS

17. The combined errors of all accounts should not exceed overall estimated materiality.

18. To illustrate how an auditor might evaluate evidence obtained in auditing current asset accounts assume that the estimated total error (direct projection plus sampling error) in cash is $1,000, in accounts receivable is $10,000, and in inventory is $49,000. Thus, the combined estimate of error for current assets is $60,000. Also, assume that allocated tolerable misstatement for these accounts established before auditing them is $70,000. The auditor would accept these accounts as being fairly

stated because the combined estimate of error is less than or equal to the allocated tolerable misstatement for these accounts.

19. Had the results in 18 above been the reverse (i.e., the combined errors exceeded the tolerable error), the auditor would have chosen one of three courses of action.
    a. Audit procedures would be extended on the belief that the indicated overstatement is incorrect.
    b. The client would be required to make an adjustment for the estimated misstatement.
    c. A qualified or adverse opinion would be issued.

OBJECTIVE 5:
DEFINE RISK IN AUDITING

20. Because there is always uncertainty whether the evidence gathered is competent, the client's internal control structure is effective, and/or the financial statements are fairly stated after completing the audit, auditors must incorporate these risks into planning the engagement.

21. Textbook figure 8-5 (page 348) shows that differences in the size and frequency of expected misstatements among transactions cycles affect the planned amount of evidence to be accumulated for each cycle.

OBJECTIVE 6:
DESCRIBE THE AUDIT RISK MODEL AND ITS COMPONENTS

22. The primary form of the **audit risk model** is AAR = IR X CR X PDR
    where **AAR** = acceptable audit risk
    IR = inherent risk
    CR = control risk
    PDR = planned detection risk.

23. Assuming that judgement has been exercised concerning the first three elements, the equation can be rearranged into a planning form to determine what detection risk is acceptable and therefore how much evidence must be accumulated.

    PDR = AAR/(IR X CR)

24. **Planned Detection risk** (PDR) is the risk the auditor is willing to take that a material misstatement exceeding a tolerable amount has not been detected by the audit process. It is dependent on the other three factors in the model. Planned detection risk and the amount of audit evidence required are inversely related; i.e., more risk, less evidence and less risk, more evidence.

25. **Inherent risk** (IR) is the likelihood, without considering the internal control structure, that a material misstatement will enter the accounting records thereby affecting the financial statements. Inherent risk and planned detection risk are inversely related.

26. **Control risk** (CR) is the auditor's assessment of the internal control structure's effectiveness in preventing or detecting a material misstatement from occurring in the financial statements. Assessing control risk at less than 100% requires that control

procedures be tested for their effectiveness. Control risk and planned detection risk are inversely related.

27. **Audit risk** is the potential that a material misstatement in the financial statements will not be detected by the audit, resulting in the auditor issuing an unqualified opinion.

28. **Acceptable audit risk** is the risk the auditor is willing to assume that a material misstatement of the financial statements remains undetected and not reported by the auditor. Theoretically, risk can fall anywhere in the range given below but as a practical matter it is always greater than zero.

	Levels of Possible Auditor Assurance	
Certainty		Complete Uncertainty
0% risk	<——————————————————————>	100% risk

29. There is a direct relationship between acceptable audit risk and planned detection risk and an inverse relationship between acceptable audit risk and planned evidence; e.g., if acceptable audit risk decreases, planned detection risk also decreases and required sample size (amount of evidence) increases.

OBJECTIVE 7:
CONSIDER THE IMPACT OF BUSINESS RISK ON ACCEPTABLE AUDIT RISK

30. Auditors also face **business risk**. Minimizing audit risk will help to minimize business risk. However, auditors can suffer losses from lawsuits arising from client business failures even though the audit report was correct. There are several factors that may influence an auditor to establish a lower level of acceptable audit risk for a specific client.
    a. **The degree to which external users rely on the statements** (consider client size, distribution of ownership, and nature and amount of liabilities).
    b. **The likelihood that a client will have financial difficulties after the audit report is issued** makes having to defend the audit as a result of the phenomena of deep-pocket liability more likely (consider liquidity position, profits (losses) in previous years, method of financing growth, nature of the client's operations, and competence of management).
    c. **The auditor's evaluation of management's integrity** (consider criminal convictions of key management; disagreements with previous auditors, the IRS, or the SEC; frequent turnover of key financial and internal audit personnel; and ongoing conflict with labor unions).

31. Establishing acceptable audit risk is a very subjective process and may be modified as additional information about the client is gathered during the course of the audit.

OBJECTIVE 8:
CONSIDER THE IMPACT OF SEVERAL FACTORS ON THE ASSESSMENT OF INHERENT RISK

32. An auditor should consider several factors in evaluating inherent risk.
    a. The nature of the client's business.
    b. The integrity of management.
    c. Results of previous audits.
    d. Initial versus repeat engagement.

e. Related parties.
f. Nonroutine transactions.
g. Judgement required to correctly record transactions.
h. Susceptibility to defalcation.
i. Makeup of the population.

33. The auditor cannot control inherent risk but can control for it in the audit risk model. Inherent risk is directly related to the amount of evidence required and indirectly related to planned detection risk. It generally is set well above 50% and at 100% if significant errors are reasonably expected.

OBJECTIVE 9: DISCUSS THE RELATIONSHIPS AMONG THE COMPONENTS OF RISK

34. Review textbook figure 8-6 (page 359) to study the factors that determine each risk and the effect each risk has on planned detection risk and planned audit evidence.
    a. As acceptable audit risk increases (↑), planned detection risk increases (↑) and planned evidence decreases (↓).
    b. As Inherent risk increases (↑), planned detection risk decreases (↓) and planned evidence increases (↑).
    c. As control risk increases (↑), planned detection risk decreases (↓) and planned evidence increases (↑).

OBJECTIVE 10: DISCUSS RISK FOR SEGMENTS AND MEASUREMENT DIFFICULTIES

35. Inherent risk and control risk are set for each segment of the audit because the factors influencing inherent risk and the controls in effect may vary from transaction cycle to transaction cycle. Acceptable audit risk is ordinarily set for the audit as a whole and is applied at the same amount for each segment.

36. The audit risk model has limitations.
    a. Acceptable audit risk, inherent risk, and control risk are subjectively determined so CPAs often express probabilities in general terms such as high, medium, and low.
    b. The model is a planning model rather than a means of evaluating results. If upon testing the internal control structure, the inherent and control risk elements prove to be misspecified such that actual risk exceeds a tolerable amount, the model should be discarded and sufficient detection procedures performed to provide a high degree of assurance that existing errors have been identified.

37. The relationship of various risk factors to evidence is shown below

SITUATION	ACCEPTABLE AUDIT RISK	INHERENT RISK	CONTROL RISK	PLANNED DETECTION RISK	AMOUNT OF EVIDENCE REQUIRED
1	high	low	low	high	low
2	low	low	low	medium	medium
3	low	high	high	low	high
4	medium	medium	medium	medium	medium
5	high	low	medium	medium	medium

OBJECTIVE 11: DISCUSS HOW MATERIALITY AND RISK ARE RELATED AND INTEGRATED INTO THE AUDIT PROCESS

38. Risk is an expression of uncertainty while materiality is a measure of size. Audit judgments about fair presentation require consideration of both factors.

39. Planned evidence is determined by planned detection risk (the planning version of the audit risk model) and tolerable misstatement. Review textbook figure 8-8 (page 365) to study the relationship between tolerable misstatement, planned detection risk, and planned evidence. If one component is changed, one or both of the other components must also change.

$$\frac{1}{\text{(tolerable misstatement)(planned detection risk)}} \Rightarrow \Rightarrow \text{planned audit evidence}$$

40. Although results can be evaluated by rearranging the risk model as follows, the results are of limited use.

AcAR = IR x CR x AcDR.

where **AcAR** = achieved audit risk
IR = inherent risk
CR = control risk
AcDR = achieved detection risk.

41. When audit evidence indicates that the original assessment of control risk or inherent risk was understated or acceptable audit risk was overstated the auditor should follow a two step process.
    a. Revise the original assessment of the appropriate risk.
    b. Consider the effect of the revision without the use of the audit risk model.

SELF-ASSESSMENT

TRUE-FALSE STATEMENTS

Indicate whether each of the following statements is true or false.

_ 1. The audit report conveys to readers the idea that there is some risk that the audit may not have detected existing material misstatements in the financial statements.

_ 2. The audit report informs users that the auditor was expressly concerned with material misstatements that might exist in the client's financial statements.

_ 3. A misstatement in the financial statements would not be considered material in size unless it is certain to affect the judgment of all users of those statements.

_ 4. An auditor's judgment about what constitutes a material amount cannot be influenced by who will most likely use the financial statement.

_ 5. There are five closely related steps in applying materiality.

_ 6. The preliminary judgment about materiality establishes the dollar amount by which the financial statements can be misstated without affecting users' decisions.

_ 7. The smaller the amount of the preliminary judgment about materiality the smaller the amount of evidence required.

_ 8. The preliminary judgment about materiality can be revised if in the auditor's professional judgment the initial amount was too large or too small.

_ 9. Clearly, materiality is a relative concept because what may be a material amount for ABC Co. may not be a material amount for XYZ Co.

_ 10. In judging what constitutes a material amount, the auditor chooses the base which gives the lowest amount and applies this to all areas of the audit.

_ 11. Qualitative factors are not relevant in deciding whether an amount is material.

_ 12. The FASB and the AICPA do not provide specific quantitative guidelines to practitioners on the measurement of materiality.

_ 13. The preliminary judgment about materiality is allocated to each audit segment so that decisions can be made about evidence accumulation.

_ 14. The portion of materiality allocated to a given account balance is referred to as the intolerable misstatement.

_ 15. The allocation of materiality to specific accounts may be done in a manner that will assign as large a tolerable misstatement as possible to those accounts for which audit costs are greatest.

_ 16. The total estimated misstatement in a segment is usually based on sampling.

_ 17. The combined estimated misstatement is determined by adding up the misstatements found in auditing specific accounts such as cash and accounts receivable.

_ 18. If the combined estimated misstatement exceeds the preliminary (or revised) judgment of materiality, the financial statements are regarded as being fairly stated.

_ 19. Audit risk is the risk that the audit will take more time and cost more than the amount agreed to by the client in the engagement letter.

_ 20. The audit risk model is discussed in the professional literature in SAS 39 and SAS 47.

_ 21. In the audit risk model, AAR = IR x CR x PDR , acceptable audit risk (AAR) is established by professional standards.

__ 22. The auditor uses the planning form of the model as an aid to determining the quantity (sufficiency) of evidence to gather.

__ 23. Legal and other sanctions, competition, and professionalism contribute to different auditors setting comparable levels of desired audit risk for similar situations.

__ 24. Inherent risk is the likelihood that material errors will occur in the financial statements after giving consideration to control risk.

__ 25. The professional literature offers little guidance in assessing inherent risk so many auditors tend to set it at a conservative level.

__ 26. In order to assess control risk at a level below 100% the auditor must test the effectiveness of the control procedures to verify that they function as the auditor's understanding of the structure indicated they would.

__ 27. If control risk and inherent risk are set at their maximum amounts the auditor controls audit risk through planned detection risk.

__ 28. After all the required audit evidence has been gathered, the audit risk model can easily be used to assess the achieved audit risk.

__ 29. As acceptable audit risk increases (inherent risk and control risk are fixed) the amount of planned detection risk increases and the amount of audit evidence required decreases.

COMPLETION STATEMENTS

Complete each of the following statements by filling in the blank space(s) with the appropriate word(s).

1. The probabilistic nature of the auditor's report is expressed by the phrases "In our __________" and "__________ assurance."

2. The auditor's report indicates that the auditor was concerned with significant financial information with the phrases "in all __________ respects" and "free of __________ misstatement."

3. A misstatement is considered to be material if it is __________ that a user's decision(s) will be __________ by the misstatement.

4. The auditor's preliminary judgment about materiality is the __________ amount by which the financial statements could be misstated and __________ affect the decisions of users.

5. The preliminary judgment about materiality will __________ during the course of the audit as more is learned about the factors which influenced the original judgment.

6. Misstatements resulting from or related to things such as __________, contractual obligations, and trends have a __________ nature which may make the materiality threshold much lower than it otherwise would be.

7. Materiality guidelines within some CPA firms might be that misstatements from 0% to 5% are not material, those from 5% to 10% require the __________ of professional judgment, and those over 10% are __________.

8. In evaluating the results of gathering evidence the auditor computes the __________ estimated misstatement from all audit segments and compares it to the __________ judgment of materiality.

9. If combined misstatements exceed the amount considered material the auditor would either __________ audit procedures or issue a qualified or __________ opinion.

10. AAR = __________ x CR x __________.

11. If acceptable audit risk were set at 5% and the expectation of errors after considering the internal control structure is 25%, planned detection risk would be __________.

12. Different auditors might choose different levels of acceptable audit risk because different auditors have different preferences for risk __________.

13. Desired audit risk is influence strongly by the __________ to which the financial statements will be used by external parties and by the likelihood that the client will experience __________ problems after the audit report is issued.

MULTIPLE-CHOICE QUESTIONS

Indicate the best answer to the following statements/questions.

1. Before applying principal substantive tests to the details of asset and liability accounts at an interim date, the auditor should
   a. Assess the difficulty in controlling incremental audit risk.
   b. Investigate significant fluctuations that have occurred in the asset and liability accounts since the previous balance-sheet date.
   c. Select only those accounts which can effectively be sampled during year-end audit work.
   d. Consider the tests of controls that must be applied at the balance-sheet date to extend the audit conclusions reached at the interim date.

2. The risk that an auditor's procedures will lead to the conclusion that a material error does **not** exist in an account balance when, in fact, such error does exist is referred to as
   a. Audit risk.
   b. Inherent risk.
   c. Control risk.
   d. Detection risk.

3. Which of the following audit risk components may be assessed in nonquantitative terms?

	INHERENT RISK	CONTROL RISK	DETECTION RISK
a.	Yes	Yes	No
b.	Yes	No	Yes
c.	No	Yes	Yes
d.	Yes	Yes	Yes

4. In performing tests of controls, the auditor will normally find that
   a. The level of risk is directly proportionate to the rate of error.
   b. The rate of deviations in the sample exceeds the rate of error in the accounting records.
   c. The rate of error in the sample exceeds the rate of deviations.
   d. All unexamined items result in errors in the accounting records.

9

THE STUDY OF THE CLIENT'S INTERNAL CONTROL STRUCTURE AND ASSESSMENT OF CONTROL RISK

CHAPTER OBJECTIVE

GAAS require the auditor to understand a client's internal control structure well enough to plan the work and to select procedures appropriate to the objectives of the engagement. To gain knowledge of the internal control structure, an auditor studies its components: **the control environment, management's risk assessment, the accounting and communication system, control activities, and monitoring.** This chapter discusses these components, the objectives of internal control, and the procedures auditors may use to satisfy this GAAS.

CHAPTER SUMMARY

OBJECTIVE 1: DISCUSS THE NATURE OF INTERNAL CONTROL AND ITS IMPORTANCE TO BOTH MANAGEMENT AND THE AUDITOR

1. Other things being equal, the less control risk (stronger the internal control structure) there is, the more planned detection risk an auditor is willing to assume, and therefore, the smaller the amount of planned evidence required.

2. A system of internal control is created to help the organization meet its goals. In designing an internal control structure which produces benefits in excess of costs management attempts to address the following concerns.
   a. Reliability of financial reporting.
   b. Compliance with applicable laws and regulations.
   c. Efficiency and effectiveness of operations.

3. The aspect of internal control that auditors are primarily concerned with is the reliability of financial reporting. Controls over compliance with applicable laws and regulations and controls affecting internal management information are important to

external auditors to the extent these controls affect the reliability of data for external reporting purposes.

4. Because account balances (output) depend in large part on input and processing, auditors tend to emphasize transaction-related controls more than balance-related controls.

OBJECTIVE 2:
DESCRIBE THE THREE KEY CONCEPTS IN THE STUDY OF INTERNAL CONTROL

5. There are three assumptions (concepts) which underlie the study of an internal control structure and assessment of control risk.
   a. It is **management's responsibility** to establish and maintain the internal control structure.
   b. **Reasonable** but not absolute **assurance** should be provided because an ideal system cannot be justified on a cost/benefit basis.
   c. Even the ideal internal control structure has **inherent limitations** because of employee carelessness, lack of understanding, or management override. As a result, control risk is always positive.

6. Control concepts, objectives, and methodology of assessment are applicable to all accounting systems regardless of the extent of computerization. All accounting systems have the following four common functions and various controls in place to assure accurate and reliable financial information.
   a. Data preparation.
   b. Data entry.
   c. Transaction processing and master file updating.
   d. Document and report generation.

OBJECTIVE 3:
IDENTIFY THE FIVE COMPONENTS OF AN INTERNAL CONTROL STRUCTURE, AND DISCUSS THEIR CHARACTERISTICS

7. Each internal control structure has five components.
   a. The control environment.
   b. Management's risk assessment.
   c. Accounting information and communication system.
   d. Control activities.
   e. Monitoring.

8. The attitudes of top management, directors, and owners of an entity towards the internal control structure is reflected in **the control environment**; i.e., the actions, policies, and procedures listed below.
   a. Integrity and ethical values.
   b. Commitment to competence.
   c. Management's philosophy and operating style reflecting their attitude.
   d. The organizational structure defining lines of responsibility and authority.
   e. The board of directors' or audit committee's effectiveness in exercising its oversight responsibilities.
   f. Assignment of authority and responsibility (formal plans, memos, job descriptions, etc.)

g. Human resource policies and practices for hiring, evaluation, training, promotion and compensation of employees.

9. **Management's risk assessment** for financial reporting involves the identification and analysis of the risk that the financial statements may not be prepared in conformity with GAAP. Generally, the more management assesses and responds to this risk the less evidence the auditor must obtain.

10. **The accounting information and communication system** must be designed to identify, assemble, classify, analyze, record, and report transactions and maintain accountability in such a way as to fulfill each of the six transaction-related control objectives.

11. **Control activities** are those policies and procedures which together with the other four components of the internal control structure, help management meet its objectives for financial reporting. The procedures may be grouped into five categories.
    a. Adequate separation of duties.
        1. Custody of assets should be separated from accounting.
        2. Authorizing transactions should be separated from custody of related assets.
        3. Operational responsibility should be separated from record-keeping.
        4. Duties within EDP should be separated. Ideally, the systems analyst, programmer, computer operator, librarian, and data control group functions should be independent.
    b. Proper procedures for authorization of transactions.
        1. General authorization is given for transactions meeting established criteria (e.g., fixed price lists).
        2. Specific authorization is required for individual transactions that don't conform to the criteria (e.g., acquisition of capital assets in excess of some amount).
    c. Adequate documents and records.
        1. Prenumbered, simple to understand documents with multiple uses should be designed to encourage timely and correct preparation.
        2. A chart of accounts should be available which encourages correct classification of transactions.
        3. Systems manuals should be available which encourage consistent application of recording procedures.
        4. Companies with complex computer systems should use of a four part standards manual which contains the following parts.
            a. Systems requirements (broad objectives including input and output).
            b. Programming documentation (writing and testing of software).
            c. Program run instructions (operating schedules and steps for operators to follow).
            d. User instructions (identification of who receives output and procedures to follow when output is not correct).
    d. Physical control over assets and records includes the use of fireproof safes and limited access storerooms and also includes computerized systems access controls, and backup and recovery procedures.
    e. Independent checks on performance by internal verification should be used (many of these can be automated in a complex EDP system).

12. **Monitoring** activities involve assessing the effectiveness of the design and operation of the internal control structure on a regular basis. For many companies, an internal audit department independent of operating and accounting activities is essential to effective monitoring.

13. Although it is more difficult to achieve separation of duties in smaller entities, control procedures can be implemented to some extent. The internal control structure of a small company is strengthened when the owner-manager (or top operating person) takes a personal interest.

OBJECTIVE 4:
DESCRIBE THE REQUIREMENTS OF UNDERSTANDING THE INTERNAL CONTROL STRUCTURE AND ASSESSING CONTROL RISK

14. Review textbook figure 9-2 (page 285) to obtain an understanding of how the auditor uses information about the internal control structure to plan the audit. An auditor's understanding of the internal control structure must be sufficient to give consideration in the planning process to **auditability**, **potential material misstatements**, **detection risk**, and **design of tests**.

15. Each component (the control environment, management's risk assessment, the accounting and communication system, control activities, and monitoring) must be studied and understood by learning how it is designed to accomplish its purpose and whether it operates as described. The extent to which control activities are identified and studied varies considerably from client to client. For a small client where the limited number of personnel make control activities ineffective resulting in a high level of control risk, only a few or possibly no controls at all would be tested.

16. After gaining an understanding of controls sufficient to plan the audit, the auditor completes the following steps.
    a. Assess whether the financial statements are auditable.
    b. Determine the assessed risk for each transaction-related control objective that material misstatements which might occur will not be prevented or detected and corrected.
    c. Assess whether it is likely that additional evidence would support a lower assessed control risk.
    d. Decide what assessed control risk to use.

17. **Procedures to gain an understanding** are applied during the understanding phase at which time the auditor gathers evidence about the design and actual implementation of controls. **Tests of controls** are required to determine the effectiveness of transaction-related controls whenever assessed transaction-related control risk is below the maximum.

OBJECTIVE 5:
KNOW HOW TO OBTAIN AN UNDERSTANDING OF THE CLIENT's INTERNAL CONTROL STRUCTURE

18. An auditor may employ several procedures to determine the design of the structure and whether it has actually been placed in operation.
    a. For continuing clients, update and evaluate the understanding of the structure gained from previous experience.

b. Make inquiries of client personnel.
c. Review the client's policy and systems manuals.
d. Examine documents and records.
e. Observe activities and operations at the client's place of business.

19. To document an understanding of the internal control structure the auditor could use narratives, flowcharts, or internal control questionnaires or any combination of these devices.

20. The questionnaire consists of a series of questions which call for yes/no/not applicable responses with "no" indicating a potential weakness. The narrative (written) and the flowchart (symbolic diagram) describe four characteristics of the internal control structure:
    a. The origin of every document and record in the system.
    b. All processing that takes place.
    c. The disposition of every document and record in the system.
    d. An indication of those control procedures pertinent to assessing control risk.

21. Relative strengths and weaknesses of these tools may be classified as follows:

	STRENGTHS	WEAKNESSES
NARRATIVE	good for simple structure	difficult to describe details of complex system sufficiently
FLOWCHART	concise pictorial overview	more difficult to update than questionnaire
QUESTIONNAIRE	can be completed quickly relatively complete coverage	doesn't provide integrated overview

OBJECTIVE 6:
KNOW HOW TO ASSESS CONTROL RISK FOR EACH MAJOR TYPE OF TRANSACTION

22. A **control matrix** may be used to assess the transaction-related control risk for each detailed transaction-related audit objective by comparing them to specific operating **key controls**.

23. Identifying and evaluating weaknesses (absence of adequate controls) involves several steps.
    a. Identify existing controls.
    b. Identify the absence of key controls.
    c. Determine potential material errors that could result.
    d. Consider whether compensating controls exist.

24. Professional standards require that any significant deficiencies (**reportable conditions**) be reported to the audit committee or, if one doesn't exist, to the person responsible for the internal control structure such as the owner-manager or the board of directors. Communicating less important deficiencies and suggestions for improving operating performance in a management letter is optional.

OBJECTIVE 7:
UNDERSTAND THE PROCESS OF DESIGNING AND PERFORMING TESTS OF CONTROLS, AS A BASIS FOR FURTHER STUDY

25. An auditor would complete the following steps to test whether controls have been operating throughout the audit period.
    a. Make inquiries of appropriate client personnel.
    b. Examine documents, records and reports.
    c. Observe control-related activities during the client's operations.
    d. Reperform the client's control procedures.

26. The lower the assessed control risk desired by the auditor the more extensive the tests of controls must be in terms of the quantity of controls tested and the depth of testing for each control. Key controls of prior periods which are still in effect may be relied on to reduce the extent of current procedures. If changes occurred in controls during a period of the year not tested by the auditor, the nature and extent of those changes would have to be determined.

27. Procedures to obtain an understanding are usually performed at one point in the audit period on one or a few transactions for all identified policies and procedures which constitute the structure. Tests of controls are applied over all or most of the audit period only to key controls where control risk is assessed below the maximum.

28. If at the outset the auditor anticipates assessing control risk below the maximum, efficiency can be achieved by performing procedures to gain an understanding and to test controls (except for reperformance) simultaneously.

APPENDIX A: ILLUSTRATIVE INTERNAL VERIFICATION PROCEDURES

29. There are many internal verification procedures which help prevent or detect errors occurring in the several phases (input, processing, output) of an EDP application.
    a. **Preprocessing authorization** - input documents are approved.
    b. **Preprocessing review** - A user department or accounting reviews documents for attributes such as completeness and correctness and initials route slip.
    c. **Batching** - documents are processed in discrete groups with the use of batch numbers, a transmittal control form, a route slip, and control totals. Control totals help to assure that no data is lost and may use one or more of the following: a **record count**, a **financial control total**, or a **hash total**.
    d. **Conversion verification** includes **key verification** in which a second data entry verifies the initial data entry, **check digits** which mathematically verify the accuracy of an identification number, **logic tests** in which the program tests for validity and format, and **control total balancing** or batching.
    e. **Input security controls** include the use of passwords, logs of activity, security codes within terminals, and physical restriction of equipment to authorized personnel.
    f. **Correct file controls** which involve the use of external labels readable by the human eye and internal labels readable by the computer are used to verify that the correct file is being used.
    g. **Programmed controls** permit 100% verification by the computer of data validity, completeness, reasonableness or limit, and matching to another field.
    h. **Postprocessing review** requires that output be compared to input.
    i. **Master file controls** involve printing out the master file for review of its contents.
    j. **Periodic internal audit** involves ongoing review of application controls.

SELF-ASSESSMENT

TRUE-FALSE STATEMENTS

Indicate whether each of the following statements is true or false.

__ 1. Control risk has a direct effect on achieving acceptable audit risk.

__ 2. The internal control structure is composed of a set of policies and procedures designed to give reasonable assurance that desired objectives are being achieved.

__ 3. The costs to develop and implement controls is of little importance.

__ 4. Although management has three broad concerns or objectives in designing an effective internal control structure, the auditor is mainly concerned with those controls which provide reliable financial reports.

__ 5. Responsibility for the establishment of an entity's controls rests with the CPA.

__ 6. Internal control structures for which costs and related benefits designed were considered in their design can only be expected to give reasonable assurance that the financial statements are not misstated.

__ 7. All internal control structures have inherent limitations because technology prevents the design of a structure capable of meeting all desired objectives.

__ 8. Employee misunderstandings, carelessness, and management override may prevent an adequately designed internal control structure from being effective.

__ 9. The concepts of reasonable assurance and inherent limitations imply that control risk will always be zero or negative.

__ 10. There are six transaction-related internal control objectives, and each of those objectives must be applied to each major transaction cycle.

__ 11. The term "control environment" is synonymous with the term "internal control structure."

__ 12. The components of an internal control structure are the control environment, management's risk assessment, the accounting information and communication system, control activities, and monitoring.

__ 13. An auditor's perception of the control environment can be influenced significantly by how effectively the audit committee discharges its oversight responsibility for financial reporting and the internal control structure.

__ 14. If the accounts receivable clerk opens the mail and lists cash receipts, there has not been adequate separation of duties.

__ 15. If the same person authorizes the payment of a vendor's invoice and signs the check in payment of that invoice, there has been inadequate separation of custody of assets from accounting for those activities.

__ 16. In order to achieve maximum accuracy it is generally desirable to have one accounting employee record all aspects of a transaction from its origin to is disposition.

__ 17. The terms "authorization" and "approval" as they relate to the concept of proper procedures for authorization are interchangeable terms.

__ 18. The use of prenumbered documents significantly increases an entity's ability to meet the internal control objective of completeness.

__ 19. Analysis indicates that using physical safeguards over documents and records is not cost justified.

__ 20. Internal verification may be accomplished in some cases by separation of duties and in other cases by reperformance.

__ 21. The effectiveness of the internal control structure in small companies with limited personnel depends on the conscientious involvement of the top operating person.

__ 22. In fulfilling the requirement to obtain an understanding of the internal control structure the auditor is not concerned with whether the various policies and procedures have been placed in operation because that step belongs in the testing phase.

__ 23. Determining that the accounting system operates as described is accomplished by "walking-through" the various accounting department offices to observe them in operation.

__ 24. Control risk is the auditor's subjective probability assessment that the internal control structure will not prevent, detect, or correct material misstatements in the financial statements.

__ 25. If the auditor believes that assessed control risk is actually less than the level supported by the evidence gathered in obtaining an understanding of the structure, he/she may exercise professional judgment and reduce assessed control risk without performing additional procedures.

__ 26. Whenever an auditor wishes to reduce tests of details of balances because of a lower assessed control risk, the effectiveness of the policies and procedures supporting the lower assessed control risk must be verified with tests of controls.

__ 27. Relying on an understanding of the internal control structure obtained by completing audits of a client in the past is not permitted because systems and controls change rapidly.

__ 28. A critical segregation of duties within EDP is to separate responsibility for systems analysis and programming from that of the computer operation.

__ 29. The librarian's main function is to maintain a written record of who checked out a computer program or a data file so that the next person who wants to use it will know where to find it.

__ 30. A standards manual is a technical document written by the computer manufacturer for use by EDP personnel to maintain hardware and debug programs.

__ 31. An understanding of general controls is usually obtained before application controls are studied because the types of application controls necessary to assess control risk at a reduced level can be seriously affected by general controls.

__ 32. Batching occurs when transactions are collected, controlled, and processed in identifiable groups.

__ 33. A hash total is a computer count of the number of hash marks which appear on the input documents.

__ 34. An effective control for assuring that all transactions are processed is to compare the program generated record count with the record count noted on the route slip by the originating department.

__ 35. Key verification is an effective technique for detecting incorrect data on the input record.

__ 36. A check digit is a unique digit which is determined by and verifies an identification number to which it has been added or appended.

COMPLETION STATEMENTS

Complete each of the following statements by filling in the blank space(s) with the appropriate word(s).

1. The common types of flowcharts are __________ flowcharts, internal control flowcharts, and __________ flowcharts.

2. Tests of controls are performed only on those key controls for which the auditor__________ control risk below __________.

3. In obtaining an understanding of the internal control structure the auditor would examine _______ or ________ transaction(s) while ______ samples would be examined in performing tests of controls.

4. If tests of controls do not cover the __________ period, the nature and extent of any __________ made in the period not tested should be determined.

5. To perform tests of controls an auditor would make inquiries of client personnel; examine documents, records, and reports; __________ selected activities; and __________ selected internal verification activities.

6. A significant weakness in the internal control structure is known as a __________ condition and must be communicated to the __________ committee.

7. The purpose of a control matrix is to __________ control risk.

8. The control matrix matches __________ internal controls with transaction-related control __________ so the auditor can determine whether each objective is partially or fully satisfied.

9. In assessing control risk the auditor considers only __________ transaction-related controls rather than all existing controls in order to improve audit __________ .

10. The internal control questionnaire provides fairly __________ coverage of each audit area for a typical company and can be completed relatively __________ .

11. A disadvantage of the internal control questionnaire is that it does not provide an integrated, __________ view of the system.

12. It is common practice in obtaining an understanding of the internal control structure to use both a __________ and a __________.

13. The purpose of obtaining an understanding of the internal control structure is to __________ the audit and __________ the nature, timing, and extent of tests to be performed.

14. The components of the internal control structure are the control __________, management's risk assessment, the __________ information and communication system, control __________, and monitoring.

15. Responsibility for releasing programs and data files only to authorized personnel rests with the __________.

16. Instructions to the computer operator on how to manage the processing of a particular application are found in the __________ __________ instructions.

17. Separating the duties of the computer __________ and the __________ is critical from an internal control standpoint.

18. Reviewing documents for completeness and correctness prior to processing is usually performed by the __________ department or the EDP __________ __________.

19. A __________ __________ is a programmed instruction which determines whether the contents of a field are the correct type of data; e.g., all numeric, or all alphabetic.

20. A matching test is a type of __________ __________.

MULTIPLE-CHOICE QUESTIONS

Indicate the best answer to the following statements/questions.

1. When considering the internal control structure, an auditor should be aware of the concept of reasonable assurance, which recognizes that the
   a. Segregation of incompatible functions is necessary to ascertain that internal control is effective.
   b. Employment of competent personnel provides assurance that the objectives of internal control will be achieved.
   c. Establishment and maintenance of an internal control structure is an important responsibility of the management and **not** the auditor.
   d. Cost of internal control should **not** exceed the benefits expected to be derived from internal control.

2. Based on a study and evaluation completed at an interim date, the auditor concludes that no significant internal control structure weaknesses exist. The records and procedures would most likely be tested again at year-end if
   a. Tests of controls were **not** performed by the internal auditor during the remaining period.
   b. The internal control structure provides a basis for reliance in reducing the extent of substantive tests of details of balances.
   c. The auditor used nonstatistical sampling during the interim period tests of controls.
   d. Inquiries and observations lead the auditor to believe that conditions have changed.

3. The auditor's communication of internal control structure related matters, a reportable condition, noted in an audit is
   a. Required to enable the auditor to state that the audit has been conducted in accordance with Generally Accepted Auditing Standards.
   b. The principal reason for studying and evaluating the internal control structure.
   c. Incident to the auditor's objective of forming an opinion as to the fair presentation of the financial statements.
   d. Required to be documented in a written report to the board of directors or the board's audit committee.

4. In a study and evaluation of the internal control structure, the completion of a questionnaire is most closely associated with which of the following?
   a. Tests of controls.
   b. Tests of details of transactions.
   c. Preliminary tests of records.
   d. Procedures to gain an understanding .

5. What is the continuing auditor's obligation concerning the discovery at an interim date of a reportable condition in the internal control structure of a client if this same reportable condition had been communicated to the client during the prior year's audit?
   a. The auditor should communicate this condition to the client immediately because the discovery of such a reportable condition in the internal control structure is the purpose of a review of interim financial information.
   b. The auditor need **not** communicate this reportable condition to the client because it had already been communicated the prior year.

c. The auditor should communicate this reportable condition to the client following completion of the examination unless the auditor decides to communicate it to the client at the interim date.
d. The auditor should extend the audit procedures to investigate whether this reportable condition had any effect on the prior year's financial statements.

6. In general, material irregularities perpetrated by which of the following are **most** difficult to detect?
   a. Internal auditor.
   b. Key-punch operator.
   c. Cashier.
   d. Controller.

7. In the evaluation of the internal control structure, the auditor is basically concerned that the components of the internal control structure provide reasonable assurance that
   a. Management **cannot** override the internal control structure.
   b. Operational efficiency has been achieved in accordance with management plans.
   c. Errors have been prevented or detected.
   d. Control procedures have not been circumvented by collusion.

8. An auditor's purpose for performing tests of controls is to provide reasonable assurance that
   a. The controls on which the auditor plans to rely are being applied as perceived when obtaining an understanding of the internal control structure.
   b. The risk that the auditor may unknowingly fail to modify the opinion on the financial statements is minimized.
   c. Transactions are executed in accordance with management's authorization and access to assets is limited by a segregation of functions.
   d. Transactions are recorded as necessary to permit the preparation of the financial statements in conformity with Generally Accepted Accounting Principles.

9. An auditor is **least** likely to test controls for a key procedure that provides for
   a. Segregation of the functions of recording disbursements and reconciling the bank account.
   b. Comparison of receiving reports and vendors' invoices with purchase orders.
   c. Approval of the purchase and sale of marketable securities.
   d. Classification of revenue and expense transactions by product line.

10. The completeness of EDP-generated sales figures can be tested by comparing the number of items listed on the daily sales report with the number of items billed on the actual invoices. This process uses
    a. Check digits.
    b. Control totals.
    c. Validity tests.
    d. Process tracing data.

11. When EDP programs or files can be accessed from terminals, users should be required to enter a(an)
    a. Parity check.

b. Personal identification code.
c. Self-diagnosis test.
d. Echo check.

12. Errors in data processed in a batch computer system may not be detected immediately because
    a. Transaction trails in a batch system are available only for a limited period of time.
    b. There are time delays in processing transactions in a batch system.
    c. Errors in some transactions cause rejection of other transactions in the batch.
    d. Random errors are more likely in a batch system than in an on-line system.

10

OVERALL AUDIT PLAN AND AUDIT PROGRAM

CHAPTER OBJECTIVE

This chapter discusses the formulation of the audit plan and audit program using the five types of audit tests.

CHAPTER SUMMARY

OBJECTIVE 1: DESCRIBE THE FIVE TYPES OF AUDIT TESTS USED TO DETERMINE THE SUFFICIENCY AND COMPLETENESS OF AUDIT EVIDENCE

1. Audit procedures can be classified into one of five basic types of tests: **procedures to obtain an understanding of the internal control structure**, **tests of controls**, **substantive tests of transactions**, **analytical procedures**, and **substantive test of details of balances**
   a. The first two types of tests are used to assess control risk.
   b. The last three types of tests are used to reduce planned detection risk.

2. In developing an audit plan and audit program, the most important consideration is that planned detection risk equals acceptable audit risk divided by the product of inherent risk and control risk.
   PDR = AAR/(IR x CR).

3. An **understanding of the internal control structure** and assurance that it operates as understood is obtained by studying its design and gathering evidence through updating and evaluating previous experience with continuing clients, inquiry, reading policy and systems manuals, documentation, and observation.

4. **Tests of controls** are performed when the auditor wishes to assess control risk for any of the transaction-related audit objectives at less than the maximum. Because evidence is needed to support that position, inquiry, documentation, observation, and reperformance are applied to each key control upon which the auditor is to rely. To gain efficiency, inquiry and documentation tests used to test controls are often an extension of those same procedures performed during the understanding phase.

5. A **substantive** test searches for dollar misstatements (monetary errors) which affect the correctness of a financial statement balance. There are three types of substantive tests.
   a. Substantive tests of transactions.
   b. Analytical procedures.
   c. Tests of details of balances.

6. **Substantive tests of transactions** determine whether the six transaction-related audit objectives have been met for a given transaction cycle so that confidence in related general ledger totals is warranted.

7. When tests of controls such as documentation and reperformance are done, the same transaction can conveniently be tested for monetary misstatement because reperformance provides evidence about the correctness of monetary amounts as well as the functioning of controls.

8. **Analytical procedures** may be used to help the auditor decide the extent to which other audit procedures should be applied. If an analytical procedure indicates no fluctuations and this was the expected condition, other tests may be reduced.

9. **Tests of details of balances** are primarily concerned with the monetary correctness of balance sheet accounts although income statement accounts are sometimes involved. These tests are discussed in depth in later chapters.

OBJECTIVE 2:
DISCUSS THE RELATIVE COSTS OF EACH TYPE OF TEST, THE RELATIONSHIPS BETWEEN TYPES OF TESTS AND TYPES OF EVIDENCE, AND THE RELATIONSHIPS AMONG TYPES OF TESTS

10. A careful study of textbook table 10-1 (page 318) indicates which types of evidence are accumulated for each of the five types of tests.
    a. Procedures to obtain an understanding (documentation, observation, inquiry, and reperformance).
    b. Tests of controls (documentation, observation, inquiry, and reperformance).
    c. Substantive tests of transactions (documentation, inquiry, and reperformance).
    d. Analytical procedures (inquiry and analytical tests).
    e. Tests of details of balances (physical examination, confirmation, documentation, inquiry, and reperformance).

11. As a general rule, the cost of obtaining evidence generally increases in the order in which the following types of tests are listed.
    a. Analytical procedures.
    b. Procedures to obtain an understanding of the internal control structure and tests of controls.
    c. Substantive tests of transactions.

d. Tests of details of balances.

12. A typical audit test of controls is to verify the presence of initials indicating independent verification of a required procedure by client personnel (e.g., quantity, price, and extension on a sales invoice). The invoice may be correct even though the independent verification did not occur (the initials are absent) because the employee creating the invoice did the work correctly. The invoice may be incorrect even though the initials are present because the second employee did not actually perform the verification. Therefore, an exception discovered in tests of controls only indicates a likelihood that dollar values are affected. Conversely, no exceptions discovered in tests of controls indicates only a likelihood that dollar values are not affected. For these reasons, many auditors want to include some reperformance procedures.

13. Review textbook figure 10-4 (page 320) to understand the trade-off between tests of controls and substantive tests. The relative cost of tests of controls and substantive tests strongly influences an auditor's decision to assess control risk at the maximum, at the minimum the auditor believes tests of controls will support, or some level of risk in between the two.

OBJECTIVE 3:
UNDERSTAND THE MEANING OF EVIDENCE MIX AND HOW IT SHOULD BE VARIED IN DIFFERENT CIRCUMSTANCES

14. The extent to which each of the five types of audit tests is used in different audits and between different transaction cycles within a given audit varies from extensive to no testing at all. The auditor exercises judgment in selecting the combination which will provide sufficient competent evidence at the minimum cost.

15. Textbook table 10-2 (page 321) illustrates four scenarios where a difference in evidence mix for each audit case is explained. For example, in a large company with a sophisticated internal control structure an auditor might choose extensive procedures at the understanding phase, extensive tests of controls, a small amount of substantive tests of transactions, extensive analytical procedures, and a small amount of tests of details of balances.

OBJECTIVE 4:
KNOW THE METHODOLOGY FOR THE DESIGN OF AN AUDIT PROGRAM

16. Specific audit procedures are listed in an audit program. As stated earlier, for greater efficiency the procedures for gaining an understanding may be performed with tests of controls and substantive tests of transactions. Thus, audit programs may be thought of as being divided into three major segments.
    a. Tests of controls and substantive tests of transactions.
    b. Analytical procedures.
    c. Tests of details of balances.

17. An auditor completes four steps in the process of designing tests of controls and substantive tests of transactions.
    a. Perform procedures to understand the internal control structure.
        1. Workpapers should include a description of the structure.
        2. Workpapers should include a description of the procedures performed to obtain the understanding.

b. Assess control risk.
c. Evaluate the cost/benefit of testing controls.
d. Design the tests of controls and substantive test of transactions to meet transaction-related audit objectives.

18. When the assessed level of control risk is planned for less than 100%, tests of controls and substantive tests must be designed to satisfy all the transaction-related audit objectives. This is usually done in a four step approach .
    a. Express detailed transaction-related audit objectives in terms of the transactions of the cycle being examined.
    b. Identify a key control(s) that should reduce control risk for each detailed transaction-related audit objective.
    c. Develop procedures to test the effectiveness of the key controls to which a reduction in control risk is attributed.
    d. Where misstatements may occur because of a weakness in the controls for a detailed transaction-related audit objective, select substantive tests of transactions which will detect expected misstatements.

19. **Analytical procedures** must be used in the planning and overall evaluation stages of the audit. They may also be used in conjunction with tests of controls, substantive tests of transactions, and tests of details of balances.

20. Designing **tests of details of balances** to meet the balance-related audit objectives requires the exercise of judgment. An auditor would generally complete the following steps
    a. Set tolerable misstatement and acceptable audit risk and inherent risk for the account balance(s) in question (the greater inherent risk or the smaller tolerable misstatement the more tests of details of balances required).
    b. Assess control risk (the greater the risk the more tests of details of balances required).
    c. Design tests of controls, substantive tests of transactions, and analytical procedures and predict the results of applying those tests.
    d. Giving due consideration to the expected results in (c) design tests of details of balances for each account to satisfy appropriate balance-related audit objectives; i.e., determine the nature, timing, and extent of tests to be performed.

21. If the actual results of performing tests of controls, substantive tests of transactions, and analytical procedures is less than acceptable, the auditor will have to redesign substantive tests of details.

22. Audit planning activities are performed from the aggregate level to the disaggregate level.
    a. Overall audit (e.g., obtaining background information).
    b. Cycle (e.g., understanding the accounting system).
    c. Account (e.g., setting tolerable misstatement).
    d. Internal control objective (e.g., setting control risk).
    e. Audit objective (e.g., designing tests of details of balances).

23. A careful study of textbook table 10-3 (page 328) shows two common relationships found in an audit program for tests of details of balances. Each audit procedure often

satisfies more than one audit objective and each audit objective is usually tested by more than one audit procedure.

OBJECTIVE 5:
UNDERSTAND THE RELATIONSHIP OF TRANSACTION-RELATED AUDIT OBJECTIVES TO BALANCE-RELATED AUDIT OBJECTIVES

24. Transaction-related audit objectives and balance sheet audit objectives may be associated as follows:

TRANSACTION-RELATED AUDIT OBJECTIVE	BALANCE-RELATED AUDIT OBJECTIVE	NATURE OF RELATIONSHIP
EXISTENCE	EXISTENCE(or completeness)	DIRECT
COMPLETENESS	COMPLETENESS(or existence)	DIRECT
ACCURACY	ACCURACY	DIRECT
CLASSIFICATION	CLASSIFICATION	DIRECT
TIMING	CUTOFF	DIRECT
POSTING/SUMMARIZATION	DETAIL TIE-IN	DIRECT
	REALIZABLE VALUE	NONE
	RIGHTS/OBLIGATIONS	NONE
	PRESENTATION/DISCLOSURE	NONE

25. Even when the internal control structure meets all transaction-related audit objectives, the auditor relies on detailed tests of balances to meet the balance-related audit objectives of realizable value, rights and obligations, and presentation and disclosure.

OBJECTIVE 6:
INTEGRATE THE FOUR PHASES OF THE AUDIT PROCESS

26. Textbook figure 10-10 (page 331) summarizes the entire audit process. The following audit time table is typical for a client with a December 31 closing.
    (a) 8-31-x1 **PHASE I**: **Plan and design an audit approach** based on an understanding of the internal control structure and preliminary analytical procedures.
    (b) 9-30-x1 **PHASE II**: Perform tests of controls and substantive tests of transactions (obtain evidence) to support assessed level of control risk and monetary correctness of transactions.
    (c)10-31-x1 & forward **PHASE III**: Perform analytical procedures and **tests of details of balances** to determine the monetary correctness of financial statement ending balances and adequacy of footnotes.
    (d) 3-15-x2 **PHASE IV**: **Complete the audit** by reviewing for contingent liabilities and subsequent events, accumulating final evidence, evaluating the results, issuing the audit report which is dated as of the last date of field work, and communicating with the audit committee and management.

<u>SELF-ASSESSMENT</u>

TRUE-FALSE STATEMENTS

Indicate whether each of the following statements is true or false.

__ 1. In the planning form of the audit risk model (PDR = AAR/(IR x CR)) the term AAR stands for applied audit risk.

__ 2. During the process of obtaining an understanding of the internal control structure the auditor is concerned with how the system is designed as well as with whether it operates as designed.

__ 3. Previous experience with continuing clients cannot be used to help obtain the required understanding because there is every reason to believe that conditions which existed in the past have been changed.

__ 4. Tests of controls document the efficiency of the controls tested.

__ 5. Tests of controls are required whenever the auditor assesses control risk at a level less than the maximum.

__ 6. Audit efficiency is increased for those controls which the auditor will assess at a reduced level if procedures to obtain an understanding and procedures to test controls are combined and completed concurrently.

__ 7. The auditor is expected to perform tests of controls of all identified weaknesses for which assessed control risk is at a maximum.

__ 8. Substantive tests are those tests which are designed to identify monetary errors in the financial statements.

__ 9. To achieve proper segregation of duties auditors generally divide the audit work so that one auditor performs tests of controls in a given transaction cycle and another auditor performs substantive tests of transactions in that cycle.

__ 10. Analytical procedures are used primarily to help the auditor analyze the debit and credit activity in an account.

__ 11. Tests of details of balances are designed to provide evidence on the monetary correctness of an ending account balance.

__ 12. The extent of tests of details of balances depends on materiality, the assessed inherent risk, assessed control risk, the results of analytical procedures, and the acceptable audit risk.

__ 13. The type of audit test known as "analytical procedures" would require accumulation of significant amounts of "documentary" evidence.

__ 14. Tests of details of balances require less accumulation of the various types of evidence than any other type of test.

__ 15. Generally, analytical procedures are the most costly type of audit test which can be performed.

__ 16. Finding a deviation in a control procedure indicates the possibility of an error in the financial statements while an exception found by completing substantive tests of transactions is a financial statement error.

__ 17. The extent to which the five types of audit tests are used varies from audit to audit because materiality, inherent risk, control risk, and the results of analytical procedures will vary from client to client.

__ 18. In an audit where extensive procedures were followed to obtain an understanding of the internal control structure, to test controls, and to complete analytical procedures, tests of details of balances would also tend to be extensive.

__ 19. One or more aspects of the planned audit program may have to be revised if the assessed levels of inherent risk and/or control risk are modified.

__ 20. There are three phases to completing an audit: phase I is planning, phase II is testing, and phase III is summarizing or completing the audit.

__ 21. Two important procedures performed to complete the audit are to review for contingent liabilities and to begin making plans for next year's audit.

__ 22. The date of the auditor's report must coincide with the date of the client's financial statements.

__ 23. The financial statement assertions of rights and obligations and disclosure are primarily tested with substantive procedures.

COMPLETION STATEMENTS

Complete each of the following statements by filling in the blank space(s) with the appropriate word(s).

1. Phase I of an audit involves obtaining an understanding of the internal control structure and preparing an audit __________ and a specific audit __________ based on the assessed level of control risk.

2. Phase II of an audit involves performing tests of __________ and substantive tests of transactions.

3. Phase III of an audit involves performing __________ procedures and detailed tests of __________.

4. Phase IV of an audit requires the auditor to review for __________ liabilities and __________ events, evaluate the results, and issue the report.

5. The effectiveness of controls is tested both for __________ and for __________.

6. The separation of duties among billing, recording sales, and handling cash receipts would be tested by __________.

7. To test whether credit is approved before shipment occurs an auditor would examine documentation for __________ initials __________ the sale.

8. Confirming the ending bank account balance directly with the depository is an example of a test of __________ of __________.

9. Inquiry may be used as a form of evidence in __________ types of audit tests.

10. The steps in designing tests of details of balances are to __________ materiality and assess acceptable audit risk and inherent risk, assess control risk, design and __________ results of tests of controls and substantive tests of transactions and evaluate the results of analytical procedures.

11. Planned tests of details of balances must be adjusted if the __________ of tests of controls and substantive tests of transactions and analytical procedures are not at least as __________ as expected.

12. Obtaining direct confirmation from debtors of balances owed the client is evidence which helps satisfy the balance-related audit objective of __________.

13. Reviewing the accounts receivable trial balance for amounts due from related parties helps satisfy the balance-related audit objective of __________.

MULTIPLE-CHOICE QUESTIONS

Indicate the best answer to the following statements/questions.

1. After completing the procedures to obtain an understanding of the internal control structure, the auditor decides **not** to assess control risk at less than the maximum. Documentation may be limited to the auditor's
   a. Understanding of the internal control structure.
   b. Reasons for deciding **not** to test controls.
   c. Basis for concluding that errors and irregularities will be prevented.
   d. Completed internal control questionnaire.

2. After completing all tests of key controls, the auditor should review the results and consider whether
   a. The planned degree of reliance on the internal control structure is justified.
   b. The evidential matter obtained from the study of the internal control structure can provide a reasonable basis for an opinion.
   c. Further study of the internal control structure is likely to justify any restriction of tests of details of balances.
   d. Sufficient knowledge has been obtained about the entity's entire internal control structure.

3. After finishing the procedures to obtain an understanding of the internal control structure, the auditor should perform tests of controls on
   a. Those key controls that have a material effect upon the financial statement balances.
   b. A random sample of the key controls that were reviewed.
   c. Those key controls upon which the auditor wishes to base an assessed control risk at less than the maximum.
   d. Those key controls in which material weaknesses were identified.

4. An auditor uses the knowledge provided by the understanding of the internal control structure and the assessed level of control risk primarily to
   a. Determine whether procedures and records concerning the safeguarding of assets are reliable.
   b. Ascertain whether the opportunities to allow any person to both perpetrate and conceal irregularities are minimized.
   c. Modify the initial assessments of inherent risk and preliminary judgments about materiality levels.
   d. Determine the nature, timing, and extent of substantive tests for financial statement assertions.

5. After obtaining an understanding of an entity's internal control structure and assessing control risk, an auditor may next
   a. Perform tests of controls to verify management's assertions that are embodied in the financial statements.
   b. Consider whether evidential matter is available to support a further reduction in the assessed level of control risk.
   c. Apply analytical procedures as substantive tests to validate the assessed level of control risk.
   d. Evaluate whether the internal control structure policies and procedures detected material misstatements in the financial statements.

6. The independent auditor selects several transactions in each functional area and traces them through the entire system, paying special attention to evidence about whether or not the control features are in operation. This is an example of
   a. A sequence test.
   b. A test of controls.
   c. A substantive test.
   d. A functional test.

11

AUDIT OF THE SALES AND COLLECTION CYCLE: TESTS OF CONTROLS AND SUBSTANTIVE TESTS OF TRANSACTIONS

CHAPTER OBJECTIVE

The purpose of this chapter is to discuss the nature of the sales and collection cycle, internal controls normally found in this cycle, and the tests of controls and substantive tests of transactions generally performed by auditors to verify the assessed level of control risk for this cycle when it is less than the maximum.

CHAPTER SUMMARY

OBJECTIVE 1: IDENTIFY THE CLASSES OF TRANSACTIONS AND ACCOUNTS IN THE SALES AND COLLECTION CYCLE

1. The objective of auditing the sales and collections cycle is to evaluate whether the account balances affected by the cycle are fairly presented in accordance with GAAP.

2. Five types of transactions are found in this cycle. Textbook table 11-1 (page 346) shows the related accounts, the business functions, and the related records for these transactions.
   a. Sales (cash and credit)
   b. Cash receipts
   c. Sales returns and allowances
   d. Bad debt expense
   e. Charge-off of uncollectible accounts.

3. Every transaction in the sales and collection cycle ultimately affects either the accounts receivable account or the allowance for uncollectible accounts. A summary of T-account relationships for this cycle shows the following:

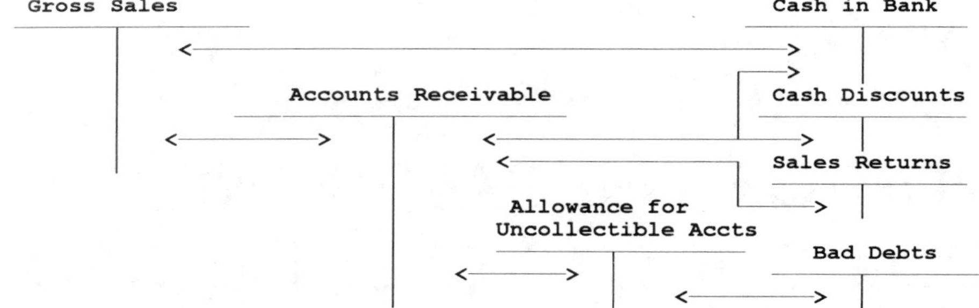

4. Auditors obtain sufficient competent evidential matter by completing a mixture of tests in order to assess control risk and manage planned detection risk (see textbook figure 11-2, page 345). This chapter is concerned with assessing control risk for the sales and collection cycle.
   a. To assess control risk (effectiveness of the internal control structure) auditors obtain an understanding of internal controls and perform tests of controls and substantive tests of transactions.
   b. To manage detection risk auditors perform substantive tests of transactions, analytical procedures, and detailed tests of balances.

OBJECTIVE 2:
DESCRIBE THE BUSINESS FUNCTIONS AND THE RELATED DOCUMENTS AND RECORDS IN THE SALES AND COLLECTION CYCLE

5. Documents, records, and files typically used in the cycle include:
   a. Customer order.
   b. Sales order.
   c. Shipping document.
   d. Sales invoice.
   e. Sales journal.
   f. Credit memo.
   g. Accounts receivable master file.
   h. Prelisting of cash receipts.
   i. Summary sales report.
   j. Monthly statement.
   k. Remittance advice.
   l. Cash receipts journal.
   m. Uncollectible accounts authorization form.
   n. Accounts receivable trial balance.
   o. Sales returns and allowances journal.

6. There are eight major activities conducted in this cycle.
   a. Processing customer orders - This legal offer to buy is the starting point of the cycle and results in the preparation of a sales order based on the customer order (written or oral).
   b. Granting credit - To minimize excessive uncollectible accounts credit sales should be approved. This step often also serves to approve shipment.
   c. Shipping goods - A shipping document (e.g., a bill of lading) should be prepared for each shipment to provide a basis for billing the customer and reducing inventory.
   d. Billing customers and recording sales - All shipments must be billed on a sales invoice at the correct amount, only once, on a timely basis with due consideration for freight charges, insurance, and payment terms.
   e. Processing and recording cash receipts - Remittance advices should be used to help assure that all cash receipts are recorded and deposited on a timely basis.

f. Processing and recording sales returns and allowances - Credit memos should be approved by authorized individuals and recorded on a timely basis.
g. Charging off uncollectible accounts receivable - Proper approval should be required to write-off an account judged to be uncollectible.
h. Providing for bad debts - The bad debt expense account estimates the amount of those sales which ultimately will not be collected.

OBJECTIVE 3:
DETERMINE THE CLIENT's INTERNAL CONTROLS OVER SALES TRANSACTIONS, DESIGN AND PERFORM TESTS OF CONTROLS AND SUBSTANTIVE TESTS OF TRANSACTIONS, AND ASSESS RELATED CONTROL RISK

7. The approach for testing controls and performing substantive tests of transactions in the sales and collection cycle is comparable to that of other cycles.
   a. Obtain an understanding of the internal control structure.
   b. Assess the planned level of control risk.
   c. Evaluate the cost/benefit of testing controls if assessed control risk could be further reduced.
   d. Where the assessed level of control risk can be further reduced design tests of controls and substantive tests of transactions to determine that transaction-related audit objectives are being achieved effectively by giving consideration to the proper procedure, sample size, items to select, and timing of the audit tests.

8. The key internal control procedures and related tests of controls are discussed below. Some of the controls discussed may actually fall under more than one classification.
   a. Adequate segregation of duties can be tested by inquiry and observing activities of client personnel.
      1. Credit-granting should be separate from the sales function.
      2. Persons performing internal comparisons such as comparing batch totals to summary reports and the master file to the general ledger should not enter data into the system.
      3. Preventing fraud is strengthened by authorizing access to cash only to people who do not authorize transactions or perform computer input for sales and cash receipts transactions.
   b. Proper procedures for authorization at three key points can be tested by examining documents for proper approval (signature or initials). Computer programmed authorizations would also be tested.
      1. Authorization for extending credit.
      2. Authorization to ship the goods.
      3. Authorization for prices, payment terms, freight, and discounts.
   c. Adequate documents and records.
      1. Prenumbered documents help prevent (a) failure to bill or record a sale (completeness) as well as (b) duplicating billings or recordings (existence) if the number sequence is accounted for. Testing the sequence of recorded sales invoices for duplicates or out of sequence numbers and tracing recorded transactions to shipping documents provides evidence of the existence objective.
      2. Multi-copied forms (sales invoice) prepared when the customer order is received can be used for credit approval, shipping authorization, and to record the quantity shipped and the amount billed to a customer. This approach reduces errors and reduces the likelihood of failing to record a

sale, assuming numeric sequence is accounted for, because all the related documents are created at the same time (completeness).

d. Mailing of monthly statements, which assists in identifying improperly stated accounts, can be verified by observation and examination of correspondence files with client customers.

e. The auditor can verify that client personnel performed internal verification procedures by examining documents for initials.

9. Normally, a significant savings of auditor time to be spent on tests of details of balances for accounts receivable and the allowance for uncollectible accounts can be achieved where the assessed level of control risk for the sales and collection cycle can be reduced through tests of controls and substantive tests of transactions.

10. A thorough study of textbook table 11-2 (page 354) [and textbook table 11-3 (page 360)] shows the key internal controls, common tests of controls, and common substantive tests of transactions for the following transaction-related audit objectives associated with the sales [and cash collection] cycle.

    a. Recorded sales [cash receipts] are for shipments [funds] actually made [received] to [from] nonfictitious customers (Existence).
    b. Existing sales [cash receipts] transactions are recorded (Completeness).
    c. Recorded sales [cash receipts] are for the amount of goods shipped [at the amount received] and are correctly billed and recorded (Accuracy).
    d. Sales [cash receipts] transactions are properly classified (Classification).
    e. Sales [cash receipts] transactions are recorded on the correct dates (Timing).
    f. Sales [cash receipts] transactions are properly included in the subsidiary records and are correctly summarized (Posting and summarization).

11. Substantive tests of transactions for sales and collections cycle transaction-related audit objectives are discussed below:

    a. Existence.
        1. Testing for recorded sales for which no shipment was made can be done by tracing recorded transactions back to shipping documents and to perpetual inventory credits.
        2. Testing for sales and shipments to fictitious customers can be done by examining related sales orders for credit approval and tracing credit entries made to accounts receivable to their source.
    b. Completeness - Tests for unbilled sales can be done by tracing shipping documents from a file in the shipping department to sales invoices and entries in the sales journal (proper direction of tests is important).
    c. Accuracy - Accuracy is generally tested by recomputation. Prices are compared to authorized amounts, extensions and footings are calculated , quantities and descriptions being billed are compared to shipping documents, and customer identification is compared against customer orders.
    d. Classification - The classification objective is generally tested concurrently with the accuracy objective by considering the nature of the transaction and the chart of accounts. Occurrences such as cash sales being charged to accounts receivable rather than cash, division A sales being credited to division B, and sales of operating assets being handled as inventory sales can be considered at that time.
    e. Timing - Again, as accuracy objective procedures are being performed, due regard can be given to dates on shipping documents compared to billing and recording dates for a reasonable relationship.

f. Posting and summarization - The sales journal should be totaled and totals traced to the general ledger and the master file.

12. The various audit procedures discussed for tests of controls and substantive tests of transactions in textbook tables 11-2 and 11-3 are structured in a design format to facilitate construction of an effective audit program, one that meets the objectives which the auditor considers important. The resulting audit program is restructured into a performance format for several reasons.
    a. Duplicate procedures are eliminated.
    b. Assures that all procedures to be performed on a document are done at the same time.
    c. Procedures are arranged in the most effective order.

13. Study the Hillsburg Hardware example of restructuring an audit program from a design to a performance format.

14. Where the assessed control risk is to be reduced further there should be at least one test of control for each key internal control to verify the effectiveness of that control. Each control can relate to one or more objectives.

15. Common substantive tests of transactions for monetary errors as shown in table 11-2 [table 11-3] relate to a specific internal control objective. The extent of substantive testing of transactions is influenced by what controls exist and the results of tests of controls.

OBJECTIVE 4:
APPLY THE METHODOLOGY FOR CONTROLS OVER SALES TRANSACTIONS TO CONTROLS OVER SALES RETURNS AND ALLOWANCES

16. The audit objectives and methods for processing credit memos differ from those for sales in two important ways.
    a. Often sales returns and allowances transactions are so immaterial that they are not audited.
    b. Particular emphasis is placed on existence of transactions to discover any diversions of cash through the use of fictitious allowances.

17. Auditors apply the same methodology used in auditing sales to audits of sales returns and allowances.

OBJECTIVE 5:
DETERMINE THE CLIENT's INTERNAL CONTROLS OVER CASH RECEIPTS TRANSACTIONS, DESIGN AND PERFORM TESTS OF THE CONTROLS AND SUBSTANTIVE TESTS OF TRANSACTIONS, AND ASSESS RELATED CONTROL RISK

18. The same methodology used for designing tests of controls and substantive tests of transactions for sales is used for cash receipts. Transaction-related audit objectives for cash are included with those listed for sales shown above.

19. Because cash is a liquid asset particular attention is directed to weaknesses that permit fraud.

a. If the auditor suspects that a cash defalcation can occur before there has been an opportunity to record the cash (accountability has not been established prior to the theft), the auditor can trace and verify the disposition of selected charges made to accounts receivable; each debit should be relieved by a credit from the cash receipts journal, the sales returns and allowances journal, or the general journal for bad debts write-off or else verified by a confirmation.
b. A four-column bank reconciliation (proof of cash) can be used to determine whether all recorded cash receipts were deposited in the bank.
c. Lapping, the theft of cash receipts from one customer which in turn is covered-up by using the cash payment made by another customer, can be discovered by comparing the details (name, amount, dates) of remittance advices with duplicate deposit tickets and entries in the cash receipts journal.

OBJECTIVE 6: APPLY THE METHODOLOGY FOR CONTROLS OVER THE SALES AND COLLECTION CYCLE TO WRITE-OFFS OF UNCOLLECTIBLE ACCOUNTS RECEIVABLE

20. Because of the possibility that accounts may be charged-off where collections from those accounts have been diverted, auditors usually consider existence of recorded write-offs the most important transaction-related audit objective in verifying the write-off of individual accounts. Proper authorization is the major control for preventing this type of misstatement.

21. Examining the written approval, credit reports, and correspondence files reduces the possibility of not discovering accounts that have been written-off and for which collections on account have been diverted.

22. In addition to the results of tests of controls and substantive tests of transactions which indicate whether it is likely that accounts receivable are misstated, internal controls for three balance-related audit objectives (realizable value, rights, and presentation and disclosure) also affect the likelihood of misstatement. These objectives are tested during tests of details of balances work.

23. The cause of all exceptions discovered in completing tests of controls and substantive tests of transactions should be analyzed and the effect on the assessed level of control risk determined.

SELF-ASSESSMENT

TRUE-FALSE STATEMENTS

Indicate whether each of the following statements is true or false.

_ 1. Except for cash sales every transaction in the sales cycle has an effect on net realizable value.

_ 2. Although the sales and collections cycle may be a major segment of an entity, the audit of this segment can be performed independently of other segments.

___ 3. A customer order initiates a series of events in the sales cycle ultimately culminating in the collection of cash or the write-off of an account receivable.

___ 4. A bill of lading is another name for an invoice.

___ 5. The person authorized to approve credit normally is the vice-president of sales or the equivalent.

___ 6. Most companies assign responsibility for receiving cash receipts and entering collection data into the computer system to the same person because that person is able to more quickly identify the proper accounts to be credited thereby making bank deposits more timely.

___ 7. A test of control has no meaning unless it tests a particular control objective.

___ 8. Normally it would be efficient for an auditor to complete an audit program following a design format.

___ 9. It is easier to make sure that audit objectives are met by preparing the planned audit program in a design format than by preparing it in a performance format.

___ 10. The only point at which a sales transaction would receive approval from an authorized person is when the credit decision is made.

___ 11. To test whether the value of a recorded sale has been internally verified an auditor would recompute the information on the sales invoices.

___ 12. To test whether the classification of a sales transaction has been internally verified an auditor would examine documents for initials of authorized personnel.

___ 13. To test whether recorded sales exist, a common substantive test of transactions would be to trace sales journal entries to duplicate sales invoices and shipping documents.

___ 14. To test whether existing sales are recorded, a common substantive test of transactions would be to trace sales journal entries to duplicate sales invoices and shipping documents.

___ 15. The procedure of accounting for the sequence of prenumbered documents can help prevent recording transactions more than once or failing to record a transaction at all.

___ 16. A common test to verify separation of duties is to observe the activities in question.

___ 17. Detecting defalcations of cash before the cash is recorded is no more difficult than detecting a defalcation occurring after the cash is recorded.

___ 18. One technique to test whether all of the client's recorded cash receipts have been deposited in the bank is to use a proof of cash.

__ 19. In lapping, a form of defalcation, the thief intercepts a customer's receipts which ultimately are replaced with the receipts intercepted from another customer.

__ 20. Lapping can be committed by any of the accounting personnel.

__ 21. Lapping is one of several types of fraud which by its very nature is permanently concealed at the time it is committed so having a policy of mandatory vacations or rotation of duties would not increase the probability of its discovery.

__ 22. The most important audit objective the auditor should keep in mind in verifying the write-off of individual uncollectible accounts is existence of the item being written-off.

__ 23. A remittance advice is the second part of a two part sales invoice which the customer is asked to return with the cash payment.

__ 24. A credit memo is issued to a customer only if the customer pays his/her account within the stipulated time period.

__ 25. Tracing entries from the cash receipts journal to the bank statements is a common substantive test of cash transactions to determine whether recorded cash receipts are for funds actually received by the company (existence).

__ 26. Tracing amounts from remittance advices or a prelisting to the cash receipts journal is a common substantive test of cash transactions to determine whether cash received is recorded in the cash receipts journal (completeness).

__ 27. If an auditor wants to test for internal verification that the classification of cash receipts transactions were reviewed and agreed to by a second person, the auditor would not examine documents for initials.

COMPLETION STATEMENTS

Complete each of the following statements by filling in the blank space(s) with the appropriate word(s).

1. A customer order is a request from a customer to purchase __________ or services.

2. A bill of lading is a type of __________ document which serves as a __________ between the carrier and the seller.

3. Excessive bad debts are likely to be the result of weak practices in __________ __________.

4. Key internal controls in any cycle should be designed to achieve the six __________ internal control __________.

5. The internal control objective for __________ is concerned with whether recorded sales are for shipments actually made to __________ customers.

6. The internal control objective for __________ is concerned with whether __________ sales transactions are recorded.

7. The direction of tests for the existence objective is from the __________ __________ to the __________ __________.

8. The direction of tests for the completeness objective is from the __________ __________ to the __________ __________.

9. A common substantive test of transactions to determine whether recorded sales transactions are for the amount of goods shipped and are correctly billed and recorded (accuracy) is to __________ information on selected sales invoices.

10. Authorized personnel should approve the processing of sales transactions for credit, __________, and __________ terms.

11. The type of audit evidence used to determine whether there is a proper separation of duties within the accounting function is to use __________ and __________.

12. A common substantive test of transactions to determine whether cash receipts are recorded on the correct dates is to __________ dates of deposits with dates in the cash receipts journal and __________ of cash receipts.

13. A defalcation of cash by someone with access to the accounting records before the receipt is recorded is the most __________ type of cash defalcation to detect because __________ for the money has not been established.

14. A proof of __________ __________ might be employed as a common substantive test of transactions to satisfy the accuracy objective that recorded cash receipts are deposited and recorded at the amount received.

MULTIPLE-CHOICE QUESTIONS

Indicate the best answer to the following statements/questions.

1. For effective internal control, employees maintaining the accounts receivable master file should not also approve
   a. Employee overtime wages.
   b. Credit granted to customers.
   c. Write-offs of customer accounts.
   d. Cash disbursements.

2. To determine whether the internal control structure operated effectively to minimize errors of failure to invoice a shipment, the auditor would select a sample of transactions from the population represented by the
   a. Customer order file.
   b. Bill of lading file.
   c. Open invoice file.
   d. Sales invoice file.

3. Which of the following might be detected by an auditor's review of the client's sales cut-off?
   a. Excessive goods returned for credit.
   b. Unrecorded sales discounts.
   c. Lapping of end-of-period accounts receivable.
   d. Inflated sales for the year.

4. Which of the following control procedures may prevent the failure to bill customers for some shipments?
   a. Each shipment should be supported by a prenumbered sales invoice that is accounted for.
   b. Each sales order should be approved by authorized personnel.
   c. Sales journal entries should be reconciled to daily sales summaries.
   d. Each sales invoice should be supported by a shipping document.

5. Alpha Company uses its sales invoices for posting perpetual inventory records. Inadequate internal control procedures over the invoicing function allow goods to be shipped that are not invoiced. The inadequate control procedures could cause an
   a. Understatement of revenues, receivables, and inventory.
   b. Overstatement of revenues and receivables, and an understatement of inventory.
   c. Understatement of revenues and receivables, and an overstatement of inventory.
   d. Overstatement of revenues, receivables, and inventory.

6. Sound internal control procedures dictate that defective merchandise returned by customers should be presented to the
   a. Purchasing clerk.
   b. Receiving clerk.
   c. Inventory control clerk.
   d. Sales clerk.

7. To achieve an effective internal control structure which department should perform the activities of matching shipping documents with sales orders and preparing daily sales summaries?
   a. Billing.
   b. Shipping.
   c. Credit.
   d. Sales order.

8. Tracing bills of lading to sales invoices will provide evidence that
   a. Recorded sales were shipped.
   b. Invoiced sales were shipped.
   c. Shipments to customers were invoiced.
   d. Shipments to customers were recorded as sales.

9. An auditor selects a sample from the file of shipping documents to determine whether invoices were prepared. This test is performed to satisfy the audit objective of
   a. Accuracy.
   b. Completeness.
   c. Control.
   d. Existence.

12

AUDIT SAMPLING FOR TESTS OF CONTROLS AND SUBSTANTIVE TESTS OF TRANSACTIONS

CHAPTER OBJECTIVE

This chapter discusses the auditor's decision regarding how many items and which specific items to select for investigation. Selection methods for nonstatistical sampling as well as statistical sampling are included. Attributes sampling (statistical sampling for specified attributes) is illustrated using the sales and collection cycle.

CHAPTER SUMMARY

OBJECTIVE 1: EXPLAIN THE CONCEPT OF REPRESENTATIVE SAMPLING

1. In selecting a sample, the auditor generally wants the sample's characteristics to approximate those of the population from which it was taken so that conclusions about the sample can validly be extended to the population. This type of sample is known as a **representative** sample.

2. **Nonsampling** risk or error occurs when an exception in the sample is not detected. This can happen because the auditor fails to recognize an exception or when the auditor performs an inappropriate audit procedure or performs an appropriate procedure ineffectively.

3. **Sampling risk** always occurs when less than 100% of the population is examined because there always is the possibility that the sample is not representative of the population.
   a. Increasing sample size reduces sampling risk.
   b. Using an appropriate selection technique; e.g., random selection reduces sampling risk.

OBJECTIVE 2:
DISTINGUISH BETWEEN STATISTICAL AND NONSTATISTICAL SAMPLING

4. Sample selection may be probabilistic or nonprobabilistic. The method for evaluating a sample depends on how it was selected. Evaluating a nonprobabilistic sample statistically would be regarded as a violation of the field work standard on evidential matter and the general standard on due professional care.

SAMPLE SELECTION	EVALUATION METHOD	
METHOD	STATISTICAL	NONSTATISTICAL
Probabilistic	Preferable	Acceptable
Nonprobabilistic	Not acceptable	Mandatory

5. Both statistical and nonstatistical sampling methods consist of four major steps. [textbook figure 12-2 (page 406) flowcharts the steps for statistically based attributes sampling.]
   a. Plan the sample (consider sampling risk and the minimization of nonsampling error).
   b. Select the sample (decide on how to select the specific sample items).
   c. Perform the tests (examine the documents, etc.).
   d. Evaluate the results (statistical sampling provides formally measured conclusions).

6. Mathematical rules applicable to statistical sampling permit quantification of sampling risk used in planning the sample (step 1) and in evaluating the results (step 4). Quantification of sampling risk is not possible with nonstatistical (nonprobabilistic) sampling.

7. There are three common approaches to **nonprobabilistic selection**.
   a. **Directed Sample selection** - Commonly used selection criteria are:
      1. Transactions most likely to contain misstatements.
      2. Transactions containing selected population characteristics.
      3. Large dollar items.
   b. **Block sampling** (taking a sequence of n items) - The fewer the number of blocks taken the greater the chance that the sample is not representative.
   c. **Haphazard selection** (taking items without regard to size, source, or other characteristics) - Most auditors have some cultural bias which results in selection of a nonrepresentative sample; e.g., items at the top of the page are more likely to be selected by some auditors than items at the bottom of the page.

8. There are four common approaches to probabilistic sample selection. Each requires the auditor to define the population of interest and the sampling unit.
   a. Simple random sample selection.
   b. Systematic sample selection.
   c. Probability proportional to size sample selection.
   d. Stratified sample selection.

OBJECTIVE 3:
SELECT REPRESENTATIVE SAMPLES

9. **Simple random selection** gives each possible combination of items in the population an equal chance of comprising the sample.

10. A **random number table** lists multitudes of independent random digits in a tabular form where each digit has an equal probability of occurring over long runs with no discernable pattern. The digits are organized in columnar groups of five digits. This grouping has no significance other than to facilitate the selection of the required number of digits.

11. Five steps are completed when using a random number table.
    a. A **numbering system** must be established for the population. If the items being sampled are not prenumbered, the auditor must devise a means of uniquely identifying them. For example, page and line numbers could be used to uniquely identify unnumbered entries in a book.
    b. A **correspondence** must be established between the random number table entries and the numbers of the population items. For example, if invoice numbers are seven digits long then five digits from the first column and the first two digits from the adjacent (second) column could be used. The remaining three digits in the second column would be ignored because the next set of numbers would start with the third column of random digits.
    c. A **route** through the table must be established and consistently followed. Usually this means going down the columns moving from left to right or else going across the rows from left to right while moving down the page.
    d. A **starting** point must be selected; e.g., the "blind stab" approach.
    e. Put the selected numbers into the appropriate **sequence**.

12. **Discards** are those random numbers in the selection path which do not qualify. For example, random number 12335 would not qualify for selection when the population numbers range from 24000 to 29000. The number of discards encountered can be reduced by carefully redefining the correspondence between random numbers and the population. In this example, by dropping the 2, any four digit number from 4000 to 9000 would qualify.

13. Most auditors use computer assistance from electronic spreadsheet programs, random number generator programs, or generalized audit software programs, when it is available, to obtain a random sample of items.
    a. Time is saved.
    b. The likelihood of auditor error is reduced.
    c. Automatic documentation is provided as a by-product of the program.

14. Using a computer random number generating program does not eliminate the need for unique identification or correspondence between the random numbers and the population items. Computer input must include the range of population numbers, the desired sample quantity, and sometimes a random number to start the program.

15. Regardless of the method of random sample selection, **Documentation** is important for future reference should the auditor be required to justify the conclusions reached. The name and page numbers of the tables used, the results of completing the five steps discussed above, and the determination of sample size should be documented.

16. Sampling with **replacement** results in a selected item being placed back into the population to possibly be selected again. In sampling **without replacement** an item

can be included in the sample only once. Auditors normally use sampling without replacement.

17. **Systematic selection** results in every n^{th} item being selected. The **interval** between the selected items is determined by dividing population size by desired sample size (N/n). It is easy to use but it can result in a **biased** sample if the characteristic of interest is not randomly distributed throughout the population.

18. The sample selection methods of probability proportional to size (PPS) and stratified sampling can be used to obtain samples that emphasize items from the population with larger recorded amounts. These are discussed in chapter 14.

19. In consideration of practicality and cost/benefit, nonprobabilistic sampling may, in some cases, be preferred to probabilistic sampling.

OBJECTIVE 4:
DEFINE AND DESCRIBE ATTRIBUTES SAMPLING

20. **Attributes sampling** estimates the proportion or **exception rate** (occurrence rate) of a characteristic or attribute of interest. For example, an auditor might be interested in the proportion of sales invoices without duplicate shipping tickets attached in the population of all sales invoices. This methodology permits the auditor to draw conclusions about the effectiveness of the client's internal control structure.

21. An exception refers to both deviations from prescribed control procedures and incorrect monetary amounts.

22. The sample exception rate will most likely differ from the true population exception rate. Auditors, therefore, determine an interval estimate (based on the sample's exception rate) of the range within which the population exception rate is likely to be with a prescribed probability.

23. The upper limit of the estimated interval within which the population's true exception rate lies is referred to as the computed upper exception rate (CUER) and is usually the part of the interval in which the auditor is primarily interested.

24. A **sampling distribution** is a probability distribution of all the possible sample results of size n that could be drawn from a population. An attribute sampling distribution is based on the binomial distribution in which there are only two possible outcomes: yes/no or true/false. Reaching a conclusion about the population based on one sample requires a knowledge about sampling distributions.

OBJECTIVE 5:
USE ATTRIBUTES SAMPLING IN TESTS OF CONTROLS AND SUBSTANTIVE TESTS OF TRANSACTIONS, AND FOR OTHER AUDIT PURPOSES

25. SAS 39 issued by the ASB in June 1981 includes the following terms
    TERMS RELATED TO PLANNING.
    a. **Attribute** - The characteristic being tested by the auditor; e.g., the attribute of interest might be the presence of initials indicating credit approval.
    b. **Acceptable risk of overreliance** (ARO) - The risk the auditor is willing to take of accepting a control as effective or a rate of monetary errors and irregularities as

tolerable, when the true population exception rate is greater than the tolerable exception rate.

c. **Tolerable exception rate**(TER) - The exception rate the auditor will permit in the population and still be willing to assess control risk at a reduced level.
d. **Estimated population exception rate**(EPER) - The exception rate the auditor expects to find in the population before testing begins.
e. **Initial sample size** - Sample size determined from the attributes sampling tables.
f. **Finite correction factor** - A factor reflecting the effect of small population sizes; used to reduce initial sample size.

TERMS RELATED TO EVALUATING RESULTS.

g. **Exception** - An exception from the attribute in a sample item.
h. **Sample exception rate**(SER) - The number of exceptions in the sample divided by the sample size.
i. **Computed upper exception rate**(CUER) - The highest exception rate in the population at a given ARO.

26. To complete an attributes sampling plan the auditor would complete the following steps.
    a. State the objectives of the audit test; e.g., to test the effectiveness of controls in the sales and collections cycle.
    b. Define attributes and exception conditions; e.g., the attribute might be that the duplicate sales invoice is approved for credit and the exception would be the absence of the initials indicating approval.
    c. Define the population - A generalization can be made only about the population from which the sample was taken so the auditor carefully considers the audit objectives when defining the population and tests the population for detail tie-in and completeness before selecting the sample.
    d. Define a sampling unit consistent with the objectives of the audit test.
    e. Specify tolerable exception rate - exercise professional judgement.
    f. Specify acceptable risk of overreliance - a lower ARO is specified for lower assessed control risk.
    g. Estimate the population exception rate - prior year's results or a preliminary sample provide a basis for an advanced estimate.
    h. Determine the initial sample size - it is based on tolerable exception rate, acceptable risk of overreliance on internal control, expected population exception rate, and only slightly on population size.
    i. Select the sample using the sample size tables for attributes sampling (textbook table 12-7 on page 400).
    j. Perform the audit procedures - maintain a record of exceptions found.
    k. Generalize from the sample to the population - calculate sample exception rate (SER) and determine computed upper exception rate (CUER) for the designated acceptable risk of overreliance (ARO) using the evaluation table for attributes sampling (textbook table 12-9 on page 403).
    l. Analyze exceptions - careless employees, misunderstood instructions, and intentional disregard for instructions are factors which affect the qualitative evaluation of the system.
    m. Decide the acceptability of the population - accept if the computed upper exception rate is less than or equal to the tolerable exception rate, (CUER <= TER).

27. Assuming an infinite population, the following relationship will help determine the effect on sample size when one of the other factors changes.

$$\text{sample size} \quad \text{----->} \quad \frac{1}{(\text{ARO})(\text{TER} - \text{EPER})}$$

28. Assuming an infinite population, the following relationship will help determine the effect on CUER when one of the other factors changes.

$$(\text{CUER}) \quad \text{----->} \quad \frac{1}{(\text{ARO})(n)} + \text{SER}$$

29. The construction of attribute sampling tables is based on the assumption that the population is infinite in size. However, accounting populations are finite so population size may have an affect on sample size and CUER whenever sample size is large relative to population size. Ten percent (10%) is a good rule-of-thumb to use in deciding when to use the finite correction factor.
   a. The finite correction factor to adjust the original sample size, n', is
      $n = n'/(1+ (n'/N))$.
   b. The finite correction factor to adjust the original computed upper exception rate (CUER') is
      $CUER = [(CUER' - SER)\sqrt{((N-n)/N)}] + SER$

30. If the CUER > TER, the auditor should analyze the exceptions and choose one of four courses of action.
   a. Revise TER or ARO after considering the difficulty of defending this action in court at a later date.
   b. Expand the sample size to reduce sampling risk and possibly CUER.
   c. Revise assessed control risk which will likely increase substantive procedures. (The choice between (b) and (c) should be based on a cost/benefit approach).
   d. Write a letter to management irrespective of actions a, b, or c.

31. **Documentation**, including the following, should be retained in the working papers.
   a. Procedures performed.
   b. Methods used to select the sample and perform the tests.
   c. Results found in the tests.
   d. The conclusions drawn.

SELF-ASSESSMENT

TRUE-FALSE STATEMENTS

Indicate whether each of the following statements is true or false.

__ 1. A random sample is always representative of the population from which it was drawn.

__ 2. Sampling risk for attributes is the likelihood that the exception rate found in the sample will be larger than or smaller than the population's exception rate.

__ 3. Nonsampling risk is the likelihood that exist

__ 4. Assuming that a random sample is to be taken, sampling risk can be controlled by the size of the sample which is drawn.

__ 5. Nonsampling risk can be controlled by the auditor's alertness, technical training and selection of appropriate procedures.

__ 6. The design of a sampling plan may combine nonprobabilistic selection with statistical evaluation in order to achieve the most efficient results.

__ 7. When a simple random sample is selected, every item in the population has an unknown chance of selection.

__ 8. If the population of invoices to be sampled has invoice numbers of six or more digits, an auditor would not be able to use the random number table in the textbook because the random numbers have only five digits.

__ 9. If an auditor followed a consistent right to left, bottom to top route through the random number table to identify sample items, the standard of due professional care would not have been followed.

__ 10. Selecting a starting point in a random number table using the "blind stab" method is acceptable.

__ 11. Each item in the population must have a unique number (identification).

__ 12. Auditors frequently use sampling with replacement because having an opportunity to look a second time at some of the selected items is quite beneficial.

__ 13. When using systematic selection the auditor calculates a selection interval by dividing sample size into population size.

__ 14. Nonprobabilistic selection can be performed with block sampling, haphazard selection, or directed sample selection.

__ 15. The exception rate or occurrence rate found in the sample is based on the proportion of exceptions to the number of items sampled.

__ 16. A sampling distribution is a frequency distribution calculated from the sample selected.

__ 17. The acceptable risk of overreliance on internal control (ARO) is the risk the auditor is willing to take that a control procedure is not effective when in fact it is.

__ 18. The computed upper exception rate (CUER) is the highest exception rate in the population at a given ARO.

__ 19. The tolerable exception rate (TER) is the highest exception rate the auditor will permit in the population and still be willing to assess level of control risk at less than 100%.

__ 20. One reason the computed upper exception rate might exceed the tolerable exception rate is that the sample is not representative.

__ 21. If the computed upper exception rate exceeds the tolerable exception rate and the auditor believes that the sample is representative, the assessed level of control risk and the planned tests of details of balances would have to be altered.

__ 22. Assuming other factors are constant, a decrease in acceptable risk of overreliance would result in a decrease in sample size.

__ 23. Assuming other factors are constant, an increase in expected sample exception rate would result in an increase in sample size.

__ 24. Assuming other factors are constant, an increase in tolerable exception rate would result in an increase in sample size.

__ 25. Assuming other factors are constant, a decrease in acceptable risk of overreliance would result in an increase in the computed upper exception rate.

__ 26. Assuming other factors are constant, an increase in sample size would result in a decrease in computed upper exception rate.

__ 27. Assuming other factors are constant, a decrease in the sample exception rate would result in an increase in the computed upper exception rate.

__ 28. If an auditor expected a exception rate of 1% from a population of 10,000 items and was willing to accept an exception rate as large as 5% with a 5% ARO, the sample size would be 93.

COMPLETION STATEMENTS

Complete each of the following statements by filling in the blank space(s) with the appropriate word(s).

1. Block sampling is the selection of several items in __________.

2. An auditor who selects sample items without regard to their size, source, or other distinguishing characteristics has completed a ________ selection.

3. Using statistical measurement techniques to evaluate a __________ sample would violate the standard of due care.

4. The __________ measures the upper-side of the interval estimate around the sample exception rate which contains the population exception rate at a given level of __________.

5. The factors which determine the size of an attributes sample are population size, __________ exception rate, acceptable risk of overreliance, and __________ population exception rate.

6. To use the sample size selection tables an auditor would select the table corresponding to ARO, locate the column with the correct __________, locate the row with the expected __________, and read the sample size at the intersection of the selected column and row.

7. For a population of 50,000, an acceptable risk of overreliance (ARO) of 10%, a tolerable exception rate (TER) of 8%, and an estimate population exception rate (EPER) of 2%, an auditor would select __________ sample items.

8. For a population of 500 , an ARO of 5%, a TER of 7% , and an EPER of 1%, an auditor would select __________ items.

9. To use the sample evaluation tables an auditor would select the table corresponding to the __________ , locate the column with the __________ of exceptions found, locate the row with the correct sample size, and read the __________ at the intersection of the selected column and row.

10. The difference between the sample exception rate and the computed upper exception rate is the computed __________ __________.

11. If more than 10% of the population has been sampled, the computed upper exception rate can ordinarily be reduced by using the __________ __________ factor to reduce the computed precision interval.

12. Assume a population of 1000 items, ARO = 5%, n = 200, and actual errors = 2. The sample exception rate is 1%, the computed precision interval before the finite correction factor is __________, and the computed upper exception rate is __________.

13. In (12) the computed precision interval after the finite correction factor is __________, and the computed upper exception rate is __________.

MULTIPLE-CHOICE QUESTIONS

Indicate the best answer to the following statements/questions.

1. When performing a test of key controls with respect to control over cash receipts, an auditor may use a systematic sampling technique with a start at any randomly selected item. The biggest disadvantage of this type of sampling is that the items in the population
   a. Must be systematically replaced in the population after sampling.
   b. May systematically occur more than once in the sample.
   c. Must be recorded in a systematic pattern before the sample can be drawn.
   d. May occur in a systematic pattern, thus destroying the sample randomness.

2. In the examination of the financial statements of Delta Company, the auditor determines that in performing tests of key controls, the exception rate in the sample does not support the assessed level of control risk when, in fact, the exception rate in the population does support the assessed level of control risk. This situation illustrates the risk of
   a. Overreliance.

b. Underreliance.
c. Incorrect rejection.
d. Incorrect acceptance.

3. The diagram below depicts the auditor's estimated exception rate compared with the tolerable rate, and also depicts the true population exception rate compared with the tolerable rate.

Auditor's Estimate Based On Sample Results	TRUE STATE OF THE POPULATION: Exception Rate Exceeds Tolerable Rate	TRUE STATE OF THE POPULATION: Exception Rate is Less Than Tolerable Rate
Exception Rate Exceeds Tolerable Rate	I.	III.
Exception Rate is Less Than Tolerable Rate	II.	IV.

As a result of tests of key controls, the auditor incorrectly revises assessed control risk to a greater level of risk and thereby increases substantive testing. This is illustrated by situation
a. I.
b. II.
c. III.
d. IV.

4. For which of the situations in the preceding question would the auditor have properly assessed control risk?
a. I.
b. II.
c. III.
d. IV.

5. An auditor plans to examine a sample of 20 purchase orders for proper approvals as prescribed by the client's internal control procedures. One of the purchase orders in the chosen sample of 20 cannot be found, and the auditor is unable to use alternative procedures to test whether that purchase order was properly approved. The auditor should
a. Choose another purchase order to replace the missing purchase order in the sample.
b. Consider this test of controls invalid and proceed with tests of details of balances since the assessed level of control risk can **not** be reduced by additional tests of controls.
c. Treat the missing purchase order as an exception for the purpose of evaluating the sample.
d. Select a completely new set of 20 purchase orders.

6. Which of the following statistical sampling methods is most useful to auditors when testing control procedures for exceptions?

a. Ratio estimation.
b. Variable sampling.
c. Difference estimation.
d. Discovery sampling.

7. An underlying feature of random-based selection of items is that each
   a. Stratum of the accounting population be given equal representation in the sample.
   b. Item in the accounting population be randomly ordered.
   c. Item in the accounting population should have an opportunity to be selected.
   d. Item must be systematically selected using replacement.

8. The expected population exception rate of client billing errors is 3%. The auditor has established a tolerable rate of 5%. In the review of client invoices the auditor should use
   a. Stratified sampling.
   b. Variable sampling.
   c. Discovery sampling.
   d. Attribute sampling.

9. Which of the following factors is generally not considered in determining the sample size for a test of controls?
   a. Population size.
   b. Tolerable rate.
   c. Risk of overreliance.
   d. Expected population exception rate.

10. An auditor who uses statistical sampling for attributes in testing internal controls should reduce the planned reliance on a prescribed control when the
    a. Sample rate of exceptions is less than the expected rate of exceptions used in planning the sample.
    b. Tolerable rate less the allowance for sampling risk exceeds the sample rate of exceptions.
    c. Sample rate of exceptions plus the allowance for sampling risk exceeds the tolerable rate.
    d. Sample rate of exceptions plus the allowance for sampling risk equals the tolerable rate.

11. Which of the following combinations results in a decrease in sample size in a sample for attributes?

	RISK OF OVERRELIANCE	TOLERABLE RATE	EXPECTED POPULATION EXCEPTION RATE
a.	Increase	Decrease	Increase
b.	Decrease	Increase	Decrease
c.	Increase	Increase	Decrease
d.	Increase	Increase	Increase

13

COMPLETING THE TESTS IN THE SALES AND COLLECTION CYCLE: ACCOUNTS RECEIVABLE

CHAPTER OBJECTIVE

This chapter discusses tests of details of balances for accounts receivable and the allowance for uncollectible accounts with particular emphasis on meeting balance-related audit objectives. Attention is given to the confirmation process and the relationship of the assessed level of control risk to audit decisions involving the use of confirmations.

CHAPTER SUMMARY

OBJECTIVE 1: RELATE THE AUDIT RISK MODEL TO ANALYTICAL PROCEDURES AND TESTS OF DETAILS OF BALANCES

1. There are three balance sheet accounts in the sales and collections cycle: cash (covered in chapter 21), accounts receivable, and the allowance for uncollectible accounts. Refer to the t-account relationships illustrated earlier in chapter 11 to review the components of the sales and collection cycle.

2. Recall that the following activities have occurred (review chapters 10, 11, and 12).
   a. The auditor has specified an acceptable audit risk and tolerable misstatement for accounts receivable.
   b. Inherent risk and control risk have been assessed.
      1. The auditor considered the nature of the client's business, management integrity, etc.
      2. The auditor obtained an understanding of the internal control structure (e.g., by reviewing an IC questionnaire and flowchart and by completing a walk-through of transactions).
      3. The auditor considered the system's ability to meet the six transaction-related audit objectives.

c. Tests of controls and substantive tests of transactions have been completed where the auditor believed that further reductions in the planned level of control risk were cost effective.

3. A review of textbook figure 13-1 (page 424), using the audit risk model, shows how auditors relate the results of tests of controls and substantive tests of transactions to analytical procedures and tests of details of balances. Planned detection risk is affected by substantive tests of transactions, analytical procedures, and tests of details of balances.

OBJECTIVE 2:
DESCRIBE THE METHODOLOGY FOR DESIGNING TESTS OF DETAILS OF BALANCES

4. After considering the results of 2 and 3 above, auditors design and perform tests of details of balances for accounts receivable and the allowance for uncollectible accounts to meet specific audit objectives. By using an evidence planning worksheet auditors are able to take into consideration when planning appropriate tests of details of balances that inherent risk, control risk, the results of substantive tests of transactions, and the results of analytical procedures may vary among the various balance-related audit objectives to be met by tests of details of balances.

5. An auditor must make several decisions and assessments as part of completing an evidence planning worksheet.
   a. A portion of the preliminary judgment about materiality must be allocated to accounts receivable.
   b. Control risk for transaction-related audit objectives must be associated with the respective balance-related audit objectives. Realizable value, rights, and presentation and disclosure are excluded from this process because they are not affected by control risk.

OBJECTIVE 3:
KNOW THE NINE ACCOUNTS RECEIVABLE BALANCE-RELATED AUDIT OBJECTIVES

6. The balance-related audit objectives applicable to accounts receivable are:
   a. Accounts receivable in the aged trial balance agree with related master file amounts, and the total is correctly added and agrees with the general ledger (detail tie-in).
   b. Recorded accounts receivable exist (existence).
   c. Existing accounts receivable are included (completeness).
   d. Accounts receivable are accurate (accuracy).
   e. Cutoff for accounts receivable is correct (cutoff).
   f. Accounts receivable are properly classified (classification).
   g. Accounts receivable is stated at realizable value (realizable value).
   h. The client has rights to accounts receivable (rights).
   i. Accounts receivable presentation and disclosure are proper (presentation and disclosure).

OBJECTIVE 4:

DESIGN AND PERFORM ANALYTICAL PROCEDURES FOR ACCOUNTS IN THE SALES AND COLLECTION CYCLE

7. Most analytical procedures for accounts receivable would be completed subsequent to year-end but prior to tests of details of balances.

8. Several analytical procedures could be performed.
   a. Review for large and unusual amounts giving particular attention to individual balances which are large, have been due for a long time, are from related parties, and/or are credit balances.
   b. Compute selected key ratios and make appropriate comparisons.
      1. Compare gross margin percentage with last years'.
      2. Compare accounts receivable turnover with last years'.
      3. Compare bad debt expense as a percentage of gross sales with previous years.
      4. Compare aging categories as a percentage of accounts receivable with previous years.

OBJECTIVE 5:
DESIGN AND PERFORM TESTS OF DETAILS OF BALANCES FOR ACCOUNTS RECEIVABLE

9. An auditor can determine the amount of evidence required to satisfy each of the balance-related objectives by completing the evidence planning worksheet.

10. To test **detailed tie-in** an auditor would foot the columns of the aged trial balance, reconcile the total column with the control account, and verify customer name, balance, and aging with the master file and supporting documents.

11. To test **existence** an auditor would confirm balances directly with customers. The existence of an account for which a confirmation has not been returned can be verified by reviewing supporting documents (customer order, shipping ticket, sales invoice, and subsequent cash receipts).

12. Other than selecting individual accounts from the master file and tracing them to the aged trial balance and using analytical procedures, testing the aged trial balance for **completeness** (the inclusion of all existing accounts) is generally satisfied by procedures performed during tests of controls and substantive tests of transactions.

13. **Testing the accuracy** of the gross receivable balance is usually accomplished with confirmations.

14. Testing the **classification** of accounts receivable is accomplished by reviewing the aged trial balance for related party accounts, notes, credit balances, etc.

15. Testing whether **transactions are recorded in the proper time period** (cutoff) involves sales, sales returns and allowances, and cash receipts cutoff. Cutoff tests are important because earnings can be significantly affected if a few material sales of the new period are erroneously included in the audit year's financial statements. There are three major steps followed by an auditor in this area.
    a. Decide what the cutoff criteria are.
    b. Evaluate the client's procedures for achieving appropriate cutoff.

c. Test the effectiveness of the procedures.

16. Cutoff for sales and sales returns and allowances should be coordinated with the inventory observation. The number of the last shipping ticket and the last receiving report prepared at year-end should be noted in the audit work papers for follow-up comparisons with the current and subsequent period's sales journal and sales returns and allowances journal. In addition, the auditor should verify that the returns received are included in inventory.

17. **Cash receipts cutoff** can be tested by tracing recorded cash receipts to bank deposits in the subsequent period noting any unusual delays.

18. Testing **rights** to accounts receivable usually involves reading minutes of board of directors' meetings, confirming with banks, reading correspondence files, and inquiring of client personnel to learn of factoring or discounting transactions.

19. Evaluating **realizable value** requires tests of the allowance for uncollectible accounts. Evaluating the allowance for uncollectible accounts usually begins with a review of the credit granting process. If the policy has changed or adherence to the policy has weakened, care must be exercised. The size and age of noncurrent accounts uncollected subsequent to year-end should be compared to that of the prior year, Dun and Bradstreet reports should be examined, correspondence with customers should be examined, and inquiries should be made of the credit manager.

20. Historical experience of accounts written-off expressed as a percentage of each age category can be applied to totals of present age categories and totaled. The allowance account's balance should be compared to this for reasonableness.

21. Auditors can test for **proper presentation and disclosure** by considering how the client has combined accounts into financial statement totals, whether required separate classifications for accounts such as related parties and segments have been made, and whether footnote discussion adequately informs statement users about the accounts in question.

22. Knowledge regarding what disclosure is appropriate comes from being alert during the course of the audit and by examining the minutes, examining contracts and agreements, reviewing bank confirmations, and discussing requirements with management.

OBJECTIVE 6:
OBTAIN AND EVALUATE ACCOUNTS RECEIVABLE CONFIRMATIONS

23. **Confirmation of accounts receivable** provides evidence that the existence, accuracy, and cutoff objectives have been satisfied. The procedure is required unless one of the following three conditions exists. Justification for not confirming accounts receivable must be documented in the working papers.
    a. Accounts receivable are immaterial.
    b. The auditor considers confirmations ineffective evidence because response rates will likely be inadequate or unreliable.
    c. The combined level of inherent and control risk is low and other substantive procedures provide sufficient competent evidence.

24. The ending balance of accounts receivable = the beginning balance + sales transactions - cash collections - writeoffs. Thus, if last year's ending balance was properly stated and audited, current writeoffs have been audited, and test of controls and substantive tests of transactions of the sales and collections cycle support a reduced level of assessed control risk, there is little likelihood of a material error in the ending balance. Under these conditions, tests of balances (confirmations) can be reduced.

25. The trade-off between increasing tests of controls and substantive tests of transactions to support a reduced level of control risk in order to reduce tests of details of balances is based on cost/benefit. However, when controls are not effective or when there is a small number of large accounts more emphasis would tend to be placed on confirmation.

26. Confirming accounts receivable is more effective than tests of controls and substantive tests of transactions in discovery of invalid accounts, disputed amounts, uncollected accounts, and overstatement misstatements, in general, but less effective in identifying omitted transactions, omitted accounts, and other types of understatements.

27. **There are two common types of confirmation requests: a positive confirmation** and a **negative confirmation request**.
    a. The positive request asks the client's customer for a response. When positive confirmations are used, auditors must resolve any disagreements and follow-up nonresponses with alternative procedures.
    b. The negative request asks for a response only if the amount stated in the confirmation is incorrect. No further action is required of the auditor when there is no response.

28. Because it is not possible to know how many and which negative requests were ignored (not responded to) follow-up procedures for nonresponses cannot be applied. As a result, positive requests are considered **more reliable** than negative requests.

29. It is acceptable to use negative confirmations when all three of the following conditions prevail.
    a. A significant portion of total receivables is comprised of a large number of small accounts.
    b. Combined assessed control risk and inherent risk is low.
    c. There is no reason to believe the recipients of the confirmations are likely to ignore them.

30. Although it is more desirable to confirm accounts at year-end, they may be confirmed up to several months prior to closing if the internal controls are adequate to permit reconciling the closing balance and activities subsequent to the confirmation with the confirmed balances. Earlier confirmation permits earlier completion of the audit.

31. The sample size for confirmation requests depends on several factors.
    a. Tolerable misstatement.
    b. Inherent risk.
    c. Assessed level of control risk.
    d. Achieved detection risk from other substantive tests (substantive tests of transactions and analytical procedures).

e. Type of confirmations being sent.
f. The number of accounts in the population.
g. Variability of account balance amounts.

32. In selecting specific accounts to confirm, auditors typically stratify the population. For example, they might confirm 100% of the accounts over a certain amount and/or all the accounts that are a certain number of days or more past due. The remaining accounts are confirmed on a random basis.

33. The **integrity** of the confirmation process depends on the auditor having complete **independence** in the selection of accounts to confirm. If the client has imposed scope restrictions, an unqualified opinion may not be possible unless three conditions prevail.
    a. The amounts involved are immaterial.
    b. The client's reasons are justifiable.
    c. Other procedures can be used to satisfy the audit objectives.

34. The **integrity** of the confirmation process can be compromised if the auditor does not maintain control of the requests and responses to ensure independent direct communication with the customers selected.

35. All confirmations returned to the auditor undelivered should be investigated because of the possibility of a fictitious account or a serious collectability problem.

36. Nonresponses to positive confirmation requests must ultimately be resolved. If no response has been received after a second or possibly a third request, **alternative procedures** would be followed.

37. Alternative procedures include examination of the following documents.
    a. Remittance advices and entries in the cash receipts journal of the new period for evidence of **subsequent cash receipt**. (Whether the sales transactions creating an account were recorded in the proper period is established by reviewing related documents.)
    b. **Customer order**.
    c. **Duplicate sales invoice**.
    d. **Shipping ticket**.
    e. **Correspondence with the client**.

38. Differences between the account balance and the amount confirmed by customers must be investigated. There are two types of differences: timing differences and exceptions.

39. There are three common timing differences.
    a. **Payment has already been made** by the customer but not received by the client.
    b. **Goods have not been received** by the customer but were shipped by the client and recorded as a sale.
    c. **The goods have been returned** but the client has not yet received the goods so the return has not been recorded.

40. All exceptions such as **clerical errors and disputed amounts** must be explained and accounted for. Often the investigation is performed by client personnel under close supervision by the auditor.

41. The effect of all misstatements on assessed internal control risk must be considered and the audit revised if necessary.

42. The results of auditing the sample of accounts selected for confirmation must be projected to the population. The auditor must decide whether sufficient competent evidence has been accumulated to make a judgement about whether the account is fairly stated in accordance with GAAP.

SELF-ASSESSMENT

TRUE-FALSE STATEMENTS

Indicate whether each of the following statements is true or false.

__ 1. Performing tests of controls and substantive tests of transactions to achieve a reduced level of control risk is always advisable.

__ 2. In the methodology to design tests of details of balances for accounts receivable, the assessment of control risk would precede the establishment of materiality and the assessment of inherent risk.

__ 3. The most important test of details of balances for accounts receivable is confirmation of individual accounts.

__ 4. The nine specific balance-related audit objectives introduced in chapter 5 are re-expressed in this chapter in terms of accounts receivable and serve as the foundation for choosing specific procedures to employ.

__ 5. A significant difference between the current year's gross margin percentage and that of prior years' may indicate possible misstatements in sales or cost of goods sold.

__ 6. A significant difference between the present number of day's sales in accounts receivable and that of prior years' may indicate a possible misstatement in the inventory.

__ 7. Detailed tie-in tests of the aged accounts receivable trial balance assures the auditor that the population being tested agrees with the general ledger and the accounts receivable master file.

__ 8. In gaining assurance that the trial balance contains the correct population the auditor should trace a sample of individual balances listed on the trial balance to the master file, but it is not necessary to trace a sample of accounts in the master file to the trial balance.

_ 9. The normal procedure to test the existence of accounts selected for audit from the accounts received trial balance is to examine the customer order, the shipping document, and subsequent cash receipts.

_ 10. The completeness objective is ordinarily tested by analytical procedures and by depending on tests of controls and substantive tests of transactions to discover any shipments which were not recorded.

_ 11. Confirmation with customers is a good way to satisfy the rights objective because a client's customer is the first to know whether the account has been sold or factored.

_ 12. Confirmation is an example of evidence which satisfies two audit objectives because in addition to testing existence it also verifies the realizable value of accounts receivable to be reported in the balance sheet.

_ 13. Evaluating the adequacy of the allowance for doubtful accounts requires the exercise of considerable professional judgment and the comparison of current conditions with experience of prior years.

_ 14. The classification objective is usually satisfied by reviewing the accounts receivable trial balance for material receivables from related parties and for significant credit balances.

_ 15. Proper cutoff for accounts receivable involves cutoff for sales, sales returns and allowances, cash receipts, and inventory.

_ 16. Confirmation of accounts receivable is an audit procedure required by professional standards unless the auditor is prepared to justify the departure because the accounts are immaterial, or the auditor believes confirmation will be ineffective, or auditor judges that the combined level of inherent and control risk is low enough that other substantive procedures can be used to accumulate sufficient competent evidence.

_ 17. Two common types of accounts receivable confirmations are the positive and the negative types.

_ 18. Negative confirmations are regarded as being more reliable than the positive confirmations.

_ 19. Assuming two, identical populations (A and B) each with some exceptions and debtors who will promptly dispose of their particular confirmation request in the waste basket, the use of positive confirmations to audit population A would be more costly than auditing population B with negative confirmations.

_ 20. When a small number of large accounts represents a significant portion of the total accounts receivable, negative confirmation requests would ordinarily be used.

_ 21. When positive accounts receivable confirmations are used the auditor is required to audit nonresponses by using alternative procedures.

__ 22. Evidence that an account receivable was paid by the customer subsequent to the confirmation date verifies that the amount was due at the confirmation date.

__ 23. Common reasons for differences being reported between the customer's records and the client's records are payments and shipments in transit.

__ 24. An auditor would lose independence if the client were asked to reconcile any differences discovered in the process of confirming accounts receivable.

__ 25. One of the final steps of auditing accounts receivable on a test basis is to generalize (project) misstatements discovered in the sample to the population as a whole.

COMPLETION STATEMENTS

Complete each of the following statements by filling in the blank space(s) with the appropriate word(s).

1. __________ is the most important test of details of accounts receivable.

2. A comparison of __________ __________ as a percentage of accounts receivable with previous years could indicate a misstatement in the allowance for uncollectible accounts.

3. Most tests of accounts receivable and the allowance for uncollectible accounts are based on the __________ __________ __________.

4. __________ __________ tests are usually performed before any other tests on accounts receivable so the auditor is assured that subsequent procedures will be performed on a population which agrees with ledger balances.

5. Follow-up procedures for positive confirmation requests may involve a __________ or possibly even a __________ request for confirmation.

6. Typical alternative procedures for nonresponses to positive confirmation requests are to examine __________ cash receipts, duplicate sales invoices, __________ documents, and correspondence with customers.

7. Commonly reported differences between account balances and confirmed amounts are that __________ has already been made, goods weren't received, and goods were __________ .

8. Although the client's personnel may prepare the confirmation requests, in order to preserve the __________ of the process the auditor must control the entire process even to the point of mailing the confirmations at facilities __________ the client's offices.

9. If the auditor believes that the internal control structure is weak and that there are many accounts in dispute, __________ confirmation requests would be used.

10. Confirmation requests clearly indicate to customers that if amounts are still owed payment __________ (should/should not) be submitted to the auditors.

11. It is acceptable to confirm receivables at an __________ date if the internal control structure is __________ and the auditor is confident that transactions subsequent to the date of confirmation through year-end will be recorded properly.

MULTIPLE-CHOICE QUESTIONS

Indicate the best answer to the following statements/questions.

1. An aged trial balance of accounts receivable is usually used by the auditor to
   a. Verify the validity of recorded receivables.
   b. Ensure that all accounts are promptly credited.
   c. Evaluate the results of tests of control procedures.
   d. Evaluate the provision for bad debt expense.

2. Confirmation is most likely to be a relevant form of evidence with regard to assertions about accounts receivable when the auditor has concerns about the receivables'
   a. Valuation.
   b. Classification.
   c. Existence.
   d. Completeness.

3. Smith is engaged in the audit of a cable TV firm which services a rural community. All receivable balances are small, customers are billed monthly, and the internal control structure is effective. To determine the validity of the accounts receivable balances at the balance sheet date, Smith would most likely
   a. Send positive confirmation requests.
   b. Send negative confirmation requests.
   c. Examine evidence of subsequent cash receipts instead of sending confirmation requests.
   d. Use statistical sampling instead of sending confirmation requests.

4. Smith Corporation has numerous customers. A customer file is kept on disk storage. Each customer file contains name, address, credit limit, and account balance. The auditor wishes to test this file to determine whether credit limits are being exceeded. The best procedure for the auditor to follow would be to
   a. Develop test data that would cause some account balances to exceed the credit limit and determine if the system properly detects such situations.
   b. Develop a program to compare credit limits with account balances and print out the details of any account with a balance exceeding its credit limit.
   c. Request a printout of all account balances so they can be manually checked against the credit limits.
   d. Request a printout of a sample of account balances so they can be individually checked against the credit limits.

5. Cooper, CPA, is auditing the financial statements of a small rural municipality. The receivable balances represent residents' delinquent real estate taxes. The internal control structure at the municipality is weak. To determine the existence of the accounts receivable balances at the balance sheet date, Cooper would most likely

a. Send positive confirmation requests.
b. Send negative confirmation requests.
c. Examine evidence of subsequent cash receipts.
d. Inspect the internal records such as copies of the tax invoices that were mailed to the residents.

6. Negative confirmation of accounts receivable is less effective than positive confirmation of accounts receivable because
   a. A majority of recipients usually lack the willingness to respond objectively.
   b. Some recipients may report incorrect balances that require extensive follow-up.
   c. The auditor can <u>not</u> infer that all nonrespondents have verified their account information.
   d. Negative confirmations do not produce evidential matter that is statistically quantifiable.

7. An auditor confirms a representative number of open accounts receivable as of December 31 and investigates respondents' exceptions and comments. By this procedure the auditor would be most likely to learn of which of the following?
   a. One of the cashiers has been covering a personal embezzlement by lapping.
   b. One of the sales clerks has not been preparing charge slips for credit sales to family and friends.
   c. One of the EDP control clerks has been removing all sales invoices applicable to his account from the data file.
   d. The credit manager has misappropriated remittances from customers whose accounts have been written off.

14

AUDIT SAMPLING FOR TESTS OF DETAILS OF BALANCES

CHAPTER OBJECTIVE

The purpose of this chapter is to discuss how auditors reach conclusions from tests of details of balances when using statistical sampling. Guidance is offered on sample selection, evaluation and auditor action when the sample results are unacceptable.

CHAPTER SUMMARY

OBJECTIVE 1: DISTINGUISH BETWEEN SAMPLING OF TRANSACTIONS AND SAMPLING OF DETAILS OF ACCOUNT BALANCES

1. When using attribute sampling in tests of controls and substantive tests of transactions the auditor's objective is to reach a conclusion about the rate of exceptions for controls being tested. When using sampling in tests of details of balances the auditor's objective is to make an inference about the population's monetary amount.

2. Two types of statistical methods are available for tests of details of balances: monetary unit sampling (MUS) and variables sampling.

3. Sample size is strongly influenced by the audit risk model (PDR = AAR / (IR x CR)) and materiality (tolerable misstatement, TM).

4. Although haphazard selection is a method which an auditor might use, scientific validation of the statistical results requires the use of a probabilistic selection technique.

5. Misstatements in the unaudited part of the population most likely will not be in the same proportion to recorded values as they are in the sample. Therefore, a range of possible population misstatements (sampling error or precision) is constructed around the point estimate of the population's misstatements.

6. Regardless of the method used, several important steps must be completed by the auditor in applying statistical sampling.
   a. Calculate the sample size.
   b. Identify and select the actual items to be audited.
   c. Determine the exception in each sample item.
   d. Summarize the sample exceptions (by stratum if stratified sampling was used).
   e. Project a point estimate of the population misstatement (by stratum and in total).
   f. Determine the sampling error (precision).
   g. Evaluate the outcome.

OBJECTIVE 2:
DEFINE AND DESCRIBE MONETARY UNIT SAMPLING

7. Monetary Unit Sampling (MUS) is the most commonly used statistical method for tests of details of balances because it combines the simplicity of attributes sampling with an expression of results in monetary terms. MUS determines the range of maximum monetary misstatement in a population at a given level of risk.

8. In MUS, the upper and lower limits of the range of probable population misstatements are known as **the upper error bound** and **the lower error bound**, respectively.

9. The population is defined as the recorded monetary amount of the account being audited. The completeness objective is not satisfied with MUS because the likelihood of sampling unrecorded items cannot be evaluated with this sampling method. Other procedures must be used for this objective such as reliance on tests of controls and substantive tests of transactions. Likewise, specific audit tests should be performed on zero, small, and negative balances.

10. The sampling unit in MUS is the individual dollar. Thus, in an account with a balance of $ 2,000,000 there are 2,000,000 sampling units. Each selected dollar results in the account of which it is a part being audited. Therefore, accounts with larger balances have a greater chance of being selected than accounts with smaller balances. Monetary unit samples are samples selected with probability proportional to size (PPS).

11. Determining tolerable misstatement for the audit of a specific account does not require preliminary allocation of materiality when using MUS. Tolerable misstatement at the financial statement level adjusted for misstatements expected to be found in other tests is used in all MUS sampling plans.

12. If the auditor accepts the population as being correct when the true misstatement is greater than the tolerable misstatement, incorrect acceptance has occurred. The auditor's decision establishing the **acceptable risk of incorrect acceptance (ARIA)** has an inverse relationship to sample size because the less risk the auditor is willing to accept the greater the sample size will be.

13. The ARIA is established by the interaction of four factors: acceptable audit risk, results of analytical procedures, inherent risk, and control risk. Assuming inherent risk is set at the maximum (1.0), then as any one of these factors differs from the expected amount there is an effect on the ARIA as shown below:

FACTOR	CHANGE IN FACTOR	CHANGE IN ARIA	CHANGE IN SAMPLE SIZE
Control Risk	Increased	Decreased	Increased
Acceptable Audit Risk	Increased	Increased	Decreased
Analytical Procedures Risk	Increased	Decreased	Increased

14. Steps for completing a MUS plan are as follows:

PLANNING THE SAMPLE.

a. State the objectives of the audit test (to determine whether the population is overstated by a material amount).
b. Define exception conditions (dollar misstatements in items sampled).
c. Define the population (the recorded population of dollars).
d. Define the sampling unit (the individual dollar).
e. Decide on tolerable misstatement (materiality at the financial statement level).
f. Specify acceptable risk of incorrect acceptance (audit risk model).
g. Estimate the exception rate in the population (must be low for MUS to be effective; e.g., less than 2%, otherwise select a different method).
h. Determine the initial sample size (select the larger sample size determined by considering the upper bound and the lower bound).

SELECTING THE SAMPLE AND PERFORMING THE TESTS.

i. Select the sample (use a random number table, systematic selection, or computer assistance to identify selected dollars which in turn are associated with physical units).
j. Perform the audit procedures (audit the physical unit associated with the dollar selected).

EVALUATING THE RESULTS.

k. Generalize from the sample to the population (make an assumption about the percent of error, use attributes sampling evaluation tables, and convert percentages to dollar amounts).
l. Analyze the exceptions (the nature and cause of all misstatements should be examined for any impact they may have on the audit risk model).
m. Decide the acceptability of the population (accept the population as fairly stated when both the lower error bound and the upper error bound fall between plus and minus the tolerable misstatement amount).

15. To determine sample size for a MUS sample, the auditor must specify the following.

a. Tolerable misstatement (assume $200,000).
b. The average percent of misstatement for population items containing misstatements (expressed for both overstatements and understatements, assume 50% and 100% respectively).
c. The ARIA (usually from the audit risk model, assume 5%).
d. The recorded population dollar value (assume $10 million).
e. An estimate of the exception rate in the population (usually a zero rate is assumed).

16. Sample size determination using the foregoing assumptions requires calculating the proportion that "adjusted tolerable misstatement" has to recorded population value,

finding that percentage in the attribute sampling table, and using the larger of the sample sizes determined for the upper and lower bound.

	UPPER BOUND	LOWER BOUND
Tolerable misstatement	$ 200,000	$ 200,000
Average percent of error assumption	÷ .50	1.00
"Adjusted tolerable misstatement"	400,000	200,000
Recorded population value	÷ 10,000,000	10,000,000
Allowable percent error bound	4 %	2 %
Required sample size from the attributes table with 5% risk of incorrect acceptance	74	149

17. To illustrate the technique of dollar selection and physical identification, consider the following accounts receivable trial balance. Note that when a systematic PPS sample is drawn, all population physical audit units with an amount equal to or greater than the amount of the interval will automatically be included in the sample.

ACCOUNT NUMBER	RECORDED AMOUNT	CUMULATIVE TOTAL
1	$425.53	$ 425.53
2	*310.00	735.53
3	53.77	789.30
4	*766.98	1,556.28
5	23.05	1,579.33
6	87.22	1,666.55
7	136.00	1,802.55
8	163.56	1,966.11
9	*202.31	2,168.42
10	43.58	2,212.00

Assume that the desired sample size is 4. Systematic selection would require a sampling interval of (2,212.00/4) = 553 and a random start between zero and 553; e.g., 434. Thus the items which contain the 434th dollar, account number 2; the 987th dollar, account number 4; the 1540th dollar, account number 4; and the 2093rd dollar, account number 9, are selected. These three accounts would be audited and the result would be projected to the population.

OBJECTIVE 3:
DETERMINE ERROR BOUNDS WHEN NO EXCEPTIONS ARE FOUND IN A SAMPLE AND WHEN EXCEPTIONS ARE FOUND IN A SAMPLE

18. Evaluating the results of sampling when no misstatements are discovered requires the determination of an allowance for sampling risk. Using the attribute sampling tables from chapter 12, a sample of 100 items at 5% ARIA with no exceptions yields a CUER of 3%. Assume that each incorrect item is in error by 100%.
    a. Thus, if all the undiscovered misstatements were overstatements, a population of $1,200,000 could be overstated by as much as 3% of its dollar value. Thus, the UEB equals $36,000.
    b. If all the undiscovered misstatements were understatements, the population could be understated by as much as 3% of its dollar value. Thus, the LEB equals $36,000.

19. The percentage of misstatement in an account is determined as follows: ((bookvalue - audited value) / bookvalue). For example,

BOOKVALUE	AUDITED VALUE	DIFFERENCE	PERCENTAGE MISSTATEMENT
$ 40	$ 400	$ 360	900 %
400	40	360	90 %

20. Evaluating the results of sampling when some misstatements are discovered requires separate consideration of overstatement and understatement misstatements and a corresponding adjustment to the allowance for sampling risk.
    a. The error rates are ranked by size (largest first) for overstatements and understatements, separately.
    b. The incremental change in CUER is calculated for each successive error.
    c. (The exception rate) X (incremental change in CUER) X (recorded value) yields the increase in the error bound.

21. Consider the discovery of two overstatement misstatements (.70 and .05 of recorded value) and one understatement misstatement (.35 of recorded value) from a population of $2,400,000. The incremental change in the CUER from the 5% ARIA table for a sample size of 100 is (4.7% - 3.0% = 1.7% and 6.2% - 4.7% = 1.5%). Computation of the Upper and Lower Error Bounds follows:

ERROR	CUER CHANGE	BOOKVALUE	%ERROR ASSUMPTION	ERROR BOUND
0	.030-.000 = .030	$ 2,400,000	1.00	$ 72,000
1	.047-.030 = .017	2,400,000	.70	28,560
2	.062-.047 = .015	2,400,000	.05	1,800
	UNADJUSTED UPPER ERROR BOUND			$ 102,360
0	.030-.000 = .030	2,400,000	1.00	$ 72,000
1	.047-.030 = .017	2,400,000	.35	14,280
	UNADJUSTED LOWER ERROR BOUND			$ 86,280

In this case, the auditor would conclude with a 5% risk of incorrect acceptance that the population is not overstated by more than $ 102,360 nor understated by more than $86,280.

22. When there are both overstatement and understatement misstatements, adjusted error bounds can be calculated by deducting a point estimate for understatements from the UEB and by deducting a point estimate for overstatements from the LEB.
    a. The point estimate for overstatements is determined by multiplying the average overstatement error percentage in the dollar units audited by the recorded value. (.7+.05) ÷ 100 = .0075 x 2,400,000 = 18,000.
    b. Similarly, the point estimate for understatements is determined by multiplying the average understatement error percentage in the dollar units audited by the recorded value.
       (.35) ÷ 100 = .0035 x 2,400,000 = 8,400.
    c. The adjusted Upper Error Bound is $102,360 - 8,400 = 93,960.
    d. The adjusted Lower Error Bound is $86,280 - 18,000 = 68,280.

OBJECTIVE 4:
TAKE APPROPRIATE ACTIONS WHEN EXCEPTIONS ARE FOUND IN THE SAMPLE

23. The acceptance/rejection decision requires a comparison of the error bounds to tolerable misstatement as shown in the following diagram.

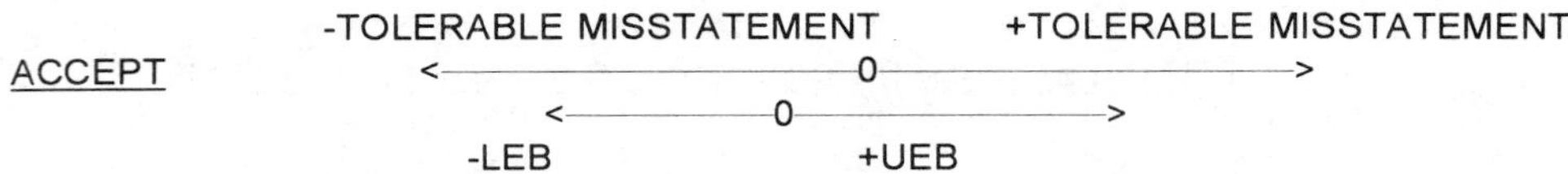

24. When either of the error bounds lies beyond tolerable misstatement the auditor has several options.
    a. **Expand audit tests** in problem areas indicated by misstatements of a particular type.
    b. **Increase sample size** because if the rate of error in the extended sample and the dollar amount and the direction of error are similar to the original sample, the error bounds should decrease.
    c. **Adjust the account balance**.
    d. **Request the client to correct the population** by analyzing individual accounts and restating the trial balance, then re-audit the account.
    e. **Refuse to give an unqualified opinion** if none of the preceding actions are taken.

25. Monetary unit sampling appeals to auditors.
    a. It automatically increases the probability of selecting larger dollar items.
    b. It may reduce the cost of the audit because several sample dollars may be contained in one physical unit which can be tested all at the same time; e.g., in statement 17 above, account number 4 contained two sample items.
    c. It is easy to apply, teach, and evaluate.
    d. The conclusion is expressed in dollars.

26. MUS has some disadvantages.
    a. The technique may be too conservative when more than a few misstatements are found because the error bounds would become quite large (greater than tolerable misstatement).
    b. Selection of dollar units from a large population may be too difficult unless there is computer assistance.

OBJECTIVE 5:
DEFINE AND DESCRIBE VARIABLES SAMPLING

27. Variables sampling is used to measure the value of a population amount or the true amount by which it is misstated. Measures made with variables sampling are termed variables estimates. There are several **variables sampling** techniques.
    a. **Difference estimation** may be used when there is a recorded value and an audited value to measure the estimated total misstatement (difference) in the population. To make the accept/reject decision this point estimate plus and minus the computed precision is compared to tolerable misstatement.
    b. **Ratio estimation** also requires both a recorded value and an audited value but is preferred to difference estimation when the size of the misstatements in the population is proportional to the recorded value of the population items. The ratio of sample dollar misstatements to the total sample value applied to the population value produces a point estimate of the total population error.
    c. **Mean-per-unit estimation** produces an average audited value which is multiplied by the number of physical units in the population to estimate the population audited value. A precision interval around this estimate is calculated and is compared to recorded value +/- tolerable misstatement to make the acceptance/rejection decision.

d. Each of the preceding methods may be further refined by **stratification** wherein the population is divided into two or more subpopulations which are tested and evaluated independently then combined for the accept/reject decision regarding the total population.

28. A sampling distribution that is constructed from a large enough sample size possesses three important characteristics.
    a. The mean of the sampling distribution equals the population mean.
    b. The shape of the sampling distribution is normally distributed so that 68.2%, 95.4%, and 99.7% of all possible sample mean values fall within one, two, and three standard errors of the population mean value, respectively. **The number of standard errors, z, is a measure of confidence**.
    c. The standard error = the population standard deviation divided by the square root of the sample size **($SE = SD \div \sqrt{n}$)**.

29. Statistical inference is accomplished by calculating a confidence interval around the point estimate of the population mean for a specified confidence level. For example, assume that the sample mean is \$50 and the standard error is \$3. The upper confidence limit for a 95.4% confidence level is (UCL) = (sample mean) + (confidence coefficient)(standard error) ; i.e., UCL = (50) + (2)(\$3) = 56 and LCL = (\$50) - (2)(\$3) = \$44. Since 95.4% of all possible sample values fall within 2 standards errors of the mean of their sampling distribution, the true population mean would lie between the UCL and the LCL 95.4 times out of every 100 times a sample is taken.

30. **Acceptable risk of incorrect rejection** (ARIR) which is controlled through Z_R is important when there is a high cost of increasing the sample or performing other tests.

31. **Acceptable risk of incorrect acceptance** (ARIA) which is controlled through Z_A is of much greater concern than ARIR because of the potential losses that can result through litigation when the financial statements contain an undetected material misstatement.

32. Some important formulas for difference estimation follow:

sample size	$n = [SD^*(Z_A + Z_R)N/(TM-E^*)]^2$
point estimate of total error	$\hat{E} = N\bar{e} = N\ (\Sigma e_j/n)$
population standard deviation of misstatements from the sample	$SD = \sqrt{[(\Sigma(e_j)^2 - n(e)^2)/(n-1)]}$
precision interval for the estimate of total error	$CPI = NZ_A\ (SD/\sqrt{n})(\sqrt{(N-n)/N})$
confidence limits at CL desired	$UCL = \hat{E} + CPI$ $LCL = \hat{E} - CPI$

where n = sample size; $\bar{e}$ = average error in sample; $\hat{E}$ = point estimate total error; N = population size; e_j = an individual sample error; SD = standard deviation

CPI = computed precision interval
UCL = computed upper confidence limit
LCL = computed lower confidence limit
Z_A = confidence coefficient for ARIA
Z_R = confidence coefficient for ARIR
SD* = estimated SD

OBJECTIVE 6:
APPLY DIFFERENCE ESTIMATION TO TESTS OF DETAILS OF BALANCES

33. The following statements outline the steps followed in completing a difference estimation sampling plan.
    a. Obtain known values and make assumptions and estimates of other required information.
        1. Tolerable misstatement, ARIA and ARIR.
        2. Population size, expected point estimate, and an estimate of the population standard deviation.
    b. Calculate the initial sample size.
    c. Take a random sample.
    d. Determine the value of each misstatement.
    e. Compute the point estimate of the total misstatement.
    f. Compute an estimate of the population standard deviation.
    g. Compute the precision interval.
    h. Compute the confidence limits.
    i. Apply the decision rule.
        1. If both confidence limits are within the range of tolerable misstatement range accept the population as being fairly stated.
        2. If either confidence limit lies outside the tolerable misstatement range, the population is considered not to be stated fairly.

SELF-ASSESSMENT

TRUE-FALSE STATEMENTS

Indicate whether each of the following statements is true or false.

_ 1. Unlike sampling for attributes where the focus of attention is the exception rate of a characteristic of interest, audit sampling for tests of details of balances is concerned with whether the monetary amount of an account balance is fairly stated.

_ 2. Stratified sampling is a method of selecting and evaluating two or more subpopulations from the population of interest.

_ 3. Stratified sampling is seldom the method used to evaluate a population because it is inefficient and does not allow the auditor the flexibility of concentrating on the types of items of greatest interest.

_ 4. By itself the point estimate of the error in the population is an adequate measure of the population error and serves as a basis for evaluating the financial statements.

_ 5. In MUS the concept of acceptable risk of incorrect acceptance is similar to the concept of acceptable risk of overreliance from attribute sampling.

_ 6. For MUS the upper limit and lower limit of the range of values within which the true population value is expected to lie are called the upper error bound (UEB) and the lower error bound (LEB), respectively.

_ 7. MUS measures the proportion of accounts in error found in the sample which is used as a basis for estimating the proportion of dollar misstatements in the population.

_ 8. MUS is particularly useful for accomplishing the completeness objective.

_ 9. The sampling unit in MUS is the individual dollar rather than a specific account.

___ 10. In MUS materiality at the financial statement level is not allocated to different segments but becomes the tolerable misstatement for each application except to the extent that it is reduced by misstatements expected to be found in non-MUS tests.

_ 11. The acceptable risk of incorrect rejection is more important to auditors than the acceptable risk of incorrect acceptance because of the strong pressure clients exert on auditors to control audit costs.

_ 12. Acceptable risk of incorrect acceptance is synonymous with the calculated detection risk from the audit risk model.

_ 13. Because MUS tends to be inefficient when the error rate is above 2% to 3%, it generally is used only when the auditor believes the population has no significant misstatements.

_ 14. When no misstatements are found in the MUS sample, the auditor can conclude that the population has no misstatements and that the difference between book value and the upper and lower error bounds is zero.

_ 15. The assumption that undetected misstatements are 100% in error for both overstatements and understatements is not conservative.

_ 16. Difference estimation does not require the existence of a recorded population value for its use.

_ 17. Ratio estimation does not require the existence of a recorded population value for its use.

_ 18. Mean-per-unit estimation can be used whether there is a recorded population value or not.

_ 19. The mean of a sampling distribution based on samples with a sufficiently large sample size (e.g., n > 30) is generally larger than the population mean.

_ 20. The standard error of a sampling distribution based on a sufficiently large sample size equals the population's standard deviation divided by the square root of the sample size.

_ 21. Statistical inference for mean-per-unit estimation is accomplished by calculating a confidence interval around the point estimate of the population mean for a specified confidence level.

_ 22. The number of standard errors, z, is a measure of confidence because it indicates the probability that a single sample will fall within a given interval around the population's true value.

_ 23. In difference estimation the decision rule for accepting the population as being fairly stated is that the -LCL must be greater than -TOLERABLE MISSTATEMENT and UCL must be less than +TOLERABLE MISSTATEMENT.

_ 24. If one or more of the error bounds of a MUS investigation lie outside the tolerable misstatement, additional sampling might decrease the error bounds enough to fall within the range of tolerable misstatement provided the error rate in the extended sample, the dollar amount and the direction of error are similar to the original sample.

_ 25. If in a MUS investigation the bookvalue is $50 and the audited value is $500, the misstatement of the item is said to be 90%.

_ 26. One disadvantage of using MUS is that it increases the probability of selecting larger dollar items.

_ 27. The point estimate of population misstatement in difference estimation is the average misstatement in the sample times the number of population items.

COMPLETION STATEMENTS

Complete each of the following statements by filling in the blank space(s) with the appropriate word(s).

1. A summary of sampling risk possibilities shows the following:

	TRUE CONDITION OF THE POPULATION	
AUDITOR'S DECISION	NOT MISSTATED BY A MATERIAL AMOUNT	MISSTATED BY A MATERIAL AMOUNT
Accept the population as being fairly stated	Correct Acceptance	(a)_________ _________
Reject the population as being materially misstated	(b)_________ _________	Correct Rejection

2. Assume the following conditions exist for the audit of ABC Co.'s accounts receivable using difference estimation: Bookvalue = $3,000,000; ARIA = 10%, ARIR = 50%, estimated SD = $80, N = 5,000 items, tolerable misstatement = $60,000, and estimated point estimate of the population misstatement = 0. Evaluation of the sample items revealed that total audited value of the sample = $262, total bookvalue of the sample = $600, and sample SD = $91. Determine each of the following unknown items. For questions b through f, assume a sample of size 169 was taken).
   a. sample size ____________.
   b. average error found in the sample ____________.
   c. point estimate of total error ____________.
   d. confidence limits at desired CL ____________.
   e. precision interval of total error ____________.
   f. the auditor's decision is to ____________.

3. Assume the following conditions exist for the audit of XYZ Co.'s accounts receivable using MUS: Tolerable misstatement = $300,000, average percent of error assumption is 100% for both under- and overstatements, bookvalue is $ 15,000,000, ARIA = 5%, and no misstatements are found in the sample. Determine each of the following unknown items.
   a. allowable percent error bound ____________.
   b. sample size ____________.
   c. upper error bound ____________.
   d. lower error bound ____________.
   e. the auditor's decision is to ____________.

4. Using systematic selection for MUS find the specific accounts the auditor would select from the following Accounts Receivable population.

ACCOUNT NUMBER	AMOUNT RECORDED	CUMULATIVE TOTAL
1	$425.53	$ 425.53
2	310.00	735.53
3	53.77	789.30
4	766.98	1,556.28
5	23.05	1,579.33
6	87.22	1,666.55
7	136.00	1,802.55
8	163.56	1,966.11
9	202.31	2,168.42
10	43.58	2,212.00

Assume that the desired sample size is 3, and the random start is with the 79th dollar.
(a)sampling interval ____________
(b)first item ____________
(c)second item ____________
(d)third item ____________

MULTIPLE-CHOICE QUESTIONS

Indicate the best answer to the following statements/questions.

1. Which of the following sampling plans would be designed to estimate a numerical measurement of a population, such as a dollar value?
   a. Discovery sampling.
   b. Numerical sampling.
   c. Sampling for variables.
   d. Sampling for attributes.

2. Auditors who prefer statistical sampling to nonstatistical sampling may do so because statistical sampling helps the auditor
   a. Measure the sufficiency of the evidential matter obtained.
   b. Eliminate subjectivity in the evaluation of sampling results.
   c. Reduce the level of tolerable misstatement to a relatively low amount.
   d. Minimize the failure to detect a material misstatement due to nonsampling risk.

3. In estimation sampling for variables, which of the following must be known in order to estimate the appropriate sample size required to meet the auditor's needs in a given situation?
   a. The qualitative aspects of misstatements.
   b. The total dollar amount of the population.
   c. The acceptable level of risk.
   d. The estimated rate of error in the population.

4. An auditor is performing substantive tests of pricing and extensions of perpetual inventory balances consisting of a large number of items. Past experience indicates numerous pricing and extension errors. Which of the following statistical sampling approaches is most appropriate?
   a. Unstratified mean-per-unit.
   b. Probability-proportional-to-size.
   c. Stop or go.
   d. Ratio estimation.

5. While performing a substantive test of details during an audit, the auditor determined that the sample results supported the conclusion that the recorded account balance was materially misstated. It was, in fact, not materially misstated. This situation illustrates the risk of
   a. Incorrect rejection.
   b. Incorrect acceptance.
   c. Overreliance.
   d. Underreliance.

15

AUDITING COMPLEX EDP SYSTEMS

CHAPTER OBJECTIVE

The purpose of this chapter is to discuss the EDP environment in which modern auditors often perform their work and to illustrate how the approach to auditing is affected by this environment.

CHAPTER SUMMARY

OBJECTIVE 1:
EXPLAIN HOW THE COMPLEXITIES OF EDP SYSTEMS AFFECT BUSINESS ORGANIZATIONS

1. Although audit concepts remain unchanged when moving from a noncomplex to a complex EDP system environment, specific methods for implementing them do change.

2. The technical complexity of an EDP system is affected by the extent to which the following occur.
   a. **On-line processing**.
   b. Connection of the computer to **communications systems**.
   c. **Distributed processing**.
   d. **Data base management systems**.
   e. **Complex operating systems**.

3. The complexity of EDP systems increases as new transaction cycles are computerized and as additional functions within those cycles are computerized.

4. Auditors are concerned with the effect of EDP on the organization, visibility of information, and the potential for misstatement.

5. The following organization changes may occur as EDP grows within the organization.
   a. Physical facilities may be modified to include separate computer rooms with special environmental controls.
   b. New personnel may be added to manage the EDP function.
   c. Data processing may be centralized to provide improved quality control while concurrently eliminating some segregation of duties.
   d. The computer may be programmed to authorize selected transactions.

6. The audit trail (i.e., the visibility of information) may be changed significantly. Source documents may not exist or may be difficult to retrieve, processing can no longer be observed, and summarization of details may eliminate detailed data.

7. The likelihood of increased material misstatement concerns the auditor. The following factors contribute to increased material misstatement.
   a. Reduced human involvement - the people who initiate transactions do not follow them through the system and many people simply accept computer output as being "correct."
   b. Uniformity of processing - the computer will process incorrect data very consistently.
   c. Unauthorized access - once the system is accessed, data can easily be changed.
   d. Loss of data - the potential for misstated financial statements and possible curtailment of operations because data is lost increases when the data is centralized.

8. On the other hand controls may improve because of uniformity of processing and because management can review and supervise the organization more effectively with expanded information and improved analytical tools.

OBJECTIVE 2: DESCRIBE EDP-RELATED INTERNAL CONTROLS IN COMPLEX SYSTEMS AND THEIR IMPACT ON EVIDENCE ACCUMULATION

9. EDP controls are often grouped into general controls and application controls.

10. General controls consist of the following:
    a. **The plan of organization** is concerned with the separation of duties within data processing into the activities of systems analysts, programmers, computer operators, librarians, and the data control group.
    b. **Procedures for documenting, reviewing, and approving systems and programs** includes documenting systems requirements (broad objectives of the system), programs (writing and testing the system), program run instructions, and user instructions.
    c. **Hardware controls** are built into the equipment to detect equipment failure but are of less concern to the auditor than how the client plans to handle misstatements identified by the computer.
    d. **Controls over access to equipment, programs, and data files** include physical controls, access controls, and backup and recovery procedures.

11. The more effective general controls are the less likely a material misstatement will occur in a computer based accounting application. The less effective general controls

are the more likely the auditor will be required to modify the tests of various computer based accounting applications to satisfy audit objectives.

12. **Application controls** which are concerned with input, processing, and output generally prevent or detect misstatements occurring in several phases of an application.
    a. Input controls assure that data entering the computer are valid, complete, and accurate.
    b. Processing controls assure that data contained within the computer are processed accurately and completely.
    c. Output controls assure that data generated by the computer are valid, accurate, complete, and distributed only to authorized people.

OBJECTIVE 3: KNOW THE SIMILARITIES AND DIFFERENCES IN OBTAINING AN UNDERSTANDING OF COMPLEX AND NONCOMPLEX INTERNAL CONTROL STRUCTURES

13. The objectives of internal control in a complex EDP system are the same as those of a noncomplex system but EDP specialists are often used to obtain an understanding of the system because of the complexities involved. Evidence is obtained to describe the system, its strengths and weaknesses, and whether the controls have actually been placed in operation.

14. Information to understand the system comes from flowcharts, EDP internal control questionnaires, and a study of error listings generated by programs. Both EDP and non-EDP controls are considered.

15. If the auditor believes that it is cost effective to further reduce assessed control risk for EDP controls, tests of controls are performed, exceptions are investigated, and a decision concerning the possible reduction of assessed control risk is made.

OBJECTIVE 4: DECIDE WHEN IT IS APPROPRIATE TO AUDIT ONLY THE NON-EDP INTERNAL CONTROLS TO ASSESS CONTROL RISK

16. **Auditing around the computer** occurs when the auditor chooses not to rely on EDP controls. Source documents in human readable form must be available and filed in such a manner that individual transactions can be traced to and from output which also must be in human readable form.

17. Although the auditor may choose to rely completely on manual controls he/she must still perform a review of EDP controls to obtain an understanding and assess whether there are significant risks that may affect the financial statements.

18. Microcomputer based accounting systems may pose special problems for auditors.
    a. Networked systems may not have adequate segregation of duties. Non-EDP controls may mitigate this weakness.
    b. Applications developed in-house may have a high risk of misstatement because developers may have little data processing knowledge, and there is often little control over access to computer records.

OBJECTIVE 5:
DESCRIBE THREE WAYS TO USE THE COMPUTER AS AN AUDIT TOOL

19. The auditor may use the computer to perform the following procedures.
    a. Use test data to test controls and processing in the client's computer system.
    b. Test computer maintained records.
    c. Perform audit tasks independent of the client's records.

20. **Test data**, both valid as well as invalid, are often used to determine whether the client's program reacts properly to each type of data. The following concerns must be addressed if this approach is to be used.
    a. **All relevant conditions** the auditor wants to challenge should be provided for in the test data. This often requires the use of a specialist.
    b. The **program tested** must be the one the client has used throughout the year.
    c. Test data may have to be **eliminated** from the client's records.

21. The output of the client's system may be tested by using an **auditor selected program**. This program may be an existing client program, one written by the auditor specifically for the present task, or a generalized audit software (GAS) routine . The following list identifies some of the tasks that GAS can perform.
    a. Verify extensions and footings.
    b. Examine records for quality, completeness, consistency, and correctness.
    c. Compare data on separate files.
    d. Summarize and sort data and perform various analyses.
    e. Compare data obtained through other audit procedures with company records.
    f. Select audit sample items for examination.
    g. Print confirmation requests and other documents.

22. **Generalized audit software (GAS)** consists of a series of utility routines for data manipulation. Advantages of GAS are that they can be quickly mastered by auditors with little formal EDP training and that they can be applied in a number of situations thereby avoiding the cost of developing specific task oriented programs. Disadvantages include large development costs and inefficient processing.

23. Using GAS requires that (1) the objectives of the application be specified, (2) the application be designed, (3) the instructions be coded, (4) the coding be keypunched (entered), and (5) the processing be completed. Generally, the required data is extracted from the client's files, entered in an auditor related file, and subsequently manipulated as desired by the auditor.

OBJECTIVE 6:
KNOW THE TYPES OF SOFTWARE AVAILABLE FOR AND USES OF MICROCOMPUTERS IN AUDITING

24. An auditor may use a microcomputer for generalized audit software applications, but it is more often used as a tool to manage the audit and to perform analyses and summarizations. The following types of microcomputer software are available for these purposes.
    a. Commercial general-use software such as electronic spreadsheets and word processors.
    b. Templates of predesigned work papers and letters which are used repetitively.

c. Special-use software developed commercially or by the accounting firm which vary in sophistication from the development of trial balance and lead schedule data to artificial intelligence and expert-systems.
d. Custom programs written by or for the auditor, usually in BASIC, to accomplish a specific task.

25. The following are examples of uses for these software packages.
    a. Trial balances and lead schedule preparation.
    b. Work paper preparation.
    c. Analytical procedures.
    d. Audit program preparation.
    e. Internal control description and testing.
    f. Audit sampling.
    g. Engagement management and time budgeting.
    h. Generalized audit software preparation.

26. Auditors using microcomputers should be wary about two quality control considerations. Input data and computational routines should be documented to facilitate supervisory review and to meet GAAS. Software should be verified as reliable so that computational and logic errors do not contaminate the results of the processing.

OBJECTIVE 7:
DISCUSS THE SPECIAL CONCERNS OF THE AUDITOR WHEN THE CLIENT's INFORMATION IS PROCESSED BY AN OUTSIDE COMPUTER COMPANY

27. Auditors of clients who have a significant level of financial data processed by a computer service center need to evaluate and test the service center's controls. As a practical matter this is usually done annually by one independent auditor whose report is relied on by the auditors of the computer center's customer.

SELF-ASSESSMENT

TRUE-FALSE STATEMENTS

Indicate whether each of the following statements is true or false.

__ 1. There is a distinct difference between the audit concepts applicable to a noncomplex EDP accounting environment and to those of a complex EDP environment.

__ 2. On-line processing and distributed processing can significantly affect the complexity of an EDP system.

__ 3. No special environmental arrangements need be made for full-scale EDP facilities.

__ 4. Complex EDP systems ordinarily have no effect on the extent of data centralization or on the elimination of some of the traditional division of duties.

__ 5. It is common in some organizations for data to be input directly into the computer without the creation of source documents.

__ 6. Traditional audit trails may be eliminated with EDP type processing because of the elimination of source documents and data summarization.

__ 7. EDP controls are classified as either general controls or application controls.

__ 8. The plan of organization and operation of the EDP function is an example of an application control.

__ 9. EDP input, processing, and output controls for updating an accounts receivable master file would be categorized as application controls.

__ 10. It is common to start the process of obtaining an understanding of the EDP internal control structure by reviewing programmed controls.

__ 11. Using the test data approach to evaluate the ability of a client's program to properly handle valid and invalid data is limited by the auditor's ability to devise tests for all the relevant types of errors that could occur.

__ 12. One of the disadvantages of generalized audit software (GAS) is the extensive and costly training required to prepare auditors to use it.

__ 13. Microcomputers tend to be used more as an audit tool rather than as a means of verifying client data stored in machine readable form.

__ 14. Completing analytical procedures, work paper preparation, and time keeping are typical tasks for which microcomputers are used by auditors.

__ 15. Computer service centers typically engage one CPA firm to obtain an understanding and test controls of the internal control structure to eliminate the redundant audits which would occur if each customer acted independently.

__ 16. Auditors are generally as concerned with hardware controls as they are with the plan of organization and operation of the EDP activity.

__ 17. Backup and recovery procedures are generally regarded as being a type of application control.

__ 18. One of the problems of using the test data approach to challenge the client's program(s) is that the test data may contaminate the client's live records.

COMPLETION STATEMENTS

Complete each of the following statements by filling in the blank space(s) with the appropriate word(s).

1. A computing function of geographically separated CPUs connected by a communication system is called a __________ __________ system.

2. Centralization of data in EDP systems permits __________ __________ controls over operations.

3. Centralization of data in an complex EDP system diminishes controls formerly achieved through __________ of __________ in complex systems.

4. EDP controls are generally classified into __________ controls and __________ controls.

5. Some segregation of duties is achieved in an EDP system through a proper __________ of __________.

6. In order to audit around the computer, source documents must be available in __________ language and must be locatable.

7. To ensure that the program used with the test data approach is the same one the client used throughout the year an auditor could process the test data on a __________ __________.

8. A convenient way to maintain control over the preparation of accounts receivable confirmations is to have them printed by the __________ __________ software.

9. Quality control concerns related to the use of microcomputers are the lack of __________ data and __________ software.

MULTIPLE-CHOICE QUESTIONS

Indicate the best answer to the following statements/questions.

1. When using a computer to gather evidence, the auditor need **not** have a working knowledge of the client's programming language. However, it is necessary that the auditor understand the
   a. Audit specifications.
   b. Programming techniques.
   c. Database retrieval system.
   d. Manual testing techniques.

2. The least likely use by the auditor of generalized audit software is to
   a. Perform analytical review on the client's data.
   b. Access the information stored on the client's EDP files.
   c. Identify weaknesses in the client's EDP control procedures.
   d. Test the accuracy of the client's computations.

3. Processing simulated file data provides the auditor with information about the reliability of controls from evidence that exists in simulated files. One of the techniques involved in this approach makes use of
   a. Controlled reprocessing.
   b. Program code checking.
   c. Printout reviews.
   d. Integrated test facility.

4. Matthews Corp. has changed from a system of recording time worked on clock cards to a computerized payroll system in which employees record time in and out with magnetic cards. The EDP system automatically updates all payroll records. Because of this change
   a. A generalized computer audit program must be used.
   b. Part of the audit trail is altered.
   c. The potential for payroll related fraud is diminished.
   d. Transactions must be processed in batches.

5. Where computer processing is used in significant accounting applications, EDP internal control procedures may be classified into two types: general and
   a. Administrative.
   b. Specific.
   c. Application.
   d. Authorization.

6. A primary advantage of using generalized audit software packages in auditing the financial statements of a client that uses an EDP system is that the auditor may
   a. Substantiate the accuracy of data through self-checking digits and hash totals.
   b. Access information stored on computer files without a complete understanding of the client's hardware and software features.
   c. Reduce the level of tests of control procedures to a relatively small amount.
   d. Gather and permanently store large quantities of supportive evidential matter in machine readable form.

7. Which of the following audit procedures would an auditor be **least** likely to perform using a generalized computer audit program?
   a. Searching records of accounts receivable balances for credit balances.
   b. Investigating inventory balances for possible obsolescence.
   c. Selecting accounts receivable for positive and negative confirmation.
   d. Listing of unusually large inventory balances.

16

AUDIT OF THE PAYROLL AND PERSONNEL CYCLE

CHAPTER OBJECTIVE

The purpose of this chapter is to discuss auditing the personnel cycle. Attention is directed to obtaining an understanding of the internal control structure of the cycle, related tests of controls, substantive tests of transactions, applying analytical procedures, and completing tests of details of balances.

CHAPTER SUMMARY

OBJECTIVE 1:
DESCRIBE THE PAYROLL AND PERSONNEL CYCLE AND THE PERTINENT DOCUMENTS AND RECORDS, FUNCTIONS, AND INTERNAL CONTROLS

1. In most entities, payroll and related expenses constitute an extremely significant dollar amount. Consequently, errors and irregularities related to payroll can materially misstate inventories, net income, and other accounts.

2. A summary of the T-account relationships for this cycle shows the following:

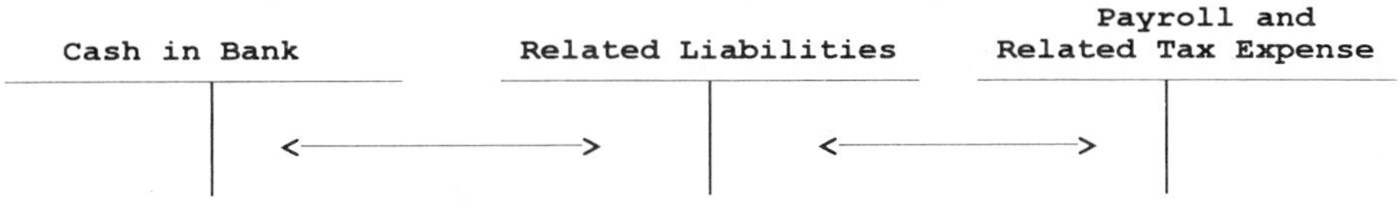

Cash in Bank		Related Liabilities		Payroll and Related Tax Expense
	<———>		<———>	

3. Because the payroll and personnel cycle typically differs from other cycles, auditors usually stress tests of controls and substantive tests of transactions and spend very little time with tests of details of balances.
   a. There is only one class of transactions for payroll.
   b. Transactions are far more important than the related balance sheet accounts.

c. Internal controls over payroll are usually effective for almost all companies regardless of size.

4. Several documents and records are typically found in this cycle.
   a. Personnel records.
   b. Deduction authorization form.
   c. Rate authorization form.
   d. Time card.
   e. Job time ticket.
   f. Payroll check.
   g. Summary payroll report.
   h. Payroll master file.
   i. Payroll journal.
   j. W-2 form.
   k. Payroll tax return.

5. To minimize misstatements and safeguard company assets, duties in this cycle are usually separated into four functions.
   a. Personnel and employment.
   b. Timekeeping and payroll preparation.
   c. Payment of payroll.
   d. Preparation of payroll tax returns and payment of taxes.

6. The **personnel and employment** department serves as a formal independent control to establish employment arrangements with each employee independent of the department in which that employee works.
   a. This arrangement provides timekeeping and payroll preparation personnel with authorization to pay employees an initial rate, subsequent increases, and to no longer pay terminated employees.
   b. It ensures that new employees are competent and trustworthy.

7. **Timekeeping and payroll preparation** activities include the following.
   a. Preparation of time cards and job time tickets by employees.
   b. The summarization and calculation of gross pay, deductions, and net pay.
   c. Preparation of payroll checks (without signatures).
   d. Preparation of payroll records.
   e. Distribution of gross payroll and related expenses to the proper accounts (i.e., work-in-process inventory, overhead, expense, etc.).

8. There are several desirable internal controls for timekeeping and payroll preparation.
   a. A time clock should be used and monitored to prevent the time stamping of cards of absent or fictitious employees.
   b. Separation of duties and independent verification of important information should be used in a non-complex EDP system. For example:
      1. An independent person might recalculate actual hours worked, review for proper approval of overtime, and examine time cards for alterations.
      2. The person who prepares the payroll checks would not have access to time cards or sign or distribute the checks.

9. **Payment of payroll** (signing and distributing the checks) should be restricted to an individual that is not involved in the other payroll functions. Unclaimed checks should be returned immediately for redeposit.

10. Using an imprest payroll account prevents the loss from payment of unauthorized payroll to no more than the balance in the imprest account. The use of an imprest account also provides other benefits.
    a. Permits delegation of duties.

b. Separates a major group of routine transactions from other transactions.
c. Facilitates cash management.
d. Simplifies the bank reconciliation process.

11. **Preparation of payroll tax returns and payment of taxes** should be controlled by an established set of procedures. An independent person should verify satisfactory completion of the required tasks.

OBJECTIVE 2:
DESIGN AND PERFORM TESTS OF CONTROLS AND SUBSTANTIVE TESTS OF TRANSACTIONS FOR THE PAYROLL AND PERSONNEL CYCLE

12. Tests of controls and substantive tests of transactions generally are the most significant audit procedure applied in the personnel cycle.
    a. There is little opportunity for confirmation from third parties of balance sheet accounts such as accrued wages, withheld taxes, etc.
    b. Verification of balance sheet accounts is relatively easy if the auditor is confident about the ability of the transaction cycle to generate correct data.

13. The approach for testing controls and performing substantive tests of transactions in the personnel cycle is comparable to that of other cycles.
    a. Gain an understanding of the internal control structure.
    b. Assess planned control risk.
    c. Evaluate the cost-benefit of testing controls.
    d. Design test of transactions (tests of controls and substantive tests) to test transaction-related audit objectives by considering procedures to apply, sample size, items to select, and timing of the procedures.

14. Several factors prompt the auditor to spend less time auditing this cycle than others despite the magnitude of annual payroll amounts.
    a. Employees will complain if their checks are understated.
    b. Payroll transactions are relatively simple and uniform.
    c. Payroll activities are subject to government and union scrutiny.

15. Direct and indirect manufacturing or construction labor can have a material effect on the valuation of inventory or construction-in-progress. Consequently, in addition to testing internal controls over payroll classification, an auditor should test for existence and completeness by tracing from job-cost records to job tickets and from job tickets to job-cost records.

16. A thorough study of textbook table 16-2 (page534) shows the key internal controls, common tests of controls, and common substantive tests of transactions for each of the following transaction-related audit objectives.
    a. Recorded payroll payments are for work actually performed by nonfictitious employees (existence).
    b. Existing payroll transactions are recorded (completeness).
    c. Recorded payroll transactions are for the amount of time actually worked and at the proper pay rate; withholdings are properly calculated (accuracy).
    d. Payroll transactions are properly classified (classification).
    e. Payroll transactions are recorded on the correct dates (timing).
    f. Payroll transactions are properly included in the payroll master file; they are properly summarized (posting and summarization).

17. Other audit concerns include testing the preparation and timely filing of payroll tax forms, payment of taxes, and reimbursement and reconciliation of the imprest payroll account.

18. The two most common types of payroll fraud involve fictitious employees and fraudulent hours.
    a. Payment of **fictitious employees** can be prevented or detected by a number of techniques.
        1. Separate duties so that the person who distributes payroll checks is not the foreman who approves time cards for payment.
        2. Compare names and signatures on paid checks to employee's signatures on withholding forms and scan endorsements for unusual or recurring second endorsements.
        3. Test the existence of employees being paid by tracing names to personnel department employment records.
    b. Payment of **fraudulent hours** is difficult for an auditor to detect but can be prevented by the employer with adequate controls.
        1. Require approval for overtime hours.
        2. Reconcile total hours paid with independently accumulated production hours.
        3. Monitor employee access to the time clock.
        4. Require foremen to approve total hours reported on job time tickets and reconcile these with time cards.

OBJECTIVE 3:
DESIGN AND PERFORM ANALYTICAL PROCEDURES FOR THE PAYROLL AND PERSONNEL CYCLE

19. Analytical procedures may be applied to data produced by the personnel cycle to identify potential misstatements of account balances.
    a. Compare the current payroll account balance with the previous year's after adjusting for rate and volume changes.
    b. Compare the current percentage of direct labor to sales with that of the prior year.
    c. Compare the current percentage of commission expense to sales with that of the prior year.
    d. Compare the current percentage of payroll tax expense to total payroll with that of the prior year.
    e. Compare the current accrued payroll tax expense with the prior year's.

OBJECTIVE 4:
DESIGN AND PERFORM TESTS OF DETAILS OF BALANCES FOR ACCOUNTS IN THE PAYROLL AND PERSONNEL CYCLE

20. Direct tests of details of balances for payroll related liabilities follow the methodology developed for other balance sheet accounts.
    a. Set materiality and assess acceptable audit risk and inherent risk for payroll liability accounts.
    b. Assess control risk for the payroll and personnel cycle.
    c. Design and perform tests of controls and substantive tests of transactions and analytical procedures for payroll and personnel cycle.
    d. Design and perform analytical procedures for payroll liability account balances.

e. Design and perform tests of details of balances for payroll liability account balances to meet audit objectives (consider what procedures are appropriate, sample size, selecting sample items, and timing).

21. Two major balance-related audit objectives related to payroll liabilities are verification that accruals are stated at the correct amounts (accuracy) and that transactions are recorded in the correct accounting period (timing). Omitted or understated accruals are of particular concern.

22. **Withheld taxes payable** can be tested by reviewing the payroll journal, subsequent cash disbursements, and related payroll tax forms and comparing them with the account balance. **Accrued payroll tax expense** can be verified by examining related tax forms filed in the subsequent period.

23. **Accrued salaries and wages** and **accrued vacation pay, sick pay, and other benefits** can be tested by recalculating the amount following the company's policy.

24. **Accrued commissions** can similarly be tested by determining the terms of the commission agreement and then recalculating the amount accrued. Consistency of application to that of the prior year should be tested and confirmation directly with employees may be appropriate in some instances.

25. **Accrued bonuses** can usually be verified by comparison with minutes of meetings of the board of directors.

26. Although testing details of balances of expense accounts should only be necessary when the internal control structure is considered weak, when tests of liability account balances reveal significant misstatements, or when analytical procedures indicate unexplained variances, details of **selected payroll** expense accounts are often tested as a matter of course.
    a. **Officers' compensation** is reported in the SEC's 10-K as well as the tax return and often can be manipulated by the very person being paid so it is common to verify each officer's salary with minutes of meetings of the board of directors.
    b. **Commissions** are generally tested in conjunction with tests of the related liability and generally involve recalculation.
    c. **Payroll tax expense** is often not tested because the audit risk does not justify the time required to complete the task. If necessary, total payroll expense can be reconciled with payroll reported on payroll tax forms which is then used to recompute payroll tax expense.
    d. **Total payroll** is often tested by reconciling the ledger accounts with the payroll tax returns. However, since the tax form most likely was prepared from the payroll journal, omissions and misclassifications would most likely not be revealed by this procedure. Tests of controls and substantive tests of transactions are more effective in this regard.

SELF-ASSESSMENT

TRUE-FALSE STATEMENTS

Indicate whether each of the following statements is true or false.

_ 1. The payroll and personnel cycle is important because it is a major expense in most companies, it is important to the valuation of inventory for some entities, and it is often handled inefficiently.

_ 2. Larger, sophisticated companies generally have one payroll account.

_ 3. In most payroll accounting systems, the accrued wages and salaries account is used at the end of each payroll period so that payroll expense accounts can be debited as salaries and wages are incurred rather than when paid.

_ 4. The cycle begins with the hiring function and ends with payments to employees for services given and to various governmental bodies for taxes withheld and accrued.

_ 5. A job time ticket is a daily record only of the time at which an employee began working and the time at which work ceased.

_ 6. A time card shows the time worked on particular jobs during a given time period.

_ 7. Labor distribution is the name given to the task of distributing the pay checks for the payroll period.

_ 8. One of the main reasons for having a personnel department is to segregate the authorization of hiring, firing, and setting of payrates from those who have access to time cards, payroll records or checks.

_ 9. An important control in timekeeping and payroll preparation is independent verification of hours worked, rate of pay, authenticity of time cards, and calculations.

_ 10. Fortunately, errors in the labor distribution will never affect inventory or other similar accounts because payroll is strictly a period cost.

_ 11. Imprest payroll bank accounts are used primarily because they make the bank reconciliation easier.

_ 12. Because there can be significant penalties for tardy and/or incorrectly prepared payroll tax forms their preparation should be verified by a competent independent person.

_ 13. In the personnel cycle, auditors generally elect to spend little time on tests of controls and substantive tests of transactions and a great deal of time on tests of details of related balances because these amounts are easily confirmed.

_ 14. One reason there is minimal risk of understatement in the payroll area is that employees are likely to complain if they are underpaid.

_ 15. A procedure useful for detecting payroll payments to fictitious employees is to trace the names of paid employees back to personnel to verify their existence, rate of pay, etc.

_ 16. Because an employer who fails to file or files incorrect payroll tax returns faces no special sanctions, auditors generally are not concerned with this minor activity.

_ 17. Ordinarily the general bank account reimbursement to the imprest payroll bank account will equal the amount of the net payroll.

_ 18. A comparison of time cards for the payroll period with an independent record of time worked such as production records is designed to help the auditor meet the completeness objective.

_ 19. Examining time cards for indication of approval is a test of controls to determine whether payroll transactions are properly authorized.

_ 20. If a comparison of direct labor as a percentage of sales with percentages of previous years indicates a large variation, direct labor might be materially misstated.

_ 21. Inherent risk for payroll related liabilities is ordinarily smaller than for other balance sheet accounts such as accounts receivable because the payroll liability accounts are generally less material.

_ 22. For an internal control structure with reduced control risk verification of withheld and accrued payroll taxes payable is usually a straight review of the payroll journal, the related payroll tax return, and subsequent cash disbursements.

_ 23. Tests of details of the officer's compensation expense account would generally only be done if control risk for the payroll and personnel cycle was set at a high level.

_ 24. For most audits the verification of payroll tax expense by recomputation is usually worth the effort expended for the information obtained.

_ 25. Auditors would extend their tests of details of balances when the possibility of material fraudulent payroll transactions existed as a result of a weak internal control structure (i.e., control risk was high).

_ 26. Generally, the detection of fraudulent payroll hours is done more effectively with adequate internal controls than by relying on the auditor.

COMPLETION STATEMENTS

Complete each of the following statements by filling in the blank space(s) with the appropriate word(s).

1. Examining time cards for initials indicating approval for payment is evidence that the __________ objective has been provided for in the internal control structure.

2. Examining internal verification indicating that the sequence of payroll checks was accounted for is evidence that the __________ objective has been provided for in the internal control structure.

3. Reviewing time cards for employee department and job tickets for job assignments, and tracing through to the labor __________ is a substantive test of transactions for the __________ objective.

4. Recomputing gross pay and net pay is a substantive test of transactions for the __________ objective.

5. A comparison of the journal entry date with the date on a paid check and the related time card is a substantive test of transactions for the __________ objective.

6. Refooting the payroll journal and tracing postings to employee earnings records and the general ledger is a substantive test of transactions for the __________ objective.

7. An important function fulfilled by the personnel and employment department is an adequate investigation of the __________ and __________ of new employees.

8. One control to prevent paying employees for time which is not worked is to require the use of __________ __________.

9. Deductions from gross pay must be supported with the existence of a __________ __________ __________.

10. A bank account with a small fixed balance maintained solely for payroll disbursements is called an __________ __________ __________.

11. There is minimal risk of material misstatement in payroll related accounts because employees will complain if underpaid, most payroll transactions are __________ and uncomplicated, and payroll transactions are audited extensively by various __________ organizations.

12. One method for testing for fictitious payroll is to request and participate in a surprise __________ __________.

13. The usual assumed deviation rate for attributes sampling in the payroll cycle is __________.

MULTIPLE-CHOICE QUESTIONS

Indicate the best answer to the following statements/questions.

1. Which of the following internal control procedures could best prevent direct labor from being charged to manufacturing overhead?
   a. Reconciliation of work in process inventory with cost records.
   b. Comparison of daily journal entries with factory labor summary.
   c. Comparison of periodic cost budgets and time cards.
   d. Reconciliation of unfinished job summary and production cost records.

2. The purpose of segregating the duties of hiring personnel and distributing payroll checks is to separate the
   a. Operational responsibility from the record keeping responsibility.
   b. Responsibilities of recording a transaction at its origin from the ultimate posting in the general ledger.
   c. Authorization of transactions from the custody of related assets.
   d. Human resources function from the controllership function.

3. The auditor may observe the distribution of paychecks to ascertain whether
   a. Payrate authorization is properly separated from the operating function.
   b. Deductions from gross pay are calculated correctly and are properly authorized.
   c. Employees of record actually exist and are employed by the client.
   d. Paychecks agree with the payroll register and the time cards.

4. An auditor would consider internal control procedures over a client's payroll to be ineffective if the payroll department supervisor is responsible for
   a. Hiring subordinate payroll department employees.
   b. Having custody over unclaimed paychecks.
   c. Updating employee earnings records.
   d. Applying pay rates to time tickets.

5. Which of the following departments should have the responsibility for authorizing payroll rate changes?
   a. Personnel.
   b. Payroll.
   c. Treasurer's.
   d. Timekeeping.

6. For an appropriate segregation of duties, journalizing and posting summary payroll transactions should be assigned to
   a. The treasurer's department.
   b. General accounting.
   c. Payroll accounting.
   d. The timekeeping department.

7. An auditor who is testing EDP controls in a payroll system would most likely use test data that contain conditions such as
   a. Deductions not authorized by employees.
   b. Overtime not approved by supervisors.
   c. Time tickets with invalid job numbers.
   d. Payroll checks with unauthorized signatures.

8. The purpose of segregating the duties of hiring personnel and distributing payroll checks is to separate the
   a. Administrative controls from the internal accounting controls.
   b. Human resources function from the controllership function.
   c. Operational responsibility from the record keeping responsibility.
   d. Authorization of transactions from the custody of related assets.

9. Tracing selected items from the payroll register to employee time cards that have been approved by supervisory personnel provides evidence that
   a. Internal controls relating to payroll disbursements were operating effectively.

b. Payroll checks were signed by an appropriate officer independent of the payroll preparation process.
c. Only bona fide employees worked and their pay was properly computed.
d. Employees worked the number of hours for which their pay was computed.

17

AUDIT OF THE ACQUISITION AND PAYMENT CYCLE

CHAPTER OBJECTIVE

The purpose of this chapter is to discuss auditing transactions arising from the acquisition and payment of goods and services obtained from third parties. Particular emphasis is given to describing the nature of the cycle, applying tests of controls and substantive tests of transactions, and applying tests of details of account balances.

CHAPTER SUMMARY

OBJECTIVE 1:
DESCRIBE THE ACQUISITION AND PAYMENT CYCLE AND THE PERTINENT DOCUMENTS AND RECORDS, FUNCTIONS, AND INTERNAL CONTROLS

1. In most companies, more accounts are affected by the acquisition and payment cycle than all other cycles combined.

2. The following summarizes the T-account relationships for this cycle.

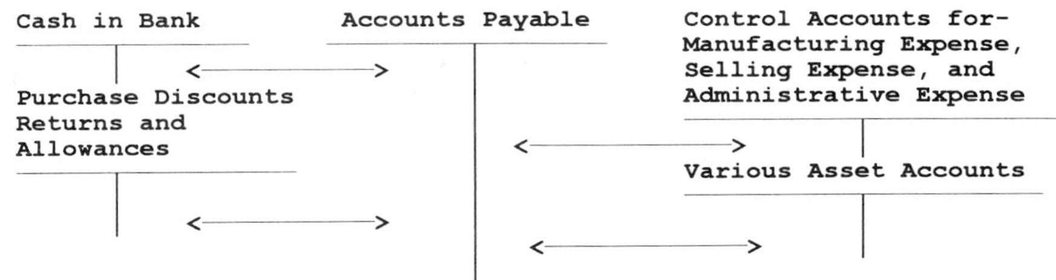

3. The process of obtaining goods and services and the related internal control principles apply equally well to manufacturing companies,

service companies, governmental units and other entities.

4. Documents and records typically used in the cycle include:
   a. Purchase requisition.
   b. Purchase order.
   c. Receiving report.
   d. Vendor's invoice.
   e. Voucher.
   f. Vendor's statement.
   g. Acquisitions journal.
   h. Debit memo.
   i. Summary acquisitions report.
   j. Check.
   k. Cash disbursements journal.
   l. Accounts payable master file.
   m. Trial balance of Accounts Payable.

5. Activities in this cycle may be classified into four primary functions.
   a. Processing purchase orders.
   b. Receiving goods and services.
   c. Recognizing the liability.
   d. Processing and recording cash disbursements.

6. **Processing purchase orders** begins with a properly approved purchase requisition originating from a department other than purchasing. The resulting purchase order legally commits the entity to buy the ordered item (description, quality, etc.) at a given price at an established location by or on a given date. Prenumbering establishes control over the purchase order document and requiring approval before submission to vendors limits the entity's exposure for improper purchases.

7. **Receiving goods and services** results in the preparation of a receiving report. This document reports the quantity, condition, and date of goods received. It also initiates the process of maintaining accountability for the goods as they move from the point of input to the point of output or consumption.

8. **Recognizing the liability** for acquisitions requires prompt and accurate recording of invoices for goods and services.
   a. Responsibility for completing the following steps should be indicated by initials.
      1. Vendor's invoices should be compared to purchase orders and receiving reports for descriptions, prices, quantities, terms, and freight charges.
      2. Arithmetical accuracy should be verified and account distribution indicated.
   b. Proper segregation of duties requires that people recording acquisitions not have access to cash, marketable securities, or other assets.
   c. Other controls include adequate documents and records, proper record keeping procedures and independent checks on performance.

9. Control over **processing and recording cash disbursements** rests heavily on having an authorized person who does not perform accounts payable functions sign prenumbered checks in payment of liabilities. Supporting documents should be cancelled to prevent reuse and blank, voided, and signed checks should be carefully controlled.

OBJECTIVE 2:
DESIGN AND PERFORM TESTS OF CONTROLS AND SUBSTANTIVE TESTS OF TRANSACTIONS FOR THE ACQUISITION AND PAYMENT CYCLE AND ASSESS RELATED CONTROL RISK

10. Significant savings of auditor time spent on tests of details of balances for inventory, permanent assets, accounts payable, and the expense accounts may be achieved if it is cost effective to further reduce assessed control risk in the acquisition cycle by testing controls and performing substantive tests of transactions.

11. The approach for testing controls and performing substantive tests of transactions in the acquisition and payment cycle is comparable to that of other cycles.
    a. Understand the internal control structure.
    b. Assess planned control risk.
    c. Evaluate cost/benefit of testing controls and performing substantive tests of transactions.
    d. Design tests of controls and substantive tests of transactions giving consideration to the proper procedure, sample size, items to select, and timing to determine that internal control objectives are being achieved effectively.

12. A thorough study of textbook tables 17-2(page 558) and 17-3(page 559)shows the key internal controls, common tests of controls, and common substantive tests of transactions for the following internal control objectives relating to the acquisition [and payment] cycle. The tables are constructed on the assumption that a separate acquisitions journal for recording all acquisitions transactions and a separate cash disbursements journal for recording all disbursement transactions exist.
    a. Recorded acquisitions [cash disbursements] are for goods and services received, consistent with the best interests of the client (existence).
    b. Existing acquisition [cash disbursement] transactions are recorded (completeness).
    c. Recorded acquisitions [cash disbursements] transactions are accurate (accuracy).
    d. Acquisition [cash disbursement] transactions are properly classified (classification).
    e. Acquisition [cash disbursement] transactions are recorded on the correct dates (timing).
    f. Acquisition [cash disbursement] transactions are properly included in the accounts payable and inventory master files and they are properly summarized (posting and summarization).

13. Typically, transactions selected for tests of acquisitions are also used for tests of payments so that audit effectiveness is maximized.

14. Tests of details for understatement of the accounts payable balance and perpetual inventory balance can be significantly reduced if the auditor is confident that the completeness objective for internal controls is effective.

15. Vouching permanent asset acquisitions for accuracy and classification and verifying expense classifications are time consuming procedures which can be significantly reduced if tests of controls and substantive tests of transactions indicate that acquisition [cash disbursement] transactions are properly classified.

16. The types of misstatements that might be found in the acquisitions and payments cycle result in a direct monetary effect on the accounts and generally misstate earnings. Consequently, tolerable deviation rates selected in applying attribute sampling are generally low. Some large and unusual items may be segregated and examined on a 100% basis.

OBJECTIVE 3:
DISCUSS THE NATURE OF ACCOUNTS PAYABLE, AND DESCRIBE THE RELATED CONTROLS

17. Accounts payable are unpaid obligations known and unpaid at the balance sheet date. Interest-bearing obligations are classified separately. Auditors usually emphasize tests for understatement of accounts payable rather than overstatement.

18. In addition to the controls discussed earlier under transaction processing, a monthly reconciliation of vendors' statements with recorded liabilities and the accounts payable master file with the general ledger should be done by an independent person.

OBJECTIVE 4:
DESIGN AND PERFORM ANALYTICAL PROCEDURES FOR ACCOUNTS PAYABLE

19. Several analytical procedures may be used in audits of the acquisitions and payment cycle.
    a. Compare acquisition-related expense account balances with prior years'.
    b. Compare individual accounts payable with previous years'.
    c. Calculate ratios such as purchases divided by accounts payable and accounts payable divided by current liabilities.

OBJECTIVE 5:
DESIGN AND PERFORM TESTS OF DETAILS FOR ACCOUNTS PAYABLE

20. There are eight audit objectives for tests of details of the accounts payable balance (realizable value is not applicable to liabilities):
    a. Accounts payable in the accounts payable list agree with the related master file, and the total is correctly added and agrees with the general ledger (detail tie-in).
    b. Accounts payable in the accounts payable list exist (existence).
    c. Existing accounts payable are in the accounts payable list (completeness).
    d. Accounts payable in the accounts payable list are accurate (accuracy).
    e. Accounts payable in the accounts payable list are properly classified (classification).
    f. The company has an obligation to pay the liability (obligations).
    g. Transactions in the acquisition and payment cycle are recorded in the proper period (cutoff).
    h. Accounts in the acquisition and payment cycle are properly disclosed (presentation and disclosure).

OBJECTIVE 6:
KNOW THE IMPORTANCE OF OUT-OF-PERIOD LIABILITY TESTS FOR ACCOUNTS PAYABLE AND COMMON TESTS

21. **Out-of-period liabilities tests** (test for understatement) include the following:
    a. **Examine underlying documentation for subsequent cash disbursements** - all disbursements made in the new period which relate to transactions of the

period being audited should be traceable to the year-end accounts payable trial balance.

b. **Examine underlying documentation for bills not paid several weeks after year end** - all unpaid invoices relating to the period being audited should be traceable to the year-end accounts payable trial balance.

c. **Trace receiving reports issued before year-end to related vendors' invoices** and to the year-end accounts payable trial balance to discover purchases erroneously omitted and recorded as new year purchases.

d. **Trace vendors' statements that show a balance due to the accounts payable list** and investigate any differences.

e. **Send confirmations to vendors with whom the client does business** to reveal vendors omitted from the accounts payable trial balance, omitted transactions, and/or misstated balances.

22. Item 20 (c), tracing receiving reports prepared prior to year-end, helps identify accounts payable understatement. Tracing receiving reports prepared during a short period immediately following year-end to related invoices and the acquisitions journal of the new period, allowing for appropriate FOB terms, will identify any which have been recorded erroneously in the year of audit.

23. **Cut-off** procedures should be coordinated with the observation of physical inventory; i.e., while observing client inventory procedures the auditor should record the number of the last receiving document prepared and determine that the client has included all last minute goods received as part of inventory and all FOB origin shipments that occurred prior to year-end.

OBJECTIVE 7:
KNOW THE RELATIVE RELIABILITY OF VENDORS' INVOICES, VENDORS' STATEMENTS AND CONFIRMATIONS OF ACCOUNTS PAYABLE

24. A vendor's statement is superior to a vendor's invoice for verifying an accounts payable balance while the vendor's invoice is superior for verifying the details of individual transactions.

25. A **confirmation of accounts payable** which is sometimes called a vendor request is considered more reliable for verifying an accounts payable balance than a vendor's statement because the confirmation comes directly from the vendor to the auditor while the statement passes through the client's hands before the auditor receives it. However, the statement is still considered relatively reliable.

26. When internal controls are regarded as being inadequate, statements are not available, or the client's integrity is suspect, accounts payable confirmation requests are usually sent to large accounts, active accounts, accounts with zero balances, and a representative sample of all others.

27. Factors which normally cause an apparent difference between the balance appearing in vendor statements or vendor confirmations and the client's accounts payable balance are inventory in transit, payments in transit, and delays in processing transactions. Documents usually needed to investigate these differences are receiving reports, vendor's invoices, and paid checks.

28. Materiality, population size, control risk, inherent risk, and desired audit risk influence the determination of sample size for accounts payable tests.

29. Variables sampling is less frequently used in auditing accounts payable because of the difficulty of determining population size. It is difficult to determine because transactions and/or balances may have been omitted. Defining the population as all potential payables solves the definition problem but may make the new population statistically unmanageable.

30. The following are two practical examples of applying variables sampling to accounts payable.
    a. Define the population to be all vendors on a list the auditor is satisfied includes all vendors.
    b. Define the population to be payments subsequent to year-end where the auditor is satisfied that all year-end payables have been paid in the new period.

SELF-ASSESSMENT

TRUE-FALSE STATEMENTS

Indicate whether each of the following statements is true or false.

__ 1. Because for most companies the acquisition and payment cycle affects more accounts than any other cycle it usually takes more time to audit than other cycles.

__ 2. A purchase requisition is a document in which the entity offers to purchase goods or services from another company under specified terms.

__ 3. A voucher is a document received from a provider of goods or services describing the item exchanged and the amount and terms of payment.

__ 4. A vendor's statement, usually received on a monthly basis, indicates the beginning balance due, purchases, payments, and the ending balance payable to the vendor.

__ 5. A receiving report is a document which describes the condition, quantity and arrival date of goods received.

__ 6. A purchasing department is seldom given general authorization for purchases of inventory.

__ 7. Requiring an approved purchase requisition as the basis for preparing and approving a purchase order is not a good internal control.

__ 8. Separation of duties is best achieved if the receiving department is independent of the storeroom, accounting, and purchasing.

_ 9. Once goods have been received it is not recommended that accounting records assign accountability for them as they move through the manufacturing process.

_ 10. Verification of detailed entries on a vendor's invoice by comparison with the purchase order and receiving report is typically done by the purchasing department.

_ 11. Responsibility for signing checks and marking supporting documents paid usually rests with the supervisor of accounts payable.

_ 12. In a typical audit four of the five most time consuming accounts to verify by tests of details of balances are found in the acquisition and payments cycle.

_ 13. Examining internal verification that the numerical sequence of receiving reports has been accounted for by client personnel is a test of controls for the completeness objective that existing acquisition transactions are recorded.

_ 14. Verifying the existence of the underlying purchase requisition, purchase order, receiving report, and vendor's invoice is a test of controls for the accuracy objective.

_ 15. As with the audit of assets, an auditor is more concerned with the possibility of overstatement of accounts payable than with understatement.

_ 16. Excluding the realizability objective, the audit objectives for auditing liabilities are basically the same as for auditing assets.

_ 17. Out-of-period liabilities tests are referred to as the search for unrecorded accounts payable.

_ 18. Assume that a cash disbursement has been made in the new period for inventory received in the year being audited. Accounts payable at the end of the period being audited would be understated if the purchase were excluded from the accounts payable trial balance.

_ 19. Examining unpaid bills through completion of the field work could not reveal any that were for goods and services received during the period being audited.

_ 20. Comparing vendors' statements and confirmations from vendors with the accounts payable trial balance may reveal misstated account balances.

_ 21. Cutoff tests should be coordinated with the physical inventory observation.

_ 22. Goods shipped FOB shipping point prior to the balance sheet date but received subsequent to year-end should be excluded from inventory and accounts payable.

_ 23. A vendor's statement is regarded as very effective evidence for verifying terms, values, etc. of individual transactions.

__ 24. The use of statistical sampling to test accounts payable for existence, accuracy, and classification might be effective if the auditor has a high degree of confidence that the accounts payable list contains the names of all vendors.

COMPLETION STATEMENTS

Complete each of the following statements by filling in the blank space(s) with the appropriate word(s).

1. The acquisition and payment cycle does not include acquisition and payment of __________ services or internal transfers and __________ of costs.

2. Acquisition transactions are usually recorded in an acquisition transactions __________.

3. A purchase __________ is a written request to the purchasing department to obtain goods or services for the department originating the document.

4. Comparing __________ of receiving reports and vendors' invoices with __________ in the acquisitions journal is a substantive test of transactions to determine whether goods are recorded on a __________ basis.

5. Tracing a canceled check to the related acquisitions journal entry and examining for payee and amount is a test of __________.

6. Reviewing the cash disbursements journal, general ledger, and accounts payable master file for __________ or unusual amounts is an __________ procedure to test for existence.

7. An auditor would send a __________ __________ confirmation request to an active vendor who does not appear on the accounts payable list as a means of searching for __________ amounts.

8. Tracing vendor names and amounts from the accounts payable list to vendors' invoices and statements is a test of __________.

9. Completing the various out-of-period liability tests provides evidence to the auditor about whether __________ accounts payable are __________ in the accounts payable list.

10. Purchases __________ information should be obtained at the time that the physical inventory count is __________.

11. Shipments under FOB __________ terms received in the very early part of the new period should be tested to determine whether those having a shipment __________ in the year being audited are included in the accounts payable list.

12. Common reconciling items which explain the difference between the balance due per a vendor's statement and the accounts payable list are __________ and __________ in transit.

13. Defining the accounts payable population is difficult because of the potential for __________ accounts payable.

MULTIPLE-CHOICE QUESTIONS

Indicate the best answer to the following statements/questions.

1. An internal control questionnaire indicates that an approved receiving report is required to accompany every check request for payment of merchandise. Which of the following procedures provides the greatest assurance that this control is operating effectively?
   a. Select and examine cancelled checks and ascertain that the related receiving reports are dated **no** earlier than the checks.
   b. Select and examine cancelled checks and ascertain that the related receiving reports are dated **no** later than the checks.
   c. Select and examine receiving reports and ascertain that the related cancelled checks are dated **no** earlier than the receiving reports.
   d. Select and examine receiving reports and ascertain that the related cancelled checks are dated **no** later than the receiving reports.

2. In a properly designed internal control structure, the same employee may be permitted to
   a. Receive and deposit checks, and also approve write-offs of customer accounts.
   b. Approve vouchers for payment, and also sign checks.
   c. Reconcile the bank statements, and also receive and deposit cash.
   d. Sign checks, and also cancel supporting documents.

3. Which of the following is the best audit procedure for determining the existence of unrecorded liabilities at year-end?
   a. Examine a sample of invoices dated a few days prior to and subsequent to year-end to ascertain whether they have been properly recorded.
   b. Examine a sample of cash disbursements in the period subsequent to year-end.
   c. Examine confirmation requests returned by creditors whose accounts appear on a subsidiary trial balance of accounts payable.
   d. Examine unusual relationships between monthly accounts payable balances and recorded purchases.

4. Purchase cutoff procedures should be designed to test whether or **not** all inventory
   a. Purchased and received before the end of the year was paid for.
   b. Ordered before the end of the year was received.
   c. Purchased and received before the end of the year was recorded.
   d. Owned by the company is in the possession of the company at the end of the year.

18

THE ACQUISITION AND PAY-MENT CYCLE: VERIFICATION OF SELECTED ACCOUNTS

CHAPTER OBJECTIVE

The purpose of this chapter is to apply the methodology presented in chapter 17 to tests of details of balances for selected other accounts. Specifically, this chapter discusses how to audit manufacturing equipment, prepaid expenses, accrued liabilities, and operating accounts.

CHAPTER SUMMARY

OBJECTIVE 1:
RECOGNIZE THE MANY ACCOUNTS BESIDES ACCOUNTS PAYABLE THAT ARE PART OF THE ACQUISITION AND PAYMENT CYCLE

1. There are a large number of accounts found in the acquisitions and payment cycle. The methodology for designing tests of details of balances for these accounts is the same as that discussed for accounts payable in chapter 17.

OBJECTIVE 2:
DESIGN AND PERFORM AUDIT TESTS OF MANUFACTURING EQUIPMENT AND RELATED ACCOUNTS

2. Manufacturing equipment was chosen to illustrate the approach to auditing all property, plant, and equipment accounts because the procedures are highly comparable among the accounts. A property master file contains detailed information on individual pieces of equipment such as the following:
   a. Descriptive information.
   b. Date acquired.
   c. Original cost.
   d. Current depreciation.
   e. Accumulated depreciation.
   f. Information on disposals.

3. Debits to manufacturing equipment have already been audited in part through obtaining an understanding of the internal control structure and tests of transactions of the acquisition and payment cycle.

4. The audit approach focuses on acquisitions rather than balances for several reasons.
   a. The number of current period equipment acquisitions is usually small.
   b. Each individual acquisition may be material in size.
   c. Each item of equipment will be used and maintained in the records for several years so omissions and errors can effect the balance sheet and the income statement for long periods of time.

5. Typical analytical procedures might include (1) comparing depreciation expense divided by gross manufacturing equipment cost with previous period's and (2) comparing monthly or annual repairs and maintenance, supplies expense, small tools expense, and similar accounts with prior year's amounts.

6. Audit objectives are very similar to those applied to other accounts.
   a. Current-year acquisitions in the acquisitions schedule agree with related property master file amounts, and the total agrees with the general ledger (detail tie-in).
   b. Current-year acquisitions as listed exist (existence).
   c. Existing acquisitions are listed (completeness).
   d. The client has rights to current-year acquisitions (rights).
   e. Current-year acquisitions as listed are accurate (accuracy).
   f. Current-year acquisitions as listed are properly classified (classification).
   g. Current-year acquisitions are recorded in the proper period (cutoff).
   h. Accounts in the acquisition and payment cycle are properly presented and disclosed (presentation and disclosure).

7. The acquisitions schedule lists each item acquired by date, vendor, expected life, whether new or used, depreciation method, cost, and description.

8. Examining purchase orders, receiving reports, and invoices is the most common audit test employed to verify additions. Usually all large and unusual transactions are verified and a sample is taken of the remainder. The objectives of existence, rights, accuracy, and classification can in large part be satisfied by this procedure.

9. Consideration should be given to the likelihood that some acquisitions may have been improperly charged to expense, especially repairs and maintenance expense. Debits to the expense account exceeding a specified size might be investigated for proper classification.

10. Controls should be in place to account for disposals of equipment.
    a. A formal system to authorize disposals should be maintained.
    b. A formal system to inform management that disposals have occurred should be maintained.
    c. Internal verification that accounting records have been properly adjusted should be required.

11. The schedule of disposals should be tested for detail tie-in and for verification of the following.
    a. Date of disposal.

b. Selling price.
c. Original cost.
d. Buyer's name.
e. Acquisition date.
f. Accumulated depreciation.
g. Any investment credit recapture.
h. Gains/losses from trade-ins.

12. The search for unrecorded disposals is influenced by the strength of controls over disposals but ordinarily would include the following.
    a. Review whether newly acquired assets replaced existing assets.
    b. Analyze gains/losses on the disposal of assets and miscellaneous income for receipts from the disposal of assets.
    c. Review plant modifications and changes in product line, taxes, or insurance coverage for indications of deletions of equipment.
    d. Make inquiries of management and production personnel about the possibility of the disposal of assets.

13. There are several important controls over existing equipment which might reduce the assessed level of control risk.
    a. The maintenance of individual fixed asset accounts in a property master file.
    b. Physical controls over easily moved equipment (tools and vehicles).
    c. Use of identification tags with assigned numbers for each asset.
    d. Periodic counts and reconciliations with recorded amounts.

14. Several audit procedures are usually applied to existing equipment.
    a. Test property master files for detail tie-in.
    b. Verify existence by examination of selected assets.
    c. Consider the need to write-down equipment no longer used (realizable value).
    d. Consider the need to disclose legal encumbrances which can be discovered by reading loan and credit agreements, bank loan confirmations, confirmations from attorneys, and client inquiry.

15. Depreciation expense is not verified during tests of controls and substantive tests of transactions because there is no exchange with external parties. Instead, the amounts for depreciation result from internal allocation for which the auditor must verify **accuracy** by inquiring about and testing whether the depreciation policy has been followed accurately and consistently from period to period considering useful life, method, salvage value, and partial year depreciation policy.

16. In some cases, reasonableness tests may be sufficient for verifying the accuracy of depreciation calculations.

17. Credits to accumulated depreciation are usually verified by virtue of having audited depreciation expense, and debits to accumulated depreciation are usually verified by virtue of having audited asset disposals.

OBJECTIVE 3:
DESIGN AND PERFORM AUDIT TESTS OF PREPAID EXPENSES

18. Audits of prepaid expenses can often be satisfied by analytical procedures because the amounts involved are immaterial. However, prepaid insurance is generally subject to additional tests because of the need to evaluate adequacy of insurance coverage.

19. Internal controls for prepaid insurance generally include the following.
    a. Controls over the acquisition and payment cycle (the audit of that cycle partially tests debits to the prepaid expense accounts).
    b. Control over the **insurance register** which lists all policies in force and the period of coverage (adequacy of coverage should be done periodically by an independent person).
    c. Use of standard monthly journal entries for expired insurance.

20. Audit emphasis for prepaid insurance is on tests of details of the prepaid balance. The expense account audit is usually done with analytical procedures and tests of the entries which credit prepaid insurance and debit expense.

21. Common analytical procedures for prepaid insurance include the following.
    a. Compare total prepaid insurance and prepaid insurance expense with prior year's.
    b. Compare the individual coverage with last year's to test for elimination or change in coverage.

22. Audit objectives relative to prepaid insurance include the following.
    a. The policies, prepaid amounts, and insurance expense in the prepaid schedule are reasonable (the remaining objectives would be considered only if a significant error were suspected or controls were inadequate).
    b. Insurance policies in the prepaid schedule exist and existing policies are listed (existence and completeness).
    c. The client has rights to all insurance policies in the prepaid schedule (rights).
    d. Prepaid amounts on the schedule are accurate and the total is correctly added and agrees with the general ledger (accuracy and detailed tie-in).
    e. The insurance expense related to prepaid insurance is properly classified (classification).
    f. Insurance transactions are recorded in the proper period (cutoff).
    g. Prepaid insurance is properly presented and disclosed (presentation and disclosure).

OBJECTIVE 4:
DESIGN AND PERFORM AUDIT TESTS OF ACCRUED LIABILITIES

23. If the auditor verifies both beginning and ending liability accruals and has audited debits to the account (payments made in the acquisition and payments cycle audit), the related expense account has been audited by virtue of being a residual amount.

24. Common factors to consider in auditing accrued property taxes include the following.
    a. In verifying accrued property taxes, only the realizable value objective is not relevant.
    b. The completeness objective is tested by (1) coordinating property tax accrual tests with the audit of current-year property tax payments and with the audit of major property additions and disposals and (2) comparing current accruals with last year's.

c. The accuracy objective is tested by (1) comparing the accrual with the tax bills and (2) recomputing amounts based on assessed valuation and the expected property tax rates.

OBJECTIVE 5:
DESIGN AND PERFORM AUDIT TESTS OF INCOME AND EXPENSE ACCOUNTS

25. Operations (income and expense accounts) are audited to determine whether they are presented in accordance with GAAP with particular concern for consistent application and proper matching. Ordinarily, auditing operating accounts is coordinated with the audit of the related balance sheet account and other parts of the audit as follows.
    a. Analytical procedures such as comparing current inventory turnover with last year's.
    b. Tests of controls and substantive tests of transactions which audit the controls and substantive aspects of many operating accounts.
    c. Review of related-party transactions which requires close scrutiny.
    d. Tests of allocations principally using tests for reasonableness and recalculation.

26. Some operating accounts are audited by performing an account analysis. This may be done even if the procedures listed in 24 above have been done. It involves examining the underlying documentation for propriety, classification, accuracy, and other pertinent information.

SELF-ASSESSMENT

TRUE-FALSE STATEMENTS

Indicate whether each of the following statements is true or false.

T 1. Assets that have expected lives of more than one year and are acquired for use in the business rather than for resale are classified as property, plant, and equipment.

T 2. The approach to auditing manufacturing equipment can generally be applied to all property, plant, and equipment.

___ 3. Because additions to manufacturing equipment are handled outside the acquisition and payment cycle, these items have not already been partially verified in earlier tests of controls and substantive tests of transactions.

F 4. When auditing manufacturing equipment auditors typically emphasize the account balance in a manner similar to the audit of current assets as opposed to investigating transactions for the year.

T 5. Acquisitions of manufacturing equipment are usually more material and fewer in number than those for current assets.

___ 6. The verification of depreciation and accumulated depreciation accounts usually is done as part of the audit of the related asset.

___ 7. Intangible assets such as patents and copyrights are audited in a manner completely different from that of manufacturing equipment.

___ 8. A comparison of monthly or annual repairs and maintenance, supplies expense, small tools expense, and similar accounts with amounts from previous years might reveal material misstatements in computing depreciation.

___ 9. Unlike misstatements in inventory compilation which are self-correcting in the short term, errors in the treatment of long-term assets can have a material effect on the financial statements over a considerable time period.

___ 10. Examining vendors' invoices and receiving reports tests whether the current-year listed acquisitions exist.

___ 11. Footing the acquisitions schedule and tracing the total to the general ledger is a test of completeness.

___ 12. Examining vendors' invoices supporting material entries to the repairs and maintenance account tests the acquisitions schedule for completeness.

___ 13. To verify rights to manufacturing equipment an auditor would examine such items as deeds and real estate tax bills.

___ 14. Physically examining manufacturing equipment additions to test the existence objective is not a common procedure.

___ 15. Verification of additions to manufacturing equipment is commonly done through confirmation.

___ 16. A formal system should be in place which requires proper authorization for disposals, trade-ins, etc., of manufacturing equipment and assures proper accounting of these activities.

___ 17. The search for unrecorded disposals will help assure that all existing disposals are recorded.

___ 18. About the only test an auditor can employ to identify unrecorded disposals of manufacturing equipment is to make inquiries of management.

___ 19. For repeat engagements where internal controls are good, auditors seldom reverify, in a subsequent period, manufacturing equipment acquired in prior years.

___ 20. Verification of depreciation expense is usually conducted as part of the regular tests of controls and substantive tests of transactions in the acquisition and payment cycle.

__ 21. Auditors are concerned with verifying that depreciation expense is accurately determined on a basis consistent with prior periods under acceptable accounting principles.

__ 22. Because of their immateriality, accounts such as prepaid expense are often tested sufficiently by analytical procedures so tests of details of balances are often not performed on these accounts.

__ 23. An essential control over the prepaid insurance schedule is the use of monthly standard journal entries.

__ 24. Periodic independent review of the adequacy of insurance coverage is an important internal control for insurance.

__ 25. Normally when the internal control structure is adequate, only analytical procedures and tests to determine that charges to insurance expense resulted from credits to prepaid insurance are necessary to verify the expense account balance.

__ 26. Many users of financial statements rely on the balance sheet more heavily than on the income statement.

__ 27. When applying analytical procedures and tests of details of balances to balance sheet accounts the auditor should be alert to the applicability of the tests to operating accounts.

__ 28. Expense account analysis, an analysis of transactions and documentation which make up an account balance, must be performed for some operating accounts; e.g., legal expense.

COMPLETION STATEMENTS

Complete each of the following statements by filling in the blank space(s) with the appropriate word(s).

1. In testing the allocation of expenditures between asset and expense categories the two most important considerations are __________ to GAAP and __________ with the preceding period.

2. It is common to verify an __________ account balance when the related __________ account is being verified.

3. Tests of controls and substantive tests of transactions often simultaneously verify __________ sheet accounts and __________ accounts.

4. An auditor would usually rely more on tests of current period __________ to audit manufacturing equipment than tests of details of balances because there are relatively __________, often __________ transactions which will affect the financial statement for __________ years.

5. A comparison of depreciation expense divided by __________ manufacturing equipment cost with the same ratios of previous years might reveal an error in computing __________.

6. To test the existence of current-year acquisitions of manufacturing equipment the auditor might examine vendors' __________ and __________ reports.

7. One test of __________ for listed acquisitions would be to evaluate total current-year acquisitions in light of business changes and economic conditions.

8. A test of detailed tie-in of the acquisitions schedule would include __________ the schedule.

9. The __________ objective is one of the __________ important audit objectives for auditing manufacturing equipment.

10. In verifying sales, trade-ins, and abandonments of manufacturing equipment auditors are concerned particularly with testing the objective that __________ disposals are recorded and __________ disposals are accurately determined.

11. Reviewing conditions surrounding the purchase of new manufacturing equipment, modifications in plant layout, and insurance coverage coupled with inquiry are means of detecting __________ __________.

12. Depreciation calculations are usually verified by __________ the expense for selected assets to determine whether a proper method has been followed __________.

13. A desirable internal control over the insurance register is __________ review of the __________ of coverage by a qualified person.

MULTIPLE-CHOICE QUESTIONS

Indicate the best answer to the following statements/questions.

1. A weakness in internal control procedures over recording retirements of equipment may cause the auditor to
   a. Inspect certain items of equipment in the plant and trace those items to the accounting records.
   b. Review the property master file to ascertain whether depreciation was taken on each item of equipment during the year.
   c. Trace additions to the "other assets" account to search for equipment that is still on hand but **no** longer being used.
   d. Select certain items of equipment from the accounting records and locate them in the plant.

2. An auditor compares 19x5 revenues and expenses with those of the prior year and investigates all changes exceeding 10%. By this procedure the auditor would be most likely to learn that
   a. Fourth quarter payroll taxes were **not** paid.
   b. The client changed its capitalization policy for small tools in 19x5.
   c. An increase in property tax rates has **not** been recognized in the client's accrual.

    d. The 19x5 provision for uncollectible accounts is inadequate because of worsening economic conditions.

3. The auditor may conclude that depreciation charges are insufficient by noting
    a. Large amounts of fully depreciated assets.
    b. Continuous trade-ins of relatively new assets.
    c. Excessive recurring losses on assets retired.
    d. Insured values greatly in excess of book values.

4. Which of the following accounts would most likely be reviewed by the auditor to gain reasonable assurance that additions to the equipment account are **not** understated?
    a. Repairs and maintenance expense.
    b. Depreciation expense.
    c. Gain on disposal of equipment.
    d. Accounts payable.

5. To strengthen internal control procedures over the custody of heavy mobile equipment, the client would most likely institute a policy requiring a periodic
    a. Increase in insurance coverage.
    b. Inspection of equipment and reconciliation with accounting records.
    c. Verification of liens, pledges, and collateralizations.
    d. Accounting for work orders.

6. The audit procedure of analyzing the repairs and maintenance accounts is primarily designed to provide evidence in support of the audit proposition that all
    a. Expenditures for fixed assets have been recorded in the proper period.
    b. Capital expenditures have been properly authorized.
    c. Noncapitalizable expenditures have been properly expensed.
    d. Expenditures for fixed assets have been capitalized.

19

AUDIT OF THE INVENTORY AND WAREHOUSING CYCLE

CHAPTER OBJECTIVE

This chapter discusses internal controls found in the inventory and warehousing cycle and auditing the various components of the cycle. Emphasis is placed on observing the count and on price testing.

CHAPTER SUMMARY

OBJECTIVE 1: DESCRIBE THE INVENTORY AND WAREHOUSING CYCLE AND THE PERTINENT FUNCTIONS, DOCUMENTS AND RECORDS, AND INTERNAL CONTROLS

1. Inventory often requires more audit time and technical skill than other parts of the audit.
   a. It usually is the largest current account and is generally a significant balance sheet item.
   b. It is often geographically distributed.
   c. It can be very diverse in its nature (jewels, chemicals, etc.) which creates observation and valuation problems.
   d. Cost allocation and obsolescence can create valuation problems.
   e. There is more than one acceptable valuation method and different methods might be used for different types of inventory.

2. On the input side, the inventory and warehousing cycle is closely related to the acquisition cycle from which debits to raw materials and manufacturing overhead come and also to the payroll and personnel cycle from which debits to direct labor and manufacturing overhead come. On the output side the debit to cost of goods sold ties-in the inventory and warehousing cycle to the sales and collection cycle.

3. The relationships discussed in (2) above are summarized by the following T-account relationships.

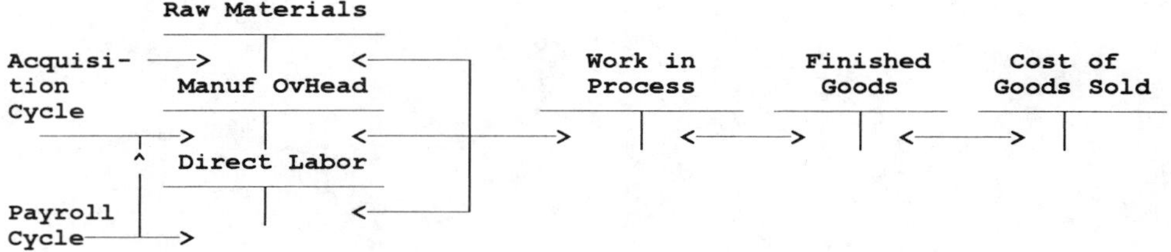

4. There are six major functions in the cycle.
   a. **Purchase requisitions** are authorized by a responsible stockroom person based on general or specific authority from management. These serve as the basis for preparing and issuing **purchase orders**.
   b. **Receiving reports** evidence inspection of goods received for quantity and quality and are distributed to stores, purchasing, and accounts payable.
   c. The stockroom hold goods received until a valid materials requisition or work order is presented indicating the type and quantity of goods needed. Stockroom personnel may recount goods received to verify quantitiesG4
   d. **Job cost** or **process cost** accounting systems account for quantities and related costs (materials, labor, and overhead) of good output and scrap.
   e. **Finished goods** are stored until a duplicate copy of the sales order authorizes release of the goods which is why many companies regard this as part of the sales and collection cycle.
   f. **Shipment** of goods is based on an authorized shipping document.

5. Perpetual inventory master files are normally maintained for raw materials and finished goods inventories. At a minimum these files would be updated for units added to and removed from each category and often would also include unit costs information.

OBJECTIVE 2:
EXPLAIN THE SIGNIFICANCE OF THE FIVE PARTS OF THE INVENTORY AND WAREHOUSING CYCLE TO THE AUDITOR

6. The audit of inventory is usually divided into manageable parts.
   a. Controls over the **acquisition of raw materials, labor, and overhead** are tested as part of the acquisition and payments cycle and the payroll and personnel cycle.
   b. **Internal transfers** from raw materials, direct labor, and overhead to work-in-process and from work-in-process to finished goods must be audited as part of the inventory cycle because they are not evaluated in any other cycle.
   c. **Shipment of goods and recording revenues and costs** are audited in the sales and collection cycle.
   d. Client personnel are **observed counting the inventory** in order to meet the existence, completeness, and accuracy objectives.

e. **Price tests** (testing costs used) and **compilation tests** (testing summarization of the inventory, quantities, extensions, and footings) are directed toward the completeness, existence, and accuracy objectives.

OBJECTIVE 3:
DESIGN AND PERFORM AUDIT TESTS OF COST ACCOUNTING

7. Cost accounting controls would generally include the following:
   a. Physical safeguards which limit access to storage areas.
   b. Use of prenumbered documents authorizing inventory movement.
   c. Maintenance of a perpetual inventory master file by independent parties.
   d. Maintenance of adequate cost records.

8. In auditing the cost accounting system auditors are concerned with four aspects of the system.
   a. **Physical controls** - tests would include observing whether there is a locked storeroom with a custodian in charge.
   b. **Documents and records transferring inventory** - test for existence, completeness, accuracy, date, and description of materials requisitions and completed production records would be completed.
   c. **Perpetual inventory master files** - tests of entries to the files would be done by examination of supporting documents.
   d. **Unit cost records** - tests in other cycles, tests of the allocation of common costs, and tests of internal transfers would be completed.

OBJECTIVE 4:
DESIGN AND PERFORM ANALYTICAL PROCEDURES FOR THE ACCOUNTS IN THE INVENTORY AND WAREHOUSING CYCLE

9. Analytical procedures are as important in auditing inventory and warehousing as they are in other cycles. Typical analytical review procedures for this cycle include the following:
   a. Compare the gross margin percentage with prior years'.
   b. Compare the inventory turnover with prior years'.

OBJECTIVE 5:
DESIGN AND PERFORM PHYSICAL OBSERVATION AUDIT TESTS FOR INVENTORY

10. Professional standards (SAS 1) require that the auditor ordinarily be present to observe the client count the inventory and test the procedures followed. The count may occur at or near year end, at a preliminary date, or on a cycle basis throughout the year.

11. However, inventory stored in public warehouses can be confirmed with the custodian. If the inventory is significant, other procedures might be necessary (e.g., review results of client's investigation of the warehouseman, review client's control procedures of the warehouseman's performance, observe inventory counts, and confirm with lenders whether inventory is being used as collateral).

12. Reliable perpetual inventory master files permit inventory tests prior to year-end, can reduce tests of details of balances work, and can produce earlier audit results.

13. Control procedures over the inventory count should include the following:
    a. Proper instructions to client personnel performing the count.
    b. Proper supervision of count by client management.
    c. Use of independent internal verification of the counts.
    d. Independent reconciliation of counts with perpetual inventory master files.
    e. Control over count tags or sheets.
    f. Submission of inventory count instructions to auditor for review prior to count.

14. The strength of internal controls greatly affects the timing decision. If assessed control risk is significantly reduced a count every year may not be required. If an interim count is done, strength of controls dictates whether the auditor needs to test perpetual inventory master files for transactions from the count date to year end. Periodic inventory of significant amount should be counted at or near year end.

15. Sample selection requires the exercise of judgement. Given limited time, most auditors would attempt to test count items of larger significance and a representative sample of all other items. Alertness for obsolete items is required.

16. An auditor considers several factors in planning for the time needed to observe the client count inventory.
    a. The quality of the control over the physical counts.
    b. The reliability of the perpetual inventory master files.
    c. The total dollar amount and type of inventory.
    d. The number and location of significant inventory locations.
    e. The nature and extent of errors discovered in prior years.

17. If the auditor observes that client personnel are not following inventory counting instructions, the auditor should contact the client's supervisor to correct the problem.

18. Because of the concern for inventory accuracy, potential obsolescence, and the possibility of consigned goods being erroneously included in the count, auditors should be thoroughly familiar with the client's instructions and with the nature of the client's business to properly observe the client's inventory count procedures.

19. Audit objectives for the observation of the physical inventory count include the following:
    a. Inventory as recorded on tags actually exists.
    b. Existing inventory is counted and tagged and tags are accounted for to make sure none are missing.
    c. The client has rights to inventory recorded on tags.
    d. Inventory is counted accurately.
    e. Obsolete and unusable inventory items are excluded or noted.
    f. Inventory is classified correctly on the tags.
    g. Cutoff information is obtained to make sure sales and purchases of inventory are recorded in the proper period.
    h. Inventory is adequately presented and disclosed.

OBJECTIVE 6:

DESIGN AND PERFORM AUDIT TESTS OF PRICING AND COMPILATION FOR INVENTORY

20. Price tests are procedures used by an auditor to determine whether unit prices used by the client are correct. Compilation procedures are used by an auditor to determine whether extensions, footings, summarizations, and postings of amounts to the general ledger are correct.

21. The following pricing and compilation controls ensure that the value of ending inventory is accurate.
    a. An adequate cost system integrated with production and accounting records.
    b. Use of standard costs with variance analysis.
    c. A formal system to review and report obsolete, slow moving items, damaged, and overstated items.
    d. Adequate documents and records for counting the inventory; e.g., prenumbered tags.
    e. Internal verification of pricing, extensions, and footings by a competent, independent person.

22. Audit objectives for inventory pricing and compilation include the following:
    a. Inventory in the inventory listing schedule agrees with the physical inventory counts, the extensions are correct, and the total is correctly added and agrees with the general ledger.
    b. Inventory items in the inventory listing schedule exist.
    c. Existing inventory items are included in the inventory listing schedule.
    d. Inventory items in the inventory listing schedule are accurate.
    e. Inventory items in the inventory listing schedule are stated at realizable value.
    f. Inventory items in the inventory listing schedule are properly classified.
    g. The client has rights to the inventory items in the inventory listing schedule.
    h. Inventory and related accounts in the inventory and warehousing cycle are properly presented and disclosed.

23. The auditor must consider the following questions when testing inventory for accuracy and realizable value.
    a. Is the method followed in accordance with GAAP including any requirements to select the lower of cost or market and to write down obsolete inventory?
    b. Has the application been applied consistently with prior years?

24. Once the auditor has identified the inventory method (LIFO, FIFO, weighted average, etc.) the client is asked to provide invoices which appropriately support the quantities and prices used in the computations. If control over perpetual inventory master files is good, they may be used in place of invoices because additions to them were already tested as part of the acquisitions and payment cycle.

25. Price testing manufactured inventory rests heavily on tests already performed on prime costs and on tests of engineering specifications or other records which indicate how much raw material and direct labor is required to manufacture a unit of finished product.

26. The manufacturing overhead application method and rate should be tested for reasonableness, consistency, and mathematical accuracy.

OBJECTIVE 7:

EXPLAIN HOW THE VARIOUS PARTS OF THE AUDIT OF THE INVENTORY AND WAREHOUSING CYCLE ARE INTEGRATED

27. A careful review of textbook figure 19-6 (page 627) shows the interrelationship between various audit tests. In large part, the audit of the inventory and warehousing cycle depends upon tests conducted in the acquisition and payment cycle (raw materials and manufacturing overhead), the payroll and personnel cycle (direct and indirect labor), and the sales and collection cycle (relief of finished goods and cost of goods sold).

SELF-ASSESSMENT

TRUE-FALSE STATEMENTS

Indicate whether each of the following statements is true or false.

_ 1. Because inventory is often the largest working capital account, diverse in nature, and geographically distributed, the audit of inventory can be complex and time-consuming.

_ 2. The inventory cycle does not interface with the acquisition and payment cycle or with the payroll and personnel cycle.

_ 3. The two basic types of cost accounting internal control structures are job cost and process cost.

_ 4. The inventory and warehousing cycle begins with the sales and collection cycle and ends with the acquisition and payment cycle.

_ 5. The functions of processing goods and storing finished goods are studied and tested as part of the audit of other cycles.

_ 6. An auditor obtains evidence about the physical existence of inventory by observing client personnel count it.

_ 7. Inventory compilation tests are those procedures applied by the CPA when the client has requested a compilation service rather than an audit.

_ 8. An inventory price test verifies that the unit costs used to value the inventory are determined correctly in accordance with GAAP and are consistent with the prior year.

_ 9. An approved materials requisition form authorizes shipment of goods to customers.

_ 10. Inventory clerks should maintain the perpetual inventory master files because their intimate knowledge of the inventory permits them to be more efficient than others.

_ 11. In auditing the transfer of inventory costs from raw materials to finished goods, the auditor will be concerned with physical controls over inventory, documents and records for transferring inventory, perpetual inventory master files, and unit cost records.

__ 12. Evidence of physical controls is obtained by observation and inquiry.

__ 13. In dealing with documents and records for transferring inventory, the concepts of completeness and existence do not apply.

__ 14. Although accurate and reliable perpetual inventory master files may permit the auditor to test inventory at an early interim date, they cannot be used as a basis for reducing the extent of physical inventory tests.

__ 15. Determining the reasonableness of manufacturing overhead costs requires the auditor to consider both the numerator and the denominator upon which the unit costs are based.

__ 16. Professional standards [SAS 1 (AU 331)] state that an auditor would ordinarily be present to observe the client count the physical inventory.

__ 17. Should the client be unable to perform the inventory count the auditor may be engaged for that purpose.

__ 18. Verification of client inventory stored in a public warehouse can be done through confirmation.

__ 19. Counting inventory on a cycle basis throughout the year is acceptable for both periodic and perpetual inventory systems.

__ 20. Observation sample sizes are generally determined in advance of the observation to allow the auditor to concentrate on detecting obsolete inventory.

__ 21. An auditor should try to make test counts of all significant items and a representative selection from all other items.

__ 22. Compilation tests verify the client's summarization of the physical counts, extensions of price times quantities, page and grand totals, and agreement with the ledger account balance.

__ 23. In price testing a FIFO inventory unit price, an auditor would not be concerned with quantities shown on the last purchase invoice of the year being audited.

__ 24. Verifying that the client has accounted for all used and unused inventory tags gives the auditor assurance that none of the counted inventory has been overlooked.

__ 25. Touring the facilities to sight untagged inventory, accounting for any movement of inventory during counting, and inquiring about other possible inventory locations gives the auditor assurance that inventory has not been omitted from the count.

__ 26. Tracing the inventory listed in the client's inventory schedule to inventory tags and to the auditor's recorded counts for existence and description gives assurance that the inventory schedule is complete.

__ 27. Tracing the inventory tags to the inventory schedule to verify inclusion of the correct quantity gives assurance that the inventory schedule is complete.

__ 28. Price tests are performed to determine that the classification objective has been met.

COMPLETION STATEMENTS

Complete each of the following statements by filling in the blank space(s) with the appropriate word(s).

1. To test whether the compiled inventory exists an auditor would trace inventory recorded on the __________ to inventory recorded on the __________.

2. To test whether existing inventory items are included in the compiled inventory an auditor would trace inventory recorded on the __________ to inventory recorded on the __________.

3. In performing price tests (especially for the FIFO evaluation method), the auditor should look at __________ invoices to account for the entire __________ of each type of inventory selected for examination.

4. To test the mechanical accuracy of the compiled inventory, an auditor would recompute the __________ of price times quantity, __________ the listing, and compare the total with the account balance.

5. Classification of inventory into raw materials, work in process, and finished goods categories can be verified by comparing the description on the inventory listing with the description on the inventory __________ and the auditor's __________ __________.

6. The client's response to __________ and being unable to find inventory tags recorded on the inventory listing for nonowned inventory provides the auditor with some assurance that the listing contains only items which are __________.

7. A comparison of inventory turnover (costs of goods sold divided by average inventory) with previous years' may indicate the presence of __________ inventory.

8. Unaccounted movement of inventory during the counting process could result in the inclusion of __________ items in the listing.

9. To determine that all the inventory has been counted an auditor might __________ the inventory to make sure that it had all been __________.

10. To test for proper sales cutoff an auditor would obtain the number of the last __________ ticket and verify that the item shipped had been __________ from the listing.

11. To test for proper purchases cutoff an auditor would obtain the number of the last __________ report and verify that the item received had been __________ in the listing.

12. The major inventory fraud committed upon __________ changed the profession's views on its responsibility relating to inventory.

MULTIPLE-CHOICE QUESTIONS

Indicate the best answer to the following statements/questions.

1. When auditing merchandise inventory at year-end, the auditor performs a purchase cutoff test to obtain evidence that
   a. All goods purchased before year-end are received before the physical inventory count.
   b. No goods held on consignment for customers are included in the inventory balance.
   c. No goods observed during the physical count are pledged or sold.
   d. All goods owned at year-end are included in the inventory balance.

2. Which of the following is a question that the auditor would expect to find on the production cycle section of an internal control questionnaire?
   a. Are vendor's invoices for raw materials approved for payment by an employee who is independent of the cash disbursements function?
   b. Are signed checks for the purchase of raw materials mailed directly after signing without being returned to the person who authorized the invoice processing?
   c. Are all releases by storekeepers of raw materials from storage based on approved requisition documents?
   d. Are details of individual disbursements for raw materials balanced with the total to be posted to the appropriate general ledger account?

3. Edwards Corp. uses the last-in, first-out method of costing for half of its inventory and the first-in, first-out method of costing for the other half of its inventory. Because of these recording and reporting methods, the auditor should issue a(an)
   a. Unqualified opinion.
   b. Disclaimer of opinion.
   c. "Except for" qualified opinion.
   d. Adverse opinion.

4. If the perpetual inventory master files show lower quantities of inventory than the physical count, an explanation of the difference might be unrecorded
   a. Sales.
   b. Sales discounts.
   c. Purchases.
   d. Purchase discounts.

5. Which of the following is **not** one of the independent auditor's objectives regarding the examination of inventories?
   a. Verifying that inventory counted is owned by the client.
   b. Verifying that the client has used proper inventory pricing.
   c. Ascertaining the physical quantities of inventory on hand.
   d. Verifying that all inventory owned by the client is on hand at the time of the count.

6. When perpetual inventory master files are maintained in quantities and in dollars, and internal control procedures over inventory are weak, the auditor would probably
   a. Want the client to schedule the physical inventory count at the end of the year.
   b. Insist that the client perform physical counts of inventory items several times during the year.
   c. Increase the extent of tests for unrecorded liabilities at the end of the year.

d. Have to disclaim an opinion on the income statement for that year.

7. Independent internal verification of inventory occurs when employees who
   a. Issue raw materials obtain material requisitions for each issue and prepare daily totals of materials issued.
   b. Compare records of goods on hand with physical quantities do not maintain the records or have custody of the inventory.
   c. Obtain receipts for the transfer of completed work to finished goods prepare a completed production report.
   d. Are independent of issuing production orders update records from completed job cost sheets and production cost reports on a timely basis.

8. An auditor's tests of controls over the issuance of raw materials to production would most likely include
   a. Reconciling raw materials and work in process perpetual inventory records to general ledger balances.
   b. Inquiring of the custodian about the procedures followed when defective materials are received from vendors.
   c. Observing that raw materials are stored in secure areas and that storeroom security is supervised by a responsible individual.
   d. Examining material requisitions and reperforming client controls designed to process and record issuances.

9. Which of the following control procedures would most likely be used to maintain accurate perpetual inventory records?
   a. Independent storeroom count of goods received.
   b. Periodic independent reconciliation of control and subsidiary records.
   c. Periodic independent comparison of records with goods on hand.
   d. Independent matching of purchase orders, receiving reports, and vendors' invoices.

20

AUDIT OF THE CAPITAL ACQUISITION AND REPAYMENT CYCLE

This chapter discusses auditing two major elements of the capital acquisition and repayment cycle, notes payable and owners' equity.

CHAPTER SUMMARY

OBJECTIVE 1: IDENTIFY THE ACCOUNTS AND THE UNIQUE CHARACTERISTICS OF THE CAPITAL ACQUISITION AND REPAYMENT CYCLE

1. Four characteristics of this cycle influence the audit.
   a. Transactions are usually **few in number.**
   b. A single transaction can be material to the financial statements.
   c. Legal requirements affecting financial statement presentation and disclosures exist.
   d. A direct relationship exists between debt and interest and between dividends and equity.

OBJECTIVE 2: DESIGN AND PERFORM AUDIT TESTS OF NOTES PAYABLE AND RELATED ACCOUNTS AND TRANSACTIONS

2. A **note payable** is an obligation to a creditor which may be secured by pledged property.

3. The objectives for the audit of notes payable are to determine the following:
   a. The internal control structure over notes payable is adequate.

b. Transactions for notes and related interest are properly authorized and recorded as defined by the six transaction-related audit objectives.

c. The liabilities for notes payable and interest payable are properly stated as defined by eight of the balance-related audit objectives (realizable value is not applicable).

4. A summary of t-account relationships for notes payable follows:

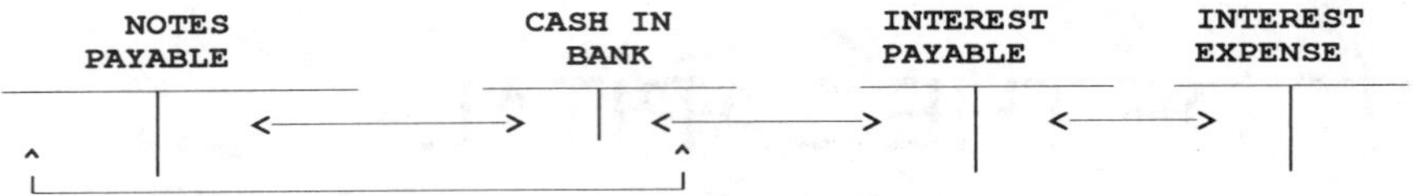

5. Four important controls over notes payable are that
   a. New notes should be **properly authorized** by the board of directors or top-level management, preferably with two signatures.
   b. There should be **adequate controls over repayment** of principal and interest as part of the acquisition and repayment cycle.
   c. There should be **proper documents and records** with subsidiary records, if necessary, and custody of properly cancelled paid notes should be vested in a responsible person.
   d. There should be **periodic independent verification** of the subsidiary record and interest expense.

6. Tests of controls and substantive tests of transactions for notes issued are included in the sales and cash collections cycle and tests of controls and substantive tests of transactions for payments are included in the acquisitions and payment cycle.

7. Analytical procedures for notes payable are advisable.
   a. They test the reasonableness of interest expense.
   b. They test for omitted notes payable.
   c. They may justify reduction or elimination of tests of details of balances.

8. The audit objectives for tests of details of balances for notes payable and interest balances includes the following (The three most important objectives are marked with an *).
   a. Notes payable in the notes payable schedule agree with the client's notes payable register or master file, the general ledger and are correctly added.
   b. Notes payable in the schedule exist.
   * c. Existing notes payable are included in the notes payable schedule.
   * d. Notes payable and accrued interest on the schedule are accurate.
   e. Notes payable in the schedule are properly classified.
   f. Notes payable are included in the proper period.
   g. The client is obligated to pay the notes payable.
   * h. Notes payable, interest expense, and accrued interest are properly presented and disclosed.

9. The schedule of notes payable provides information on all transactions for the year and includes the following information.
   a. Principal and interest.
   b. Beginning and ending balances for notes and interest payable.

c. Descriptive information (due date, interest rate, collateral).

OBJECTIVE 3:
DESCRIBE THE PRIMARY CONCERNS IN THE DESIGN AND PERFORMANCE OF AN AUDIT OF OWNER's EQUITY

10. For publicly held companies verification of owners' equity is normally much more complex than for privately held companies because of the volume and complexity of the transactions involved.

11. A summary of the t-account relationships for owners' equity follows:

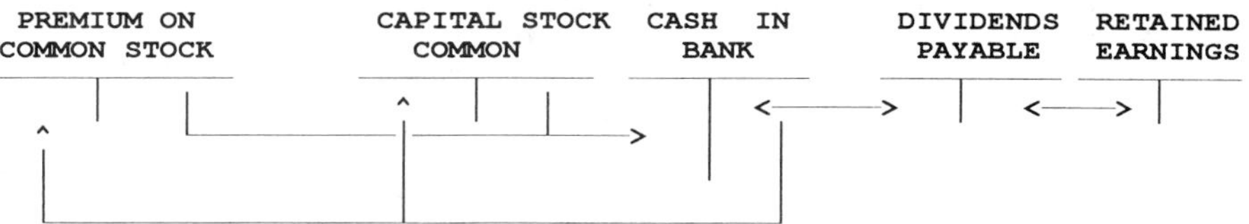

12. The objectives for the audit of owner's equity are to determine the following:.
    a. Internal controls over capital stock and related dividends are adequate.
    b. Owners' equity transactions are recorded properly as defined by the six transaction-related audit objectives.
    c. Owners' equity balances are properly stated and disclosed as defined by the balance-related audit objectives (excluding rights/obligations and realizable because they are inapplicable).

13. Owner equity transactions should be properly authorized. The following transactions require authorization by the board of directors.
    1. Issuances of capital stock.
    2. Repurchases of capital stock.
    3. Declaration of dividends.

14. There should be proper recordkeeping and segregation of duties of owner equity transactions.
    a. The control structure of a company that maintains its own records for owners' equity transactions should meet the following goals
        1. Recognize the actual owners of capital stock.
        2. Disburse dividend payments to holders of record.
        3. Minimize the potential for employee fraud (e.g., use an imprest dividend account).
    b. The control system normally includes (1) well-defined policies for preparing stock certificates and recording capital stock transactions in **the capital stock certificate book** and **the shareholders' capital stock master file** and (2) independent internal verification of information in the records. Particular attention should be given to compliance with state laws regarding par value, number of shares authorized, and state transaction taxes.

15. Companies whose shares are publicly traded must use an **independent registrar** who issues new stock and receives retired stock in accordance with the corporate charter and applicable laws. **Stock transfer agents** are used to maintain stockholder records.

OBJECTIVE 4:
DESIGN AND PERFORM TESTS OF CONTROLS, SUBSTANTIVE TESTS OF TRANSACTIONS AND TESTS OF DETAILS OF BALANCES FOR CAPITAL STOCK AND RETAINED EARNINGS

16. There are several audit concerns regarding capital stock and additional paid-in capital.
    a. Existing capital stock transactions are recorded (confirm with registrar or transfer agent and review minutes to board of directors' meetings).
    b. Recorded capital stock transactions exist and are accurately recorded (examine minutes, confirm with transfer agent, trace to cash receipts journal, verify allocation between par value and premium, consider adherence to GAAP; e.g., stock involved in purchase vs. pooling of interests).
    c. Capital stock is accurately recorded (confirm number of shares outstanding with transfer agent, multiply by par value, and recompute weighted average shares outstanding for EPS).
    d. Capital stock is properly presented and disclosed (consult legal documents, corporate charter, minutes, and GAAP to verify proper presentation and disclosure for capital stock, options, warrants, convertible securities, etc.).

17. The audit emphasis for dividends is on transactions rather than balances. Dividends are typically audited 100%. The more important audit objectives in this area are listed below.
    a. Recorded dividends exist (examine board minutes for authorization and audit work papers for possible restrictions).
    b. Existing dividends are recorded (examine board minutes).
    c. Dividends are accurately recorded (recompute, confirm with transfer agent, and trace to cash disbursements).
    d. Dividends as paid to stockholders exist (trace payments to dividends records and recompute accuracy of checks).
    e. Dividends payable are recorded.
    f. Dividends payable are accurately recorded.

18. The audit of retained earnings begins with an analysis of the account. The credit for earnings is traced to the income statement. The charge for dividends was audited as explained above. Other entries should be evaluated in terms of GAAP (e.g., prior-period adjustments) and in terms of their classification, accuracy, and presentation and disclosure.

19. Transactions erroneously omitted from retained earnings might include stock dividends and appropriations or reversals of previous appropriations.

20. Presentation and disclosure regarding retained earnings requires a knowledge of agreements made which restrict dividend payments and/or require appropriations of retained earnings.

SELF-ASSESSMENT

TRUE-FALSE STATEMENTS

Indicate whether each of the following statements is true or false.

_ 1. An important characteristic of the capital acquisition and repayment cycle is that there are many transactions which individually are immaterial.

_ 2. A significant legal relationship exists between the entity and the holder of the stock or bond being audited which could affect the financial statements and related required presentation and disclosure.

_ 3. No audit efficiency is gained by auditing interest expense concurrently with notes payable or dividends concurrently with related equity accounts.

_ 4. Responsibility for issuance of new notes should generally rest with the board of directors or high-level management.

_ 5. Audit tests completed in the tests of controls and substantive tests of transactions for cash receipts includes tests for notes payable transactions involving the issuance of notes.

_ 6. Audit tests completed in the tests of controls and substantive tests of transactions for cash disbursements include tests for notes payable transactions involving repayment of interest and principal.

_ 7. Because of the tests of controls and substantive tests of transactions completed in other cycles an auditor would not normally perform additional tests of controls and substantive tests of transactions for notes payable.

_ 8. The three most important objectives in auditing notes payable are that the items listed in the schedule of notes payable and accrued interest exist, that the notes are properly classified, and that overall reasonableness is achieved.

_ 9. Common restrictions which would require footnote disclosure are requirements for compensating balances and restrictions of dividend payments.

_ 10. A standard bank confirmation could not be used to test the notes payable schedule for completeness.

_ 11. An analysis of interest expense and a review of the minutes of the board of directors meetings could not be used to test the notes payable schedule for completeness.

_ 12. Confirmation with holders of notes payable of the principal amount due, interest rates, and the last date for which interest has been paid tests the accuracy objective.

_ 13. The existence of listed notes payable can be tested by confirmation and by reviewing approval recorded in minutes to board of directors meetings.

_ 14. Verifying owners' equity accounts of publicly traded companies is much more difficult than for closely held companies because of the volume of transactions involved.

__ 15. Because of the unique nature of transactions in this cycle, the six transaction-related audit objectives are not relevant to the proper recording of transactions.

__ 16. Because issuance and repurchase of capital stock are usually material transactions, board approval authorizing these transactions is generally required.

__ 17. A capital stock book is a record of balances of the outstanding shares held by individual stockholders.

__ 18. A stockholders' ledger is a record of the capital stock issued and repurchased over the life of the entity.

__ 19. The stock exchanges require each listed company to have one of its employees serve as a stock registrar to assure the proper issuance of stock certificates.

__ 20. Because independent stock transfer agents maintain stockholder records and disburse cash dividends to shareholders the internal control structure over these transactions is improved.

__ 21. The objective of determining that existing capital stock transactions are recorded can easily be satisfied by confirming transactions with the registrar or transfer agent.

__ 22. Verifying the existence and accuracy of capital stock transactions ordinarily begins with an examination of minutes to directors' meetings.

__ 23. Auditing the achievement of the six transaction-related audit objectives for dividend transactions is ordinarily done on a test basis.

__ 24. Verification of dividends begins with an examination of board approval in the meeting minutes and recomputation of the amounts involved.

COMPLETION STATEMENTS

Complete each of the following statements by filling in the blank space(s) with the appropriate word(s).

1. The exclusion of a __________ transaction occurring in the capital acquisition and repayment cycle could be __________ in itself.

2. A note payable is a __________ __________ to a creditor. It may be secured or unsecured by assets.

3. An important control over notes payable is periodic __________ verification.

4. The normal starting point for the audit of notes payable is with a schedule of __________ payable and __________ __________.

5. To test the notes payable schedule for completeness an auditor might review the __________ __________ for new notes credited directly to the bank account.

6. To test an individual entry in the notes payable schedule for existence an auditor might examine a __________ copy of the note for __________.

7. To test the notes payable schedule for __________ an auditor might examine notes paid after year-end to determine whether they were included in liabilities at the balance sheet date.

8. The amount of time spent auditing owners' equity for a closely held corporation is likely to be __________ because the types of transactions likely to be found are for __________ earnings and the __________ of dividends.

9. The most important procedures for preventing misstatements in owners' equity accounts are (1) adequate controls to assure proper preparation of stock certificates and __________ capital stock transactions and (2) independent __________ __________ of information in the records.

10. The use of a separate __________ __________ bank account limits the amount of money paid for dividend checks to no more than the funds in that account.

11. The four main concerns with auditing capital stock and paid-in capital in excess of par are that __________ capital stock transactions are recorded, that the recorded transactions exist and are __________ recorded, that capital stock is accurately recorded, and that capital stock is properly presented and ______________.

12. The audit of entries to retained earnings may require considerable knowledge of __________ opinions and __________ statements.

13. A common item requiring disclosure relative to retained earnings is any __________ on the payment of __________.

14. Existing capital stock transactions can be __________ with the registrar or __________ agent.

MULTIPLE-CHOICE QUESTIONS

Indicate the best answer to the following statements/questions.

1. An auditor's program for the examination of long-term debt should include steps that require the
   a. Inspection of the accounts payable subsidiary ledger.
   b. Investigation of credits to the bond interest income account.
   c. Verification of the existence of the bondholders.
   d. Examination of any bond trust indenture.

2. Two months before year end the bookkeeper erroneously recorded the receipt of a long-term bank loan by a debit to cash and a credit to sales. Which of the following is the most effective procedure for detecting this type of misstatement?
   a. Analyze the notes payable journal.
   b. Analyze bank confirmation information.
   c. Prepare a year-end bank reconciliation.
   d. Prepare a year-end bank transfer schedule.

3. In connection with the examination of bonds payable, an auditor would expect to find in a trust indenture
   a. The issue date and maturity date of the bond.
   b. The names of the original subscribers to the bond issue.
   c. The yield to maturity of the bonds issued.
   d. The company's debt to equity ratio at the time of issuance.

4. During an examination of a publicly held company, the auditor should obtain written confirmation regarding debenture transactions from the
   a. Debenture holders.
   b. Client's attorney.
   c. Internal auditors.
   d. Trustee.

5. Which of the following is the most important consideration of an auditor when examining the stockholders' equity section of a client's balance sheet?
   a. Changes in the capital stock account are verified by an independent stock transfer agent.
   b. Stock dividends and/or stock splits during the year under audit were approved by the stockholders.
   c. Stock dividends are capitalized at par or stated value on the dividend declaration date.
   d. Entries in the capital stock account can be traced to a resolution in the minutes of the board of directors' meetings.

6. An audit program for the examination of the retained earnings account should include a step that requires verification of the
   a. Market value used to charge retained earnings to account for a two-for-one stock split.
   b. Approval of the adjustment to the beginning balance as a result of a write-down of an account receivable.
   c. Authorization for both cash and stock dividends.
   d. Gain or loss resulting from disposition of treasury shares.

7. The auditor is concerned with establishing that dividends are paid to client corporation stockholders owning stock as of the
   a. Issue date.
   b. Declaration date.
   c. Record date.
   d. Payment date.

21

AUDIT OF CASH BALANCES

CHAPTER OBJECTIVE

This chapter discusses audit procedures employed for tests of details of balances for three types of cash accounts: general cash accounts, payroll bank accounts, and petty cash. In addition, the relationship between the transactions cycle and audit decisions in the cash area are mentioned.

CHAPTER SUMMARY

OBJECTIVE 1: DESCRIBE THE MAJOR TYPES OF CASH ACCOUNTS MAINTAINED BY BUSINESS ENTITIES

1. The general cash account ordinarily functions as one side of all journal entries in both the sales and collections cycle and the acquisitions and cash payments cycle. Furthermore, activity in most other cash accounts is ultimately recorded in general cash.

2. Many companies improve control over payroll disbursements by using an imprest payroll account which makes payments only for payroll, receives deposits from general cash in the amount of the payroll, and maintains some minimum fixed account balance.

3. Control over branch operations is enhanced by using an imprest disbursements account which functions like an imprest petty cash fund. In both cases a working fund balance is established. The fund is replenished when receipts for disbursements are presented.

4. There are two other typical types of cash accounts.

a. Imprest petty cash funds are used for small cash acquisitions.
b. Cash equivalents such as time deposits, certificates of deposit, and money market funds are used to earn a return on temporary excess funds.

OBJECTIVE 2: DESCRIBE THE RELATIONSHIP OF CASH IN THE BANK TO THE VARIOUS TRANSACTION CYCLES

5. Study textbook figure 21-2 (page 662). It shows the interrelationship between cash and the transaction cycles. Cash is usually an important account to audit because of its integral relationship with the major transaction cycles, the material amount of money which flows through the account, and the fact that it is the most desirable asset to steal.

6. A bank reconciliation will disclose differences which exist between the bank's records and the company's records, but it cannot be depended upon to reveal whether all transactions related to cash were recorded properly. For example, the following would not be discovered by a bank reconciliation.
    a. Failure to bill a customer.
    b. Billing a customer at a lower price than established by policy.
    c. Payment for raw materials that were not received.

OBJECTIVE 3: DESIGN AND PERFORM AUDIT TESTS OF THE GENERAL CASH ACCOUNT

7. In auditing the year-end cash balance, the auditor determines whether six of the nine balance-related audit objectives have been met. Rights to general cash, classification, and realizable value are not problems.

8. Controls over cash transactions have already been discussed in earlier chapters so the focus of control in this chapter is on independent bank reconciliations. They should be completed by a person independent of recording and handling cash receipts and cash disbursements so that the reconciliation can be used to **internally verify** the ending cash balance as well as cash receipts and disbursements transactions.

9. A competent bank reconciliation should include (* indicates procedures related to tests of controls and substantive tests of transactions discussed earlier) the following.
    - * a. Compare canceled checks with the cash disbursements journal for date, payee, and amount.
    - * b. Examine canceled checks for signature, endorsement, and cancellation.
    - * c. Compare deposits in the bank with recorded cash receipts for date, customer, and amount.
    - * d. Account for the numerical sequence of checks and investigation the missing ones.
    - e. Reconcile all items causing a difference between the book and bank balances and the verification of their propriety.
    - f. Reconcile total debits on the bank statement with the totals in the cash disbursements journal.
    - g. Reconcile total credits on the bank statement with the totals in the cash receipts journal.
    - h. Review month-end interbank transfers for propriety and proper recording.

   i. Follow-up on outstanding checks and stop-payment notices.
   j. Review of the completed reconciliation by an independent responsible employee.

10. Balance-related audit objectives for the general cash account are listed below (* indicates the three most important objectives). Ownership and classification objectives are excluded because they are not a problem.
   a. Cash in the bank as stated on the reconciliation foots correctly and agrees with the general ledger.
   * b. Cash in the bank as stated on the reconciliation exists.
   * c. Cash in the bank as stated on the reconciliation is accurate.
   * d. Existing cash in the bank is included.
   e. Cash receipts and cash disbursements transactions are recorded in the proper period.
   f. Cash in the bank is properly presented and disclosed.

11. Auditors generally send a **standard bank confirmation** request to each bank with which the client does business. Replies should be made directly to the auditor. Second requests may be necessary in some cases. The following information is requested.
   a. The balances in all accounts held by that bank.
   b. The rate of interest paid on interest-bearing accounts.
   c. Information on various forms of debt (notes, mortgages) owed to the bank (amount, date of loan, due date, interest rate, and collateral).

12. All information reported by the bank is traced to the appropriate working papers.

13. A **cutoff bank statement** is a bank statement for a partial period of time (usually the first 7 to 10 days of the new period) which is mailed by the bank directly to the auditor. This external document is used to verify reconciling items. If a cutoff statement cannot be obtained, the integrity of the first bank statement of the new period is established by reviewing it for alterations and testing it for arithmetic accuracy.

14. The following procedures are used to test the bank reconciliation.
   a. Trace the balance per the cutoff statement to the reconciliation.
   b. Trace checks returned with the cutoff statement to the outstanding check list and the cash disbursements journal noting dates and other information.
   c. Investigate all outstanding checks not included with checks returned in the cutoff bank statement by discussion with the client and possibly by confirmation with the payee.
   d. Trace all deposits in transit to the cutoff bank statement noting date of deposit for reasonableness.
   e. Investigate and verify propriety of other reconciling items.
   f. Verify that the client's bank reconciliation is mathematically accurate.

OBJECTIVE 4:
RECOGNIZE WHEN TO EXTEND AUDIT TESTS OF THE GENERAL CASH ACCOUNT TO TEST FURTHER FOR MATERIAL FRAUD

15. When the controls over cash activities are weak and/or when the auditor suspects material errors or irregularities in cash balances, fraud-oriented procedures may be

applied; e.g., extended tests of the bank reconciliation, proofs of cash, and tests for kiting.

16. **Extended tests of the bank reconciliation** results in verification that all entries in the journal for the last month of the year are properly reflected in or excluded from the bank reconciliation and vice-versa. All uncleared items from the November reconciliation would be included in the December reconciliation.

17. **A proof of cash** (four-column bank reconciliation) helps the auditor determine whether the following objectives were achieved.
    a. All cash receipts recorded in the cash receipts journal were deposited.
    b. All deposits recorded by the bank were recorded in the accounting records.
    c. All recorded cash disbursements were paid by the bank.
    d. All payments made by the bank were recorded by the client.

18. The proof of cash combines substantive tests of transactions and tests of details of balances auditing because beginning and ending balances are reconciled as well as cash receipts and cash disbursements for the period covered by the beginning and ending dates.

19. **Kiting** is the transfer of money from one bank to another close to year-end for the purpose of overstating the ending balance of cash on deposit. The deposit is recorded in one bank, often with a corresponding credit to revenue, but it is not recorded as a disbursement in the other bank during the period being audited. Consequently, the same money appears as an asset twice.

20. A bank transfer schedule listing transfers just before and after year-end should be prepared. Information from the bank transfer schedule, bank statements, and the cash receipts and disbursements journals are compared for correct accounting in the proper time period.
    a. The accuracy of the information on the bank transfer schedule should be verified.
    b. The date of the recording of the disbursements and receipts for each transfer must be in the same fiscal year.
    c. Disbursements on the bank transfer schedule should be correctly included in or excluded from year-end bank reconciliations as outstanding checks.
    d. Receipts on the bank transfer schedule should be correctly included in or excluded from year-end bank reconciliations as deposits in transit.

21. Even if fraud is not suspected, bank transfer schedules are often prepared when there have been numerous transfers close to year-end.

22. Several other audit procedures might uncover cash fraud.
    a. Confirmation of accounts receivable.
    b. Tests of accounts receivable for lapping.
    c. Scanning the general ledger cash account and both cash journals for large or unusual transactions.
    d. Examining supporting documentation for the write-off of bad debts and sales returns and allowances.
    e. Tracing customer orders to billings and ultimately to cash receipts.

OBJECTIVE 5:

DESIGN AND PERFORM AUDIT TESTS OF THE PAYROLL BANK ACCOUNT

23. The audit of the payroll bank account is principally done by reconciliation following the procedures outlined above for the general account.

OBJECTIVE 6: DESIGN AND PERFORM AUDIT TESTS OF PETTY CASH

24. Control over petty cash begins by establishing an imprest fund for which one person is responsible. Disbursements from the fund should be supported by receipts and properly authorized, prenumbered petty cash forms. Internal auditors should periodically perform surprise examinations of the fund. Limits on the amount and nature of qualified expenditures should be established.

25. Although auditors generally emphasize tests of controls and substantive tests of transactions of the petty cash fund rather than tests of the ending balance, it is common for them to count the fund balance. When examining selected reimbursement transactions auditors usually complete the following steps.
    a. Foot the selected petty cash vouchers supporting the reimbursements.
    b. Account for the numerical sequence of the petty cash vouchers.
    c. Examine the select vouchers for authorization.
    d. Examine all supporting documents for reasonableness, propriety, and cancellation.

SELF-ASSESSMENT

TRUE-FALSE STATEMENTS

Indicate whether each of the following statements is true or false.

_ 1. The chapter on auditing cash balances was placed near the end of the textbook because it is one of the least important audit areas.

_ 2. Imprest payroll bank accounts are used to maximize the amount of interest income earned on deposited money.

_ 3. An imprest disbursements bank account for branch operations improves controls over cash receipts and disbursements.

_ 4. As a general rule, all cash transactions either originate from or terminate with an entry to general cash.

_ 5. A bank reconciliation will reveal differences which exist between the bank's records and the company's records in addition to errors in recording transactions such as failing to bill a customer.

_ 6. Verification of the ending cash balance with the bank reconciliation assures the auditor that all cash transactions that took place during the year are correctly reflected in the ending balance.

_ 7. The bank reconciliation should be completed by someone independent of the cash receipts and cash disbursements functions.

_ 8. The audit objectives for tests of details of balances of rights, classification, and realizable value are not generally a problem over which the auditor needs to be concerned.

_ 9. Reasonableness tests are employed in the cash area because auditors frequently audit bank reconciliations on a test basis.

_ 10. Existence, accuracy and completeness are the most important audit objectives for cash in the bank.

_ 11. Counting the cash on hand on the last day of the year provides the auditor with evidence of the classification objective.

_ 12. Having recorded the last check written at year-end permits the auditor to test cutoff for cash disbursements.

_ 13. Tracing deposits in transit and outstanding checks to the subsequent period bank statement provides evidence about the cutoff objective.

_ 14. There are no presentation and disclosure considerations relative to cash balances in bank accounts.

_ 15. The integrity of the standard bank confirmation is enhanced if it is mailed directly to the auditor.

_ 16. As the name standard bank confirmation implies, the form would not be used to verify such things as contingent liabilities and collateral security interests.

_ 17. A cutoff bank statement is just like a regular bank statement except that it covers a shortened period of time such as the first seven to ten days of the first month following year end.

_ 18. The purpose of sending the cutoff bank statement directly to the auditor is to provide him/her with evidence needed for the bank reconciliation sooner in the audit, thereby facilitating early completion of the engagement.

_ 19. When a cutoff bank statement is not available the auditor must perform tests of the propriety of the regular monthly bank statement in order to use it to verify reconciling items on the bank reconciliation.

_ 20. All paid checks returned with the cutoff bank reconciliation which were written in the year being audited should appear on the list of outstanding checks.

_ 21. There are no additional procedures the auditor can take to verify the outstanding checks not returned with the cutoff bank statement.

_ 22. Ordinarily, all deposits in transit should appear as deposits on the cutoff bank statement.

_ 23. The auditor has the responsibility to extend tests of the bank reconciliation if he/she believes the reconciliation to be intentionally misstated.

_ 24. Kiting occurs when money is transferred from one bank to another and the receipt is recorded in the account of the receiving bank but the disbursement is not recorded in the account of the paying bank which results in the asset being counted twice.

_ 25. Tests for kiting are performed using a bank reference schedule.

COMPLETION STATEMENTS

Complete each of the following statements by filling in the blank space(s) with the appropriate word(s).

1. Virtually all cash __________ and __________ transactions flow through general cash at some point in time.

2. With an __________ disbursements bank account, reimbursement to the branch is based on the presentation of __________ documentation.

3. The amount of cash flowing __________ and __________ of the cash account is often larger than the activity for any other account.

4. Preparation of a bank reconciliation __________ (would/would not) detect payment made for raw materials not received.

5. Preparation of a bank reconciliation __________ (would/would not) detect the direct payment of a note by the bank charged against the company's account for which the company has not yet made an entry.

6. Factors the auditor must consider in auditing cash are that (1)it can be __________ by conditions found in other cycles, (2) a large volume of transactions flows through the account, and (3) it is the __________ __________ asset to steal because of its liquidity.

7. Counting the cash on hand on the __________ day of the year and subsequently __________ the amount to deposits in transit is a test of the cash account balance for __________.

8. Tracing __________ checks to the subsequent period bank statement is a test of the cash account balance for __________.

9. The three most important audit objectives for the cash in bank account balance are __________, __________, and __________.

10. The validity of the standard bank confirmation could be seriously affected if it is not __________ __________ by the auditor.

11. The purpose of the cutoff bank statement is to __________ the ___________ items on the client's year-end bank reconciliation with evidence that is __________ to the client.

12. Other reconciling items which the auditor might have to account for are __________ __________ charges, bank errors and corrections, and transactions debited or credited directly by the bank not yet recorded by the client.

13. A proof of cash provides evidence about ___________ and __________.

14. If a client maintains an __________ payroll account and requires that an ___________ employee reconcile the account on a regular basis the audit time required for this account should be relatively small.

MULTIPLE-CHOICE QUESTIONS

Indicate the best answer to the following statements/questions.

1. On receiving the bank cutoff statement, the auditor should trace
   a. Deposits in transit on the year-end bank reconciliation to deposits in the cash receipts journal.
   b. Checks dated prior to year-end to the outstanding checks listed on the year-end bank reconciliation.
   c. Deposits listed on the cutoff statement to deposits in the cash receipts journal.
   d. Checks dated subsequent to year-end to the outstanding checks listed on the year-end bank reconciliation.

2. An auditor ordinarily should send a standard confirmation request to all banks with which the client has done business during the year under audit, regardless of the year-end balance, because this procedure
   a. Provides for confirmation regarding compensating balance arrangements.
   b. Detects kiting activities that may otherwise **not** be discovered.
   c. Seeks information about indebtedness to the bank.
   d. Verifies securities held by the bank in safekeeping.

3. An auditor would be most likely to identify a contingent liability by obtaining a(an)
   a. Related party transaction confirmation.
   b. Accounts payable confirmation.
   c. Transfer agent confirmation.
   d. Standard bank confirmation.

4. When counting cash on hand the auditor must exercise control over all cash and other negotiable assets to prevent
   a. Theft.
   b. Irregular endorsement.
   c. Substitution.
   d. Deposits-in-transit.

5. To gather evidence regarding the balance per bank in a bank reconciliation, an auditor would examine all of the following **except**
   a. Cutoff bank statement.

b. Year-end bank statement.
c. Bank confirmation.
d. General ledger.

6. For the most effective internal control procedure, monthly bank statements should be received directly from the banks and reviewed by the
   a. Controller.
   b. Cash receipts accountant.
   c. Cash disbursements accountant.
   d. Internal auditor.

7. Which of the following cash transfers results in a misstatement of cash at December 31, 19x7?

Bank Transfer Schedule

	Disbursement		Receipt	
Transfer	Recorded in books	Paid by bank	Recorded in books	Received by bank
a.	12/31/x7	1/4/x8	12/31/x7	12/31/x7
b.	1/4/x8	1/5/x8	12/31/x7	1/4/x8
c.	12/31/x7	1/5/x8	12/31/x7	1/4/x8
d.	1/4/x8	1/11/x8	1/4/x8	1/4/x8

8. On the last date of the fiscal year, the cash disbursements clerk drew a company check on bank A and deposited the check in the company account bank B to cover a previous theft of cash. The disbursement has not been recorded. The auditor will best detect this form of kiting by
   a. Comparing the detail of cash receipts as shown by the cash receipts records with the detail on the confirmed duplicate deposit tickets for three days prior to and subsequent to year-end.
   b. Preparing from the cash disbursements book a summary of bank transfers for one week prior to and subsequent to year-end.
   c. Examining the composition of deposits in both bank A and B subsequent to year-end.
   d. Examining paid checks returned with the bank statement of the next accounting period after year-end.

9. Wald, Inc. has a June 30, year-end. Its bank mails bank statements each Friday of every week and on the last business day of each month. For a year-end on Saturday, June 30, the auditor should have the client ask the bank to mail directly to the auditor
   a. Only the June 29 bank statement.
   b. Only the July 13 bank statement.
   c. Both the June 29 and July 6 bank statements.
   d. Both the July 6 and 13 bank statements.

22

COMPLETING THE AUDIT

CHAPTER OBJECTIVE

This chapter discusses how auditors obtain information concerning contingent liabilities, review for subsequent events, accumulate final evidence, evaluate the results, and communicate with the audit committee and management.

CHAPTER SUMMARY

OBJECTIVE 1:
CONDUCT A REVIEW FOR CONTINGENT LIABILITIES AND COMMITMENTS

1. A contingent liability is created under the following conditions.
   a. An existing condition creates the potential for making a future payment to an outside party.
   b. The amount of the future payment is uncertain.
   c. A future event will determine the outcome.

2. Either of the following conditions requires disclosure of a material contingent liability in the footnotes.
   a. A reasonable estimate of a probable loss is not possible.
   b. The likelihood of an estimatable loss is only reasonably possible.

3. A contingent liability footnote discloses the following:
   a. A description of the nature of the contingency.
   b. An opinion of management or legal counsel about the expected outcome.

4. Auditors are particularly concerned about the following contingencies.
   a. Pending litigation for patent infringement and product liability.
   b. Income tax disputes.

c. Guarantees of obligations of others and discounted notes receivable.

5. An auditor would search for contingent liabilities using the following procedures.
   a. Inquire of management orally and in writing.
   b. Review reports of internal revenue agents for income tax settlements.
   c. Scan minutes of directors' and stockholders' meetings.
   d. Analyze legal expense accounts and supporting documentation.
   e. Correspond with all major attorneys for status of legal activities.
   f. Review existing working papers for potential contingent liabilities (e.g., confirmation letters from bank indicating discounted notes receivable, etc).
   g. Examine letters of credit and confirm used and unused balances.

6. Purchase, sales and other commitments agreeing to a set of fixed terms must be disclosed in the footnotes.

OBJECTIVE 2:
OBTAIN AND EVALUATE LETTERS FROM THE CLIENT'S ATTORNEYS

7. Management prepares confirmation letters requesting attorneys to respond directly to the auditors about contingencies with which they have had significant involvement. The letter addresses the following:
   a. Lists or requests that the attorney list significant pending threatened litigation, claims, or assessments.
   b. Lists material unasserted claims and assessments.
   c. Requests that the attorney discuss the status of each claim or assessment (what legal action is intended, potential for an unfavorable outcome, and the estimated range of potential loss).
   d. Asks that unlisted pending or threatened legal actions be identified.
   e. Requests the attorney to avow directly to the auditor the attorney's responsibility to inform management of any legal matters which require disclosure in the financial statements.
   f. Asks the attorney to discuss any factors which limited his/her responses to the foregoing.

8. An auditor shouldn't be unusually concerned if because of a lack of knowledge about these matters an attorney refuses to indicate whether he/she is aware of pending litigation or required financial statement disclosure.

9. SAS 12 (AU 337) indicates, however, that if an attorney with knowledge of these matters refuses to respond to an auditor's inquiry concerning pending litigation and/or required financial statement disclosure, the audit report should be qualified.

OBJECTIVE 3:
CONDUCT A POST-BALANCE-SHEET REVIEW FOR SUBSEQUENT EVENTS

10. SAS 1 (AU 560) requires the auditor to investigate whether events occurring from year-end to the date of the audit report have any effect on the financial statements or related disclosures. These events fall into one of two categories.

11. The first type of event are those which have **a direct effect on the financial statements and requires an adjustment** to them because additional information is provided about

a condition which existed at the balance sheet date. An example would be the settlement of a lawsuit for an amount which is different than the recorded amount.

12. The second type of event are those which **have no direct effect on the financial statements but for which disclosure is required** because they are so significant. An example would be the issuance of bonds or equity securities subsequent to year end.

13. In addition to procedures done as part of the tests of details of balances the following procedures are completed to discover **subsequent events**.
    a. Inquire of management.
    b. Correspond with attorneys.
    c. Review internal statements prepared subsequent to the balance sheet.
    d. Review records prepared subsequent to the balance sheet date.
    e. Examine minutes issued subsequent to the balance sheet date.
    f. Obtain a letter of representation from management.

14. An audit report would be **dual dated** if after leaving the field the auditor was required to review the details of a material subsequent event which became known to the auditor before the audit report was issued.

OBJECTIVE 4:
DESIGN AND PERFORM THE FINAL STEPS IN THE EVIDENCE-ACCUMULATION SEGMENT OF THE AUDIT

15. Late in the audit, final evidence accumulation procedures are completed.
    a. Typically the partner performs final analytical procedures to review for possible misstatements and to obtain a final objective look at the financial statements.
    b. The going concern assumption is evaluated again after proposed adjustments have been incorporated into the financial statements.
    c. The client provides the auditor with a letter of representation.
    d. The auditor reads the other information contained in the annual report.

16. The purpose of the letter of representation is to remind management of its responsibility for the representations contained in the financial statements and to document those responses.

17. Although the letter of representation cannot be used as reliable audit evidence, SAS 19 (AU 333) requires the auditor to obtain it and requires that a qualified opinion or disclaimer of opinion be issued when the client refuses to provide it.

18. SAS 8 (AU 550) requires that the auditor read other information, outside of the financial statements, that is contained in the annual report for consistency with the financial statements. A material inconsistency which the client refuses to change may require the auditor to withdraw or issue a modified unqualified opinion.

OBJECTIVE 5:
INTEGRATE THE AUDIT EVIDENCE GATHERED AND EVALUATE THE OVERALL AUDIT RESULTS

19. To reach an overall conclusion on the financial statements (i.e., evaluate the results) the auditor completes five steps.

a. Consider whether the evidence accumulated is sufficient (complete the engagement checklist).
b. Determine whether the audit opinion is supported by competent evidence (review the unadjusted error worksheet).
c. Evaluate financial statement disclosures (complete a financial statement disclosure checklist).
d. Review the working papers.
e. Submit the audit working papers to independent review.

20. Immaterial errors discovered during the audit are aggregated on an **unadjusted error worksheet** or **summary of possible adjustments worksheet**.

21. Management is responsible for the financial statements and the related disclosure even in those cases where the auditor drafted the financial statements because management must approve them for issuance.

22. Although auditors accumulate disclosure information on each area being examined during the course of the audit, most auditors also use a financial statement disclosure checklist to avoid overlooking an item and to assist in performing the final review.

23. An independent review of the working papers is performed by another member of the audit firm.
    a. The reviewer evaluates the performance of inexperienced personnel.
    b. The reviewer evaluates whether the audit meets the CPA firm's standards.
    c. The reviewer attempts to counteract any bias that may enter into the field auditor's judgment.

OBJECTIVE 6:
COMMUNICATE EFFECTIVELY WITH THE AUDIT COMMITTEE AND MANAGEMENT

24. In addition to the audit report, the auditor communicates other information to the client's audit committee and senior management.
    a. Communicate all irregularities and illegal acts, regardless of materiality.
    b. Communicate reportable internal control structure deficiencies.
    c. Communicate other items of interest.
        1. Auditor's responsibilities under GAAS.
        2. Significant accounting policies selected and applied.
        3. Significant adjustments proposed to management.
        4. Disagreements with management concerning audit scope, accounting principles, and wording of the audit report.
        5. Difficulties encountered in performing the audit.

25. A management letter is optional. It is written for two reasons.
    a. It fosters good relations between management and the auditor as a result of the suggestions made for improving the client's business.
    b. It informs the client of other services (tax and management advisory services) which the CPA can provide.

OBJECTIVE 7:
IDENTIFY THE AUDITOR's RESPONSIBILITIES WHEN FACTS AFFECTING THE AUDIT REPORT ARE DISCOVERED AFTER ITS ISSUANCE

26. Occasionally, an auditor will learn that the financial statements are materially misleading after the statements and related audit report have been issued. If the evidence for this condition existed at or prior to the date of the audit report and the client refuses to take the appropriate action (notify the SEC and appropriate regulatory agencies and recall and reissue the financial statements), the auditor must notify the board of directors, any appropriate regulatory agencies, and each person relying on the financial statements. When the company's securities are publicly traded, the SEC and the stock exchange are asked to notify third party users.

SELF-ASSESSMENT

TRUE-FALSE STATEMENTS

Indicate whether each of the following statements is true or false.

_ 1. A contingent liability is a potential future obligation to an outside party for an unknown amount resulting from activities that have already taken place.

_ 2. Proper footnote disclosure of a contingent liability is to describe the nature of the contingency and to refrain from mentioning any expected outcome because of the uncertainty involved.

_ 3. Ordinarily, auditors search for contingent liabilities throughout the entire course of the audit and conduct a final review at or near the completion of the audit.

_ 4. An important source of information concerning contingent liabilities is a letter of confirmation from the client's legal counsel.

_ 5. It is unlikely that an attorney would ever refuse to respond to the request to make statements about the client's contingent liabilities because of a lack of knowledge.

_ 6. There is no affect on the auditor's opinion if an attorney of record refuses to respond to the request to make statements about a material existing lawsuit against the client.

_ 7. The standard letter of confirmation from the client's legal counsel should extend from year end to as close to the audit report date as possible.

_ 8. The responding attorney ordinarily would not be asked to acknowledge responsibility for informing management about legal matters that require financial statement disclosure.

_ 9. If an auditor believes that the client's legal counsel has lost perspective about a contingent liability, a separate evaluation may be obtained from the CPA's legal counsel.

_ 10. Purchase commitments are entered into as a matter of course in some industries and require no special attention from the auditor.

___ 11. Professional standards require the auditor to conduct a review for subsequent events near the completion of the engagement.

___ 12. Subsequent events which require adjustment to the financial statements provide additional information about conditions which already existed at the balance sheet date.

___ 13. Subsequent events for which no adjustment is made but which require disclosure provide information about significant events/conditions which did not exist at the balance sheet date.

___ 14. Evidence obtained in a subsequent events review that equipment not being used in operations was disposed of at a price significantly below the current book value would not require an adjustment to the financial statements.

___ 15. Evidence obtained in a subsequent events review that an uninsured loss of inventories had resulted after year end as a result of a fire would require an adjustment to the financial statements.

___ 16. Reviewing interim internal financial statements and examining minutes to board of director's meetings subsequent to the balance sheet date are common procedures conducted during a subsequent events review.

___ 17. Dual dating occurs when there is a long delay between completing the field work and issuing the report because the auditor must date the report with both the date at which the field work was completed and the date at which the report was issued.

___ 18. An important part of evaluating the results of the audit is to review the audit program to verify completion of all parts with adequate documentation for all audit objectives.

___ 19. If in evaluating the results of the audit an auditor concludes that sufficient, competent evidence has not been gathered, the only alternative at this point is to withdraw from the engagement.

___ 20. Professional standards make it optional for the auditor to obtain a letter of representation from the client.

___ 21. If a client representation letter is received it can be regarded as highly reliable evidence because it is signed by client officials who are independent of the accounting function.

___ 22. One purpose of the client representation letter is to document the responses received from management about various aspects of the audit.

___ 23. The unadjusted error worksheet should be reviewed at the conclusion of the audit to determine whether the combined effect of the unadjusted errors might be significant enough to warrant an adjusting entry.

___ 24. Because auditors are engaged to examine the financial statements and the related footnotes, they have no responsibility for information contained elsewhere in the annual report.

___ 25. One reason that an independent review of the working papers is conducted by another member of the CPA firm is to make sure that the audit meets the firm's standard of performance.

COMPLETION STATEMENTS

Complete each of the following statements by filling in the blank space(s) with the appropriate word(s).

1. Auditors write management letters to encourage better __________ with the client and to __________ additional services the CPA firm can provide.

2. Financial statements must be __________ or reissued when information is discovered after the audit report is issued that already __________ at the audit report date which indicates that the financial statements were not fairly presented.

3. The auditor has __________ for taking appropriate steps upon subsequent discovery of an existing material fact __________ of who was initially at fault in failing to discover the fact.

4. Contingent liability footnotes should describe the __________ of the contingency and express either legal counsel's or management's __________ as to the expected outcome.

5. Tests of contingent liabilities near the end of the audit is more a __________ than an __________ search.

6. A common test for contingent liabilities is to __________ __________ expense for the period under audit and review invoices and statements from legal counsel for indications of contingent liabilities.

7. A review for subsequent events is sometimes referred to as a __________ balance __________ review.

8. The declaration subsequent to year end of bankruptcy due to deteriorating financial conditions by a major customer with a significant outstanding account receivable balance at the balance sheet date __________ (would/would not) require an adjustment to the financial statements because the condition __________ (did/did not) exist at the appropriate point in time.

9. The issuance of bonds or equity securities in the new period has no __________ effect on the financial statements but disclosure of such an event is __________.

10. One source of information about subsequent events is the letter of __________ obtained from management.

11. If a subsequent event is brought to the auditor's attention after completion of the field work but prior to issuing the audit report the auditor may __________ the period for all subsequent events or __________ additional review to matters related to the new subsequent event.

MULTIPLE-CHOICE QUESTIONS

Indicate the best answer to the following statements/questions.

1. Which of the following auditing procedures is ordinarily performed last?
   a. Obtaining a management representation letter.
   b. Testing the purchasing function.
   c. Reading the minutes of directors' meetings.
   d. Confirming accounts payable.

2. A client acquired 25% of its outstanding capital stock after year end and prior to completion of the auditor's field work. The auditor should
   a. Advise management to adjust the balance sheet to reflect the acquisition.
   b. Issue pro forma financial statements giving effect to the acquisition as if it had occurred at year-end.
   c. Advise management to disclose the acquisition in the notes to the financial statements.
   d. Disclose the acquisition in the opinion paragraph of the auditor's report.

3. Subsequent to the issuance of the auditor's report, the auditor became aware of facts existing at the report date that would have affected the report had the auditor then been aware of such facts. After determining that the information is reliable, the auditor should next
   a. Notify the board of directors that the auditor's report must **no** longer be associated with the financial statements.
   b. Determine whether there are persons relying or likely to rely on the financial statements who would attach importance to the information.
   c. Request that management disclose the effects of the newly discovered information by adding a footnote to subsequently issued financial statements.
   d. Issue revised pro forma financial statements taking into consideration the newly discovered information.

4. A secondary objective of the auditor's consideration of the internal control structure is to provide
   a. A basis for determining the nature, extent, and timing of audit tests.
   b. Assurance that management's procedures to detect irregularities are properly functioning.
   c. A basis for constructive suggestions concerning improvements in the internal control structure.
   d. Evidence that incompatible functions for accounting control purposes have been eliminated.

5. Hall accepted an engagement to audit the 19x5 financial statements of XYZ Company. XYZ completed the preparation of the 19x5 financial statements on February 13, 19x6, and Hall began the field work on February 17, 19x6. Hall

completed the field work on March 24, 19x6, and completed the report on March 28, 19x6. The client's representation letter normally would be dated

a. February 13, 19x6.
b. February 17, 19x6.
c. March 24, 19x6.
d. March 28, 19x6.

6. The primary objective of analytical procedures used in the final review stage of an audit is to
   a. Obtain evidence from details tested to corroborate particular assertions.
   b. Identify areas that represent specific risks relevant to the audit.
   c. Assist the auditor in assessing the validity of the conclusions reached.
   d. Satisfy doubts when questions arise about a client's ability to continue in existence.

7. In an audit of contingent liabilities, which of the following procedures would be least effective?
   a. Reviewing a bank confirmation letter.
   b. Examining customer confirmation replies.
   c. Examining invoices for professional services.
   d. Reading the minutes of the board of directors.

23

OTHER AUDIT, ATTESTATION SERVICES, AND COMPILATION ENGAGEMENTS

CHAPTER OBJECTIVE

This chapter discusses other types of engagements a CPA may perform. The nature of the engagement, the procedures required, the reporting requirements, and reasons for each type of service are addressed.

CHAPTER SUMMARY

OBJECTIVE 1: UNDERSTAND COMPILATION AND REVIEW SERVICES THAT MAY BE OFFERED TO CLIENTS

1. **Compilation** and **review** services are provided to nonpublic clients. Standards for these services are established by The Accounting and Review Services Committee. The amount of evidence accumulation required for these services is significantly less than that required for an audit, and therefore, the level of assurance expressed in a practitioner's report for a review or a compilation is accordingly much less than that given in an audit report.

2. A review engagement requires the accountant to perform inquiry and analytical procedures that provide a reasonable basis for expressing limited assurance on the financial statements.

3. CPAs are required to follow professional standards for **review** services.
   a. Have knowledge of the client's business and accounting practices.
   b. Have knowledge of the accounting principles and practices of the industry in which the client functions.
   c. Perform analytical procedures.
   d. Direct inquiries to management to learn

1. How the entity records, classifies, and summarizes transactions, and discloses information in the financial statements.
2. About actions taken at board of directors' and stockholders' meetings which have a relationship to the financial statements,and
3. Whether GAAP has been followed in the preparation of the financial statements.

e. Obtain a letter of representation from management who are knowledgeable about financial matters.
f. Read the financial statements and consider whether they appear to be in conformity with GAAP.
g. Obtain reports from other accountants, if applicable.
h. State on all pages of the review report that readers should "See accountant's review report."

4. The following statements are made in a review report.
   a. AICPA standards for review services were followed.
   b. The financial statements are representations of management.
   c. A review consists principally of inquiry and analytical procedures.
   d. The scope of a review is substantially less than that of an audit and, therefore, no opinion is expressed.
   e. The CPA is not aware of any material modifications needed to make the financial statements conform to GAAP except those which are included in the reviewer's report. (The effect of these departures from GAAP do not need to be estimated).

5. A compilation is the presentation of financial statements based on management's representations without expressing any assurance about them.

6. A CPA is required to exercise due care in performing a **compilation**.
   a. The CPA must have knowledge of the accounting principles and practices of the client's industry.
   b. The CPA must have knowledge of the client's business and accounting practices.
   c. The CPA must read the compiled financial statements being watchful for omissions or errors in arithmetic and the application of GAAP, including disclosure and make inquiries where appropriate.
   d. The CPA must disclose in the report any known omissions or departures from GAAP (except as noted in item 7B, below).
   e. State on all pages of the compilation report that readers should "See accountant's compilation report."

7. One of three forms of compilation can be provided.
   a. Compilation with full disclosure.
   b. Compilation that omits substantially all disclosures. Third party users must be advised that the financial statements are not designed for those who are not informed about the omitted disclosures.
   c. Compilation when the CPA is not independent. Third parties must be advised that the CPA is not independent.

8. The following statements are made in a compilation report.
   a. The financial statements were compiled according to AICPA standards.
   b. The financial statements are the representation of management.

c. The financial statements were not audited or reviewed.
d. The CPA offers no form of assurance about the financial statements.

OBJECTIVE 2:
DESCRIBE ENGAGEMENTS TO REVIEW INTERIM FINANCIAL INFORMATION FOR PUBLIC COMPANIES

9. The SEC requires public entities to report quarterly **interim financial information** in Form 10-Q (typically without being associated with a CPA firm's name) and again as selected financial data in an unaudited footnote to the annual audited financial statements.

10. In reviewing interim financial information contained in the footnote, a CPA is required to perform three procedures in addition to those required for a review of a nonpublic company's financial statements.
    a. Obtain sufficient information about the internal control structure to complete the review (usually acquired as part of the annual audit).
    b. Use the results of the annual audit in considering the scope and results of inquiries and analytical procedures performed in the review.
    c. Read the minutes of directors' and stockholders' meetings.

11. The following statements are made in a report on interim financial statements.
    a. The review was conducted according to standards established by the AICPA.
    b. A review of interim financial information consists principally of analytical procedures and inquiry.
    c. A review is substantially less in scope than an audit and no opinion is expressed.
    d. The CPA is not aware of any material modifications needed to make the financial statements conform to GAAP except those which are included in the reviewer's report (the dollar effect of any departures from GAAP must be stated, if practicable).

OBJECTIVE 3:
DESCRIBE OTHER ATTESTATION ENGAGEMENTS FOR FINANCIAL STATEMENTS PREPARED ON A COMPREHENSIVE BASIS OTHER THAT GAAP

12. Auditors are frequently engaged to provide attestation services other than to financial statement prepared in accordance with GAAP.
    a. Other comprehensive basis of accounting.
    b. Specified elements, accounts, or items.
    c. Information accompanying basic financial statements.

OBJECTIVE 4:
DESCRIBE SPECIAL ENGAGEMENTS TO ATTEST TO FINANCIAL STATEMENTS PREPARED ON A COMPREHENSIVE BASIS OTHER THAN GAAP

13. Financial statements may be prepared in accordance with several **other comprehensive bases of accounting** (OCBA) than GAAP.
    a. Cash or modified cash basis.
    b. A basis required by a regulatory agency.

c. Income-tax basis.

14. GAAS are adhered to in audits of OCBA financial statements. Auditors must be knowledgeable about the OCBA. When an OCBA is followed, financial statement titles are appropriately modified with titles such as "Statement of Income-Statutory Basis" to reflect the OCBA.

15. An auditor's unqualified report on financial statements prepared under an OCBA would include the following sections.
    a. An introductory paragraph equivalent to that given for GAAP financial statements.
    b. A scope paragraph equivalent to that given for GAAP financial statements.
    c. A middle paragraph stating that the basis of presentation is a comprehensive basis of accounting other than GAAP and referring to a footnote in the financial statements which
        1. Describes the basis of accounting followed.
        2. Describes how the basis differs from GAAP.
    d. An opinion paragraph which expresses the auditor's opinion concerning the financial statement's conformity with the OCBA.
    e. A paragraph restricting distribution for reports on financial statements prepared in conformity with the requirements of a governmental regulatory agency.

16. Circumstances which require the audit report on GAAP financial statements to depart from an unqualified opinion or to add an explanatory paragraph also apply to audit reports on OCBA financial statements and specific elements, etc.

OBJECTIVE 5:
DESCRIBE SPECIAL ENGAGEMENTS TO ATTEST TO SPECIFIED ELEMENTS, ACCOUNTS, OR ITEMS CONTAINED IN FINANCIAL STATEMENTS

17. A CPA may report on one or more **specified elements, accounts, or items** of a financial statement as a result of an examination or the application of agreed-upon procedures. The first standard of reporting under GAAS does not apply, and the materiality threshold is adjusted.

18. A report on the audit of a specific element, etc. resembles the standard audit report but includes additional statements.
    a. The element, etc. is identified.
    b. The basis on which the item is presented is identified.
    c. The source of any significant interpretations is identified.
    d. Distribution of the report is restricted whenever the specific element, etc. is not in conformity with GAAP or another comprehensive basis of accounting.

19. The report resulting from applying agreed-upon procedures to a specific element, etc. would include the following statements.
    a. The specified elements, accounts, or items are identified.
    b. Distribution of the report is limited to identified parties.
    c. The procedures performed are listed.
    d. The accountant's findings are stated.
    e. A disclaimer of an opinion is made.
    f. A statement relates the report only to the specific element and does not extend to the financial statements taken as a whole.

g. (optional) Negative assurance may be given about the specific element.

OBJECTIVE 6:
EXPLAIN THE AUDITOR'S ROLE AND RESPONSIBILITIES IN ATTESTING TO INFORMATION ACCOMPANYING THE BASIC FINANCIAL STATEMENTS

20. In response to a client request, several additional items of information such as the following may be submitted by an auditor (*SAS 29*, *Information Accompanying the Basic Financial Statements in Auditor-submitted Documents*).
    a. Details of comparative statement control totals such as cost of goods sold and operating expenses.
    b. Supplementary information required by the FASB or SEC.
    c. Details on insurance coverage.
    d. Statistical data for selected ratios and trends.
    e. Specific comments regarding changes that have taken place in the statements.

21. Reporting standards require the auditor to clearly indicate the degree of responsibility being assumed for the additional information by giving a positive opinion or a disclaimer.

22. The CPA should be careful that the additional information is not necessary for the proper interpretation of the basic financial statements.

OBJECTIVE 7:
UNDERSTAND THE AICPA ATTESTATION STANDARDS AND THE LEVELS OF ASSURANCE AND TYPES OF ENGAGEMENTS

23. External accountants have expanded the types of client **assertions** to which they apply procedures and about which they attest. Attestations dealing with historical financial statements are addressed by auditing standards. Except for reviews of historical financial statements, all other attestations are dealt with by attestation standards established by the Auditing Standards Board.

24. The following summarizes the **Attestation Standards**.
    a. To comply with the General Standards a practitioner must
        1. Have adequate technical training and proficiency.
        2. Have adequate knowledge in the subject matter.
        3. Believe that
            a. The assertion(s) can be evaluated against reasonable criteria.
            b. The assertion(s) can be reasonably and consistently measured.
        4. Maintain an independent mental attitude.
        5. Exercise due professional care.
    b. Work which complies with the Field Standards should
        1. Be planned and assistants should be supervised.
        2. Produce sufficient evidence to support the conclusion.
    c. The Reporting Standards require that the report state
        1. The assertions about which the auditor is reporting and the character of the engagement.
        2. Whether the assertion(s) conform to the criteria.
        3. Any significant reservations about the engagement and the presentation of the assertion(s).

4. That distribution is restricted for a report on an engagement to evaluate the conformity of assertions with agreed-upon criteria or to apply agreed-upon procedures.

25. Specific attestation standards have been developed for three areas of practice.
    a. Prospective financial statements.
    b. Reports on internal controls over financial reporting.
    c. Compliance with laws and regulations.

26. A practitioner is required to perform some procedures and accumulate some evidence whenever he/she is **associated** with a set of client assertions.

27. The level of **assurance** (none, moderate, high) given by a CPA varies directly with the amount of competent, relevant evidence gathered to support the attestation.

28. An **examination** requires the reporting CPA to make a positive, direct statement of conclusion concerning conformity of the assertions with the applicable criteria.

29. **Review** and **agreed-upon procedures** engagements require the reporting CPA to make indirect, negative assurance that nothing came to the practitioner's attention to indicate that the assertions do not conform to the applicable criteria. Distribution of reports on agree-upon procedures is restricted.

OBJECTIVE 8: DESCRIBE SPECIAL ENGAGEMENTS TO ATTEST TO PROSPECTIVE FINANCIAL STATEMENTS

30. There are two types of **prospective financial statements**. A **forecast** reports the entity's expected financial position, results of operations, and cash flows to the best of management's knowledge and belief and may be prepared either for general or limited distribution. A **projection** reports the entity's expected financial position, results of operations, and cash flows to the best of management's knowledge and belief based on one or more hypothetical assumptions and is prepared for limited distribution.

31. Only examinations, compilations, and agreed-upon procedures are permitted for prospective financial statements. A review of prospective financial statements is not permitted by professional standards.

32. Several procedures would be performed for an examination of prospective financial statements.
    a. Evaluate the preparation of the forecast or projection.
    b. Evaluate the underlying assumptions.
    c. Assess conformity with AICPA presentation guidelines.
    d. Issue a report on the examination.

33. Several statements are made by the auditor in a report on prospective financial statements.
    a. Identify the prospective financial statements.
    b. State that the examination was performed in accordance with AICPA standards which should be briefly described.

c. Opine on conformity of the statements with AICPA presentation guidelines and on the reasonableness of the underlying assumption as a basis for the forecast or projection.
d. State that the result may not be achieved.
e. State that no responsibility is assumed by the CPA to update the report.

OBJECTIVE 9:
DESCRIBE SPECIAL ENGAGEMENTS TO ATTEST TO A CLIENT'S INTERNAL CONTROL STRUCTURE

34. Reports on an **internal control structure** may be issued for several different reasons.
    a. The report may be directed to management for internal use only.
    b. A report may be directed to management and a regulatory agency that the internal control structure meets the internal control structure requirements of a regulatory agency.
    c. The report, such as one regarding an EDP center's internal control structure, may be prepared for distribution to third parties.

35. When engaged to report on the internal control structure under the attestation standards, an auditor examines all significant areas of the structure unless specifically excluded by agreement.

36. Auditors are required to complete five major steps during an examination of an internal control structure.
    a. Plan the scope of the audit.
    b. Obtain an understanding of the design of the internal control structure.
    c. Test controls to determine conformity with prescribed procedures.
    d. Evaluate the results of 16(b) and 16(c).
    e. Issue the appropriate report.

OBJECTIVE 10:
DESCRIBE SPECIAL ENGAGEMENTS TO ATTEST TO A CLIENT's COMPLIANCE WITH LAWS AND REGULATIONS

37. A compliance attestation engagement is undertaken to report whether an entity has complied with specific laws, regulations, or other requirements.

38. A common example of this type of report is a report on compliance with provisions of a debt agreement, compliance with which is necessary for the loan to continue.

39. To minimize serious misunderstandings between the auditor and users of compliance attestation reports the following conditions should be met.
    a. Management must provide a written assertion about which the auditor provides assurance.
    b. There must be reasonable criteria against which management's assertion can be evaluated.
    c. Management's assertion is capable of reasonably consistent estimation or measurement using such criteria.
    d. Management accepts responsibility for the entity's compliance with specified requirements.

40. Compliance attestation engagements may either be examinations or agree-upon procedures. Agree-upon procedures are encouraged by professional standards whenever a user's needs are met by this approach because there is less likelihood of the client's misunderstanding the attestor's opinion.

SELF-ASSESSMENT

TRUE-FALSE STATEMENTS

Indicate whether each of the following statements is true or false.

_ 1. The *Statement on Standards for Attestation Engagements* supersedes previous detailed standards relating to audits of financial statements.

_ 2. The greater the amount of competent, relevant evidence the CPA accumulates the higher the level of assurance attained.

_ 3. When no assurance is given about the client's assertions, the CPA does not have any procedures or requirements to fulfill.

_ 4. The three basic types of engagements for attestation engagements are examinations, reviews, and compilations.

_ 5. The first standard of reporting under GAAS does not apply to a report on an examination of specified elements, accounts or specified items.

_ 6. Materiality defined for an examination of elements, accounts, or specified items generally differs from that defined for an examination of the financial statements taken as a whole.

_ 7. In an agreed-upon procedures engagement for which there are no proposed adjustments the auditor is required to state that "...no matters came to our attention that caused us to believe that the (specified elements, accounts, or items) should be adjusted."

_ 8. Because they are clearly recognized and commonly understood, terms established to identify financial statements prepared under GAAP should also be used to identify financial statements prepared under OCBA.

_ 9. If an auditor has obtained an understanding of the internal control structure to the extent necessary to complete an audit of the financial statements, sufficient evidence has been gathered to issue an opinion on that structure for public distribution.

_ 10. The objectives of an internal control structure described in an auditor's report on an internal control structure conform closely with the definition found in the professional standards.

_ 11. Readers of the auditor's report on an internal control structure are cautioned about inherent limitations of any internal control structure and the risk of projecting an evaluation into the future.

_ 12. Statistical data for past years in the form of ratios and trends would commonly be included in information accompanying basic financial statements.

_ 13. The auditor's report on the information accompanying basic financial statements may be added to the standard report on the basic financial statements or it may appear separately in the document submitted by the auditor.

_ 14. Compilation and review services may be provided to all clientele of a CPA firm.

_ 15. Statements on Standards for Accounting and Review Services are issued by the Auditing Standards Board, the senior technical committee recognized under Rule 204 of the Rules of Professional Conduct of the AICPA to issue such standards.

_ 16. Since no opinion is offered in a compilation, the CPA has no requirements to fulfill.

_ 17. Procedures required in a review of interim financial information include reading the minutes of the board of directors' and stockholders' meetings, obtaining a letter of representation from management, and inquiring about any changes in the internal control structure.

_ 18. Forecasts and Projections are interchangeable terms used to represent prospective financial statements.

COMPLETION STATEMENTS

Complete each of the following statements by filling in the blank space(s) with the appropriate word(s).

1. To audit an assertion made by a responsible party, the assertion must be capable of evaluation against some reasonable and understandable __________.

2. In an audit, the CPA issues a __________ form or direct statement report.

3. When the scope of the audit of specified elements, accounts, or items is limited, it is known as an __________ __________ engagement.

4. The middle paragraph of the auditor's report on OCBA financial statements should include a statement that a __________ basis of accounting other than GAAP has been used and it should refer to a footnote which explains the basis and states how it differs from __________.

5. The auditor's opinion on information accompanying basic financial statements may indicate either a __________ __________ of assurance or __________ assurance.

6. __________ is defined in SSARS as presenting, in the form of financial statements, information that is the __________ of management without undertaking to express any __________ on the statements.

7. A CPA firm (can/cannot) __________ issue a compilation report if it is not independent with respect to the client, as defined by the Code of Professional Ethics.

8. In a review engagement of a nonpublic company the primary procedures required of a CPA are __________ and __________ procedures.

9. As a result of performing a review engagement, the CPA is able to express a __________ degree of assurance that no material modifications should be made to the financial statements for them to be in conformity with GAAP.

10. The SEC (does/does not) __________ require that the quarterly 10-Q reports be reviewed by independent accountants.

11. Now that the AICPA has issued authoritative guidance to preparers and auditors of prospective financial statements the auditor (can/cannot) __________ vouch for the achievability of the forecasted amounts.

12. Whenever a practitioner is associated with a set of assertions, he/she must perform some __________ and accumulate some __________.

MULTIPLE-CHOICE STATEMENTS/QUESTIONS

Indicate the best answer to the following statements/questions.

1. Given one or more hypothetical assumptions, a responsible party may prepare, to the best of its knowledge and belief, an entity's expected financial position, results of operations, and changes in financial position. Such prospective financial statements are known as
   a. Pro forma financial statements.
   b. Financial projections.
   c. Partial presentations.
   d. Financial forecasts.

2. Which of the following best describes the auditor's reporting responsibility concerning information accompanying the basic financial statements in an auditor-submitted document?
   a. The auditor should report on all the information included in the document.
   b. The auditor should report on the basic financial statements but may not issue a report covering the accompanying information.
   c. The auditor should report on the information accompanying the basic financial statements only if the auditor participated in the preparation of the accompanying information.
   d. The auditor should report on the information accompanying the basic financial statements only if the document is being distributed to public shareholders.

3. The accountant's report expressing an opinion on an entity's internal control structure would not include a

a. Brief explanation of the broad objectives and inherent limitations of an internal control structure.
b. Specific date that the report covers, rather than a period of time.
c. Statement that the entity's internal control structure is consistent with that of the prior year after giving effect to subsequent changes.
d. Description of the scope of the engagement.

4. When reporting on financial statements prepared on a comprehensive basis of accounting other than generally accepted accounting principles, the independent auditor should include in the report a paragraph that
   a. States that the financial statements are not intended to be in conformity with Generally Accepted Accounting Principles.
   b. States that the financial statements are not intended to have been examined in accordance with Generally Accepted Auditing Standards.
   c. Refers to the authoritative pronouncements that explain the comprehensive basis of accounting being used.
   d. Justifies the comprehensive basis of accounting being used.

5. The objective of a review of interim financial information is to provide the CPA with a basis for
   a. Expressing a limited opinion that the financial information is presented in conformity with Generally Accepted Accounting Principles.
   b. Expressing a compilation opinion on the financial information.
   c. Reporting whether material modifications should be made to such information to make it conform with Generally Accepted Accounting Principles.
   d. Reporting limited assurance to the board of directors only.

6. Auditor's reports issued in connection with which of the following are generally not considered to be special reports or special purpose reports?
   a. Specified elements, accounts, or items of a financial statement.
   b. Compliance with aspects of contractual agreements related to audited financial statements.
   c. Financial statements prepared in conformity with the price-level basis of accounting.
   d. Compiled financial statements prepared in accordance with appraised liquidation values.

7. An accountant has been asked to compile the financial statements of a nonpublic company on a prescribed form that omits substantially all the disclosures required by Generally Accepted Accounting Principles. If the prescribed form is a standard preprinted form adopted by the company's industry trade association, and is to be transmitted only to such association, the accountant
   a. Need not advise the industry trade association of the omission of all disclosures.
   b. Should disclose the details of the omissions in separate paragraphs on the compilation report.
   c. Is precluded from issuing a compilation report when all disclosures are omitted.
   d. Should express limited assurance that the financial statements are free of material misstatements.

24

INTERNAL AND GOVERNMENTAL FINANCIAL AUDITING AND OPERATIONAL AUDITING

CHAPTER OBJECTIVE

This chapter discusses the role of internal and governmental auditors and the differences and similarities between financial and operational auditing.

CHAPTER SUMMARY

OBJECTIVE 1: UNDERSTAND THE ROLE OF INTERNAL AUDITORS IN FINANCIAL AUDITING

1. Internal auditors work for a single entity and devote their professional efforts to auditing the affairs of that employer.

2. The Institute of Internal Auditors (IIA) establishes ethical and practice standards, offers continuing education, maintains the Certified Internal Auditor program, and encourages professionalism for its members.

3. IIA practice standards provide guidance in five areas of concern.
   a. Internal auditors should be independent of the activities they audit.
   b. Internal audits should be performed with proficiency and due professional care.
   c. The scope of the internal audit should encompass the examination and evaluation of the adequacy and effectiveness of the organization's system of internal control and the quality of performance in carrying out assigned responsibilities.
   d. Audit work should include planning the audit, examining and evaluating information, communicating results, and following up.
   e. The director of internal audit should properly manage the internal audit department.

4. Internal and external auditors differ in that external auditors are primarily responsible to financial statements users while internal auditors are responsible to management.

5. Internal and external auditors are similar in that both must be competent and remain objective in their work and both use the audit risk model and materiality in planning and evaluating their work.

6. External auditors can assess control risk at a lower amount and therefore reduce substantive testing if internal auditors are competent, objective and independent in the conduct of their work.

7. *SAS 65 (AU 322)* permits external auditors to receive direct assistance from internal auditors thereby reducing audit fees. The external auditors must have confidence in the internal auditor's competence, independence and objectivity.

OBJECTIVE 2: UNDERSTAND THE NATURE OF GOVERNMENTAL FINANCIAL AUDITING

8. The General Accounting Office's (GAO's) **Government Auditing Standards** (the yellow book) sets standards for financial and performance audits of governmental units.

9. The **Single Audit Act** provides that the audit requirements for federally funded agencies be satisfied with a single coordinated audit.
   a. The single Audit Act and *OMB Circular A-128*, a companion publication, stipulate that audits subject to their requirements must also follow the Yellow Book's standards.
   b. The audit may be performed by external governmental auditors or CPAs who meet the independence and qualification standards.

10. Several additions and modifications to the Yellow Book distinguish its standards from Generally Accepted Auditing Standards established by the Auditing Standards Board of the AICPA.
   a. Thresholds of acceptable risk and tolerable misstatement may be lower.
   b. Participating auditors must have an appropriate system of internal quality control and participate in an external quality control review program.
   c. Field work standards require that tests be made for compliance with applicable laws and regulations.

11. The Yellow Book imposes additional reporting requirements beyond those required by GAAS. The auditor must report the following:
   a. Whether the audit was performed in accordance with GAAS and government auditing standards.
   b. The results of tests of compliance with applicable laws and regulations (may be in a separate report).
   c. The results of the auditor's obtaining an understanding of the internal control structure and assessment of control risk (may be in a separate report).

12. The Act (Single Audit Act and Circular A-128) includes the following provisions.
   a. Requires the completion of a single, coordinated audit for entities receiving more than $100,000 in any fiscal year.
   b. Permits an entity receiving between $25,000 and $100,000 to elect implementation of the Audit Act requirements.

c. Exempts entities receiving less than $25,000 from the Act.

13. The Act expands on the Yellow Book's requirements.
    a. An applicable law or regulation is defined as one which has a material effect on a major federal financial assistance program.
    b. A representative number of charges from each major program must be tested for compliance.
    c. The *Compliance Supplement* identifies compliance requirements for various federal programs.
    d. Several reports are required by the Yellow Book and the Act.
        1. A report on the audit of the financial statements.
        2. A report on the internal control structure of the entity.
        3. A report on compliance with laws and regulations.
        4. A report on a supplementary schedule of the entity's expenditures for each federal financial assistance program.
        5. A report identifying all findings of noncompliance and questioned costs (the Yellow Book's scope is less rigorous).
        6. A report on internal controls used to administer federal financial assistance programs.
        7. A report on fraud, abuse, illegal acts, or indications of illegal acts.

14. Auditing governmental units is a complex task.
    a. The Yellow Book recognizes this complexity by requiring auditors responsible for a significant portion of a governmental audit to attend at least 24 hours of governmental audit education in the two-year period prior to the audit.
    b. The AICPA helps auditors deal with the complex nature of governmental audits through two publications.
        1. *SAS 68, Compliance Auditing Applicable to Governmental Entities and Other Recipients of Governmental Financial Assistance.*
        2. *Audit and Accounting Guide for Audits of State and Local Governmental Units.*

OBJECTIVE 3:
DISTINGUISH OPERATIONAL AUDITING FROM FINANCIAL AUDITING

15. Operational audits, sometimes known as **management audits** or **performance audits**, are designed to evaluate the efficiency and effectiveness of operating methods and procedures.

16. Operational audits differ from financial audits in terms of the purpose of the audit, the users (readers) of the resulting reports, and the inclusion of nonfinancial items in the operational audit.

OBJECTIVE 4:
GIVE AN OVERVIEW OF OPERATIONAL AUDITS AND OPERATIONAL AUDITORS

17. **Effectiveness** is concerned with whether defined goals are achieved and **efficiency** is concerned with whether the goals are achieved with a minimum use of resources.

18. Financial auditors obtain an understanding of the internal control structure for the purpose of determining the extent of tests of details of balances needed to express

an opinion about the financial statements, but an operational audit of the internal control structure assesses its effectiveness and efficiency and is therefore concerned with both financial and nonfinancial aspects of the structure.

19. Operational audits are often categorized as functional (such as payroll or production engineering), organizational (such as a branch or subsidiary), or special assignments (such as studying and recommending ways to reduce product costs).

20. Operational audits may be performed by internal auditors, government auditors, or CPA firms.

21. The Yellow Book defines and sets standards for performance (operational) audits.
    a. **Economy and efficiency audits**.
        1. Determine whether resources are acquired, protected, and used economically and efficiently.
        2. Determine the causes of inefficiencies or uneconomical practices.
        3. Determine whether the entity has complied with laws and regulations concerning economy and efficiency.
    b. **Program audits**.
        1. Determine the extent to which program objectives are being achieved.
        2. Determine the effectiveness of a program.
        3. Determine whether an entity has complied with the applicable laws and regulations for a program.

22. As a result of financial audits CPA firms often suggest improvements which clients could make in their method of operations. Occasionally, the management services group of a CPA firm will be engaged to perform an operational audit for a client.

23. **Independence and competence** are essential characteristics for an operational auditor to possess.

24. The following conditions can compromise an operational auditor's independence.
    a. The auditor reports to the person who manages the function being audited.
    b. The auditor audits operating functions which the auditor performs.
    c. The auditor corrects the deficiencies found.
    d. The auditor has the authority to require implementation of suggestions for improvement.

25. **Competence of the operational audit staff** may require the use of several people who each possess expertise in different areas of interest.

OBJECTIVE 5:
PLAN AND PERFORM AN OPERATIONAL AUDIT

26. There often is no well defined criteria for evaluating effectiveness and efficiency. Some suggested criteria for evaluating operations include the following:
    a. **Historical performance** which indicates whether things are getting better or worse.
    b. **Comparable performance** to similar elements within the entity or outside of it.
    c. **Engineered standards** such as time and motion studies.
    d. **Discussion and agreement** on criteria by all parties concerned.

27. Each operational audit has three phases: planning, accumulation and evaluation of evidence, and reporting and follow-up.

28. **Planning** requires determining the scope of the audit, staffing, gathering background information, and establishing evaluation criteria as a basis for identifying the appropriate evidence to gather.

29. Operational audits require the **accumulation and evaluation** of **evidence** similar to that required for financial audits. Documentation, confirmation, mechanical accuracy, observation, and inquiry are commonly used.

30. **Operational audit reports** are tailored to the scope, findings, and recommendations of each audit and are usually sent only to management and the unit being audited.

31. Examples of audit findings in operational audits discussed in the periodic literature (e.g., *The Internal Auditor*) seem to be predominantly efficiency related rather than effectiveness related. Most likely, the reason for this is that people are more interested in learning how large dollar savings were accomplished than how much more effective an operation became based on audit findings.

SELF-ASSESSMENT

TRUE-FALSE STATEMENTS

Indicate whether each of the following statements is true or false.

__ 1. Operational auditing is concerned with the effectiveness and/or the efficiency of any part of an organization selected for audit.

__ 2. The purposes of financial auditing and operational auditing are generally the same.

__ 3. The Yellow Book standards for performance audits cover economy and efficiency audits as well as program audits.

__ 4. Effectiveness refers to the resources used to achieve objectives while efficiency refers to the accomplishment of those objectives.

__ 5. The maintenance of identical production records by accounting and production because they are unaware of each other's activities is an example of inefficiency.

__ 6. The scope of internal control evaluation for financial audits is restricted to matters affecting financial statement accuracy, whereas operation auditing is concerned with any control affecting efficiency or effectiveness.

__ 7. An operational audit of the payroll and personnel cycle would be an example of an organizational operational audit.

__ 8. Operations audits are completed only by internal auditors and government auditors.

__ 9. Internal auditors may perform financial, compliance, or operational audits.

__ 10. *Standards for the Practice of Internal Auditing* were issued by the AICPA in 1978.

__ 11. *Governmental Auditing Standards* is referred to as the yellow book and is followed extensively by GAO auditors.

__ 12. The two most important qualities for an operational auditor to possess are independence and competence.

__ 13. Operational auditing employs the use of generally accepted operating standards as the criteria against which to judge and report on efficiency and effectiveness.

__ 14. Historical performance is one source of evaluation criteria for completing an operational audit.

__ 15. Discussion and agreement cannot serve as the basis for evaluation criteria to be used in an operational audit because these criteria are undefined.

__ 16. It is common for some operational auditors to have a non-accounting background.

__ 17. Successful completion of the operational audit and adoption of its recommendations is better accomplished if the auditor and the auditee have a clear understanding of and agree about the objectives and criteria used.

__ 18. Standard wording is required in the operational audit report because of the involvement of a significant number of third party users.

__ 19. The Yellow Book prohibits CPAs from auditing state or local governmental units receiving federal financing.

__ 20. Reporting requirements for the Yellow Book and GAAP are essentially identical.

__ 21. The Single Audit Act requires an audit for recipients of federal financial assistance in amounting to $100,000 or more.

COMPLETION STATEMENTS

Complete each of the following statements by filling in the blank space(s) with the appropriate word(s).

1. Many people do not differentiate between operational auditing, __________ auditing, and __________ auditing.

2. Operational audits differ from financial audit in __________, __________ of reports, and inclusion of __________ areas.

3. An operational audit is completed by reviewing a part of an organization's operating procedures and methods for the purpose of evaluating __________ and __________.

4. Effectiveness refers to accomplishing a given set of __________ while efficiency refers to how __________ were used to accomplish desired goals.

5. The __________ and __________ of internal control evaluation and testing differ significantly between financial and operational auditing.

6. The three broad categories of operational audits are __________, functional, and __________ __________.

7. Effectiveness of the internal audit function is enhanced if it reports to the audit committee of the __________ of directors or the company's __________.

8. The __________ of __________ __________ is the professional trade association for internal auditors.

9. Personal qualities that all operational auditors should possess to be effective are __________ and __________.

10. Sources for developing specific evaluation criteria to use in an operational audit are __________ performance, __________ performance, engineered standards, and discussions and __________.

11. Each operational audit consists of the __________ phase, the evidence accumulation and __________ phases, and the reporting and __________ phases.

12. If a CPA firm is engaged to perform an operational audit for a client it would most often be completed by the __________ __________ staff of the CPA firm.

13. The Yellow Book requires that the auditor responsible for significant portions of the audit attend at least 24 hours of governmental audit education in the __________ period prior to the audit.

14. The Single Audit Act requires that the audit include the selection and testing of a representative number of charges from each major __________ for compliance.

15. An audit report following Yellow Book standards would state that the audit was done in __________ with both Generally Accepted Auditing Standards and __________ auditing standards.

MULTIPLE-CHOICE QUESTIONS

Indicate the best answer to the following statements/questions.

1. Operational auditing is primarily oriented toward
   a. Future improvements to accomplish the goals of management.
   b. The accuracy of data reflected in management's financial records.
   c. The verification that a company's financial statements are fairly presented.
   d. Past protection provided by existing internal control structure.

2. A primary purpose of an operational audit is to provide
   a. The results of internal examinations of financial and accounting matters to a company's top-level management.
   b. A measure of management performance in meeting organizational goals.
   c. A means of assurance that the internal control structure is functioning as planned.
   d. Aid to the independent auditor, who is conducting the examination of the financial statements.

3. A governmental audit may extend beyond an audit leading to the expression of an opinion on the fairness of financial presentation to include

	Program Results	Compliance	Economy & Efficiency
a.	Yes	Yes	No
b.	Yes	Yes	Yes
c.	No	Yes	Yes
d.	Yes	No	Yes

4. Which of the following bodies promulgates standards for audits of federal financial assistance recipients?
   a. Governmental Accounting Standards Board.
   b. Financial Accounting Standards Board.
   c. General Accounting Office.
   d. Governmental Auditing Standards Board.

5. Governmental effectiveness (program) auditing seeks to determine whether the desired results are being achieved and objectives are being met. The first step in performing such an audit would be to
   a. Evaluate the system used to measure results.
   b. Determine the sampling frame to use in studying the system.
   c. Collect and analyze quantifiable data.
   d. Identify the legislative intent of the program being audited.

6. When performing an audit of a city that is subject to the requirements of the single Audit Act of 1984, an auditor should adhere to
   a. Governmental Accounting Standards Board General Standards.
   b. Governmental Finance Officers Association Governmental Accounting, Auditing, and Financial Reporting Principles.
   c. General Accounting Office Standards for Audit of Governmental Organizations, Programs, Activities, and Functions.
   d. Securities and Exchange Commission Regulation S-X.

7. When an internal auditor plans to perform an operational audit and finds that no performance standards have been established, the auditor should
   a. Eliminate the test from the audit program since field work implies measurement and an auditor cannot measure without standards.
   b. Develop a set of standards and proceed with the examination.
   c. Develop a set of standards, work with the auditee to gain acceptance of the standards, and then proceed with the examination.
   d. Develop a set of standards, and after obtaining the audit supervisor's approval, proceed with the examination.

8. Which of the following is an appropriate audit objective for a program-results audit in a not-for-profit organization?
   a. Establish the need for the goods or services provided.
   b. Verify the reasonableness of costs incurred.
   c. Determine whether the organization's objectives are being accomplished.
   d. Verify that the use of resources is proper.

APPENDIX-SOLUTIONS

CHAPTER 1

True-false Statements

1.	F	8.	T	15.	F	22.	T
2.	F	9.	F	16.	F	23.	F
3.	T	10.	T	17.	F	24.	T
4.	F	11.	F	18.	T	25.	T
5.	T	12.	T	19.	T	26.	T
6.	F	13.	F	20.	T	27.	F
7.	F	14.	T	21.	T	28.	F
						29.	F

Completion Statements

1.	technical	proficiency	
2.	independence		
3.	professional	preparing	
4.	planned	supervised	
5.	understanding	plan	
6.	sufficient	competent	
7.	accordance	generally	
8.	Principles	consistently	
9.	disclosures	adequate	
10.	express		
11.	securities	registration	
12.	profession		
13.	regulation S-X	series	
14.	criteria		
15.	economic	time	
16.	efficiency	effectiveness	
17.	criteria		
18.	within		
19.	internal	revenue	agents
20.	provider	transactions	
21.	six	regional	local
22.	tax	accounting	
23.	compilation	review	

Multiple-choice Questions

1.	B	5.	A
2.	B	6.	D
3.	C	7.	A
4.	D	8.	C

CHAPTER 2

True-false Statements

1.	T	8.	T	15.	F	22.	T
2.	F	9.	F	16.	T	23.	T
3.	T	10.	T	17.	F	24.	T
4.	F	11.	F	18.	T	25.	F
5.	F	12.	T	19.	T	26.	T
6.	F	13.	F	20.	T	27.	F
7.	T	14.	T	21.	F		

Completion Statements

1.	associated	
2.	explanatory	
3.	factual	conclusion
4.	responsibility	auditor
5.	GAAS	reasonable
6.	guarantee	
7.	three	is not
8.	are not	
9.	related	
10.	qualified	disclaimer
11.	unlikely	reasonable
12.	pervasive	
13.	disclaimer	rules
14.	nature	
15.	qualifying	scope
16.	observation	confirmation
17.	prevent	misstated
18.	fees	
19.	neutralizes	

Multiple-choice Questions

1.	D	5.	C	9.	A
2.	A	6.	C	10.	B
3.	D	7.	D		
4.	C	8.	A		

CHAPTER 3

True-false Statements

1.	T	8.	T	15.	T	22.	T
2.	T	9.	T	16.	F	23.	T
3.	F	10.	F	17.	F	24.	F
4.	F	11.	F	18.	F	25.	F
5.	T	12.	F	19.	T	26.	T
6.	T	13.	T	20.	F		
7.	F	14.	T	21.	F		

Completion Statements

1.	expulsion	
2.	remedial	joint
3.	board	
4.	professional	
5.	auditor	
6.	commission	service
7.	smaller	larger
8.	prohibited	deceptive
9.	income	tax
10.	non-attestation	
11.	contingent	
12.	authorized	permission
13.	permission	
14.	violation	conduct
15.	unqualified	unusual
16.	professional	competence
17.	fact	appearance
18.	all	involved
19.	unbiased	
20.	principles	interpretations

Multiple-choice Questions

1. B
2. C
3. D
4. D

CHAPTER 4

True-false Statements

1.	T	8.	T	15.	T	22.	F
2.	T	9.	T	16.	T		
3.	F	10.	F	17.	F		
4.	F	11.	T	18.	T		
5.	F	12.	T	19.	T		
6.	T	13.	F	20.	T		
7.	T	14.	T	21.	T		

Completion Statements

1.	integrity	
2.	engagement	
3.	legal	counsel
4.	knowingly	
5.	structure	objectives
6.	substance	facts
7.	knowledge	intent

8.	reliance	
9.	adequate	occur
10.	negligence	privity
11.	relying	negligence
12.	contributory	

Multiple-choice Questions

1.	D	5.	B
2.	D	6.	C
3.	A	7.	C
4.	C	8.	A

CHAPTER 5

True-false Statements

1.	T	8.	T	15.	T	22.	T
2.	T	9.	F	16.	T	23.	T
3.	F	10.	F	17.	T	24.	F
4.	T	11.	T	18.	T	25.	F
5.	F	12.	T	19.	F		
6.	F	13.	F	20.	F		
7.	F	14.	F	21.	T		

Completion Statements

1.	professional	reasonable
2.	auditor's	report
3.	responsible	structure
4.	managements'	responsibility
5.	reasonable	assurance
6.	economically	feasible
7.	errors	irregularities
8.	employee	management
9.	employee	fraud
10.	management	fraud
11.	intended	deception
12.	expanded	
13.	expanded	
14.	violation	laws
15.	three	
16.	does not	assurance

Multiple-choice Questions

1. C
2. B
3. A
4. A

CHAPTER 6

True-false Statements

1.	T	8.	T	15.	F	22.	T
2.	T	9.	F	16.	T	23.	T
3.	F	10.	F	17.	F	24.	F
4.	T	11.	F	18.	T	25.	T
5.	F	12.	T	19.	T	26.	T
6.	T	13.	F	20.	F	27.	T
7.	F	14.	T	21.	T		

Completion Statements

1.	procedures	particular	
2.	judgment		
3.	one	three	
4.	persuasive	sufficient	
5.	relevant		
6.	reasonable	doubt	
7.	external	internally	
8.	quantity		
9.	persuasive	entire	
10.	observation		
11.	examination	documentation	analytical
12.	review		

Multiple-choice Questions

1.	C	5.	A
2.	B	6.	A
3.	A		
4.	D		

CHAPTER 7

True-false Statements

1.	F	8.	F	15.	F	22.	T
2.	T	9.	F	16.	T	23.	T
3.	T	10.	T	17.	F		
4.	F	11.	T	18.	T		
5.	F	12.	F	19.	F		
6.	T	13.	F	20.	F		
7.	F	14.	T	21.	T		

Completion Statements

1.	costs	misunderstandings
2.	standing	stability
3.	lawsuit	

4.	publicly	debt
5.	continuity	
6.	technical	proficiency
7.	type	services
8.	timing	time
9.	related	party
10.	inquiring	filings
11.	layout	answers
12.	minutes	legal

Multiple-choice Questions

1.	A	5.	B
2.	C	6.	C
3.	D	7.	D
4.	C	8.	A

CHAPTER 8

True-false Statements

1.	T	8.	T	15.	T	22.	T
2.	T	9.	T	16.	T	23.	T
3.	F	10.	F	17.	F	24.	F
4.	F	11.	F	18.	F	25.	T
5.	T	12.	T	19.	F	26.	T
6.	T	13.	T	20.	T	27.	T
7.	F	14.	F	21.	F	28.	F
						29.	T

Completion Statements

1.	opinion	reasonable
2.	material	material
3.	probable	influenced
4.	maximum	not
5.	change	
6.	irregularities	qualitative
7.	exercise	material
8.	combined	preliminary
9.	extend	adverse
10.	IR	PDR
11.	20%	
12.	avoidance	
13.	degree	financial

Multiple-choice Questions

1.	A	3.	D
2.	D	4.	B

CHAPTER 9

True-false Statements

1.	T	10.	T	19.	F	28.	T
2.	T	11.	F	20.	T	29.	F
3.	F	12.	T	21.	T	30.	F
4.	T	13.	T	22.	F	31.	T
5.	F	14.	T	23.	F	32.	T
6.	T	15.	F	24.	T	33.	F
7.	F	16.	F	25.	F	34.	T
8.	T	17.	F	26.	T	35.	F
9.	F	18.	T	27.	F	36.	T

Completion Statements

1.	systems	program	
2.	assessed	100%	
3.	one or two	larger	
4.	entire	changes	
5.	observe	reperform	
6.	reportable	audit	
7.	assess		
8.	key	objectives	
9.	key	efficiency	
10.	complete	quickly	
11.	overall		
12.	questionnaire	flowchart	
13.	plan	determine	
14.	environment	accounting	activities
15.	librarian		
16.	program	run	
17.	operator	programmer	
18.	user	control	group
19.	format	test	
20.	programmed	control	

Multiple-choice Questions

1.	D	5.	C	9.	D
2.	D	6.	D	10.	B
3.	C	7.	C	11.	B
4.	D	8.	A	12.	B

CHAPTER 10

True-false Statements

1.	F	8.	T	15.	F	22.	F
2.	T	9.	F	16.	T	23.	T
3.	F	10.	F	17.	T		

4.	F	11.	T	18.	F
5.	T	12.	T	19.	T
6.	T	13.	F	20.	F
7.	F	14.	F	21.	F

Completion Statements

1.	plan	program
2.	controls	
3.	analytical	balances
4.	contingent	subsequent
5.	design	operation
6.	observation	
7.	authorized	approving
8.	details	balances
9.	all	
10.	set	predict
11.	results	favorable
12.	existence	
13.	disclosure	

Multiple-choice Questions

1.	B	5.	B
2.	A	6.	B
3.	C		
4.	D		

CHAPTER 11

True-false Statements

1.	T	8.	F	15.	T	22.	T
2.	T	9.	T	16.	T	23.	T
3.	T	10.	F	17.	F	24.	F
4.	F	11.	F	18.	T	25.	T
5.	F	12.	T	19.	T	26.	T
6.	F	13.	T	20.	F	27.	F
7.	T	14.	F	21.	F		

Completion Statements

1.	merchandise			
2.	shipping	contract		
3.	credit	approval		
4.	detailed	objectives		
5.	existence	nonfictitious		
6.	completeness	existing		
7.	sales	journal	shipping	document
8.	shipping	documents	sales	journal
9.	recompute			

10.	shipment	pricing
11.	inquiry	observation
12.	compare	prelisting
13.	difficult	accountability
14.	cash	receipts

Multiple-choice Questions

1.	C	5.	C	9.	B
2.	B	6.	B		
3.	D	7.	A		
4.	A	8.	C		

CHAPTER 12

True-false Statements

1.	F	8.	F	15.	T	22.	F
2.	T	9.	F	16.	F	23.	T
3.	F	10.	T	17.	F	24.	F
4.	T	11.	T	18.	T	25.	T
5.	T	12.	F	19.	T	26.	T
6.	F	13.	T	20.	T	27.	F
7.	F	14.	T	21.	T	28.	T

Completion Statements

1.	sequence		
2.	haphazard		
3.	nonprobabilistic		
4.	CUER	confidence	
5.	tolerable	estimated	
6.	TER	SER	
7.	48		
8.	59		
9.	ARO	number	CUER
10.	precision	interval	
11.	finite	correction	
12.	2.1%	3.1%	
13.	1.9%	2.9%	

Multiple-choice Questions

1.	D	5.	C	9.	A
2.	B	6.	D	10.	C
3.	C	7.	C	11.	C
4.	D	8.	D		

CHAPTER 13

True-false Statements

1.	F	8.	F	15.	F	22.	F
2.	F	9.	F	16.	T	23.	T
3.	T	10.	T	17.	T	24.	F
4.	T	11.	F	18.	F	25.	T
5.	T	12.	F	19.	T		
6.	F	13.	T	20.	F		
7.	T	14.	T	21.	T		

Completion Statements

1.	confirmation		
2.	aging	categories	
3.	aged	trial	balance
4.	Detail	tie-in	
5.	second	third	
6.	subsequent	shipping	
7.	payment	returned	
8.	integrity	outside	
9.	positive		
10.	should not		
11.	interim	adequate	

Multiple-choice Questions

1.	D	5.	A
2.	C	6.	C
3.	B	7.	A
4.	B		

CHAPTER 14

True-false Statements

1.	T	8.	F	15.	F	22.	T
2.	T	9.	T	16.	F	23.	T
3.	F	10.	T	17.	F	24.	T
4.	F	11.	F	18.	T	25.	F
5.	T	12.	T	19.	F	26.	F
6.	T	13.	T	20.	T	27.	T
7.	F	14.	F	21.	T		

Completion Statements

1. a. incorrect acceptance
   b. incorrect rejection
2. a. 169
   b. -2
   c. -10,000
   d. 44,800

e. LCL = -54,800 UCL = 34,800
f. Accept

3. a. 2%
b. 149
c. 300,000
d. 300,000
e. Accept

4. a. 737.33
b. 1
c. 4
d. 4

Multiple-choice Questions

1.	C	4.	D
2.	A	5.	A
3.	C		

CHAPTER 15

True-false Statements

1.	F	8.	F	15.	T
2.	T	9.	T	16.	F
3.	F	10.	F	17.	F
4.	F	11.	T	18.	T
5.	T	12.	F		
6.	T	13.	T		
7.	T	14.	T		

Completion Statements

1.	distributed	processing
2.	higher	quality
3.	separation	duties
4.	general	application
5.	plan	organization
6.	nonmachine	
7.	surprise	basis
8.	generalized	audit
9.	visible	unreliable

Multiple-choice Questions

1.	A	5.	C
2.	C	6.	B
3.	D	7.	B
4.	B		

CHAPTER 16

True-false Statements

1.	T	8.	T	15.	T	22.	T
2.	F	9.	T	16.	F	23.	F
3.	F	10.	F	17.	T	24.	F
4.	T	11.	F	18.	F	25.	T
5.	F	12.	T	19.	T	26.	T
6.	F	13.	F	20.	T		
7.	F	14.	T	21.	T		

Completion Statements

1.	existence		
2.	completeness		
3.	distribution	classification	
4.	accuracy		
5.	timing		
6.	posting and summarization		
7.	competence	trustworthiness	
8.	time	cards	
9.	deduction	authorization	form
10.	imprest	payroll	account
11.	uniform	governmental	
12.	payroll	payoff	
13.	zero		

Multiple-choice Questions

1.	B	5.	A	9.	D
2.	C	6.	B		
3.	C	7.	C		
4.	B	8.	D		

CHAPTER 17

True-false Statements

1.	T	8.	T	15.	F	22.	F
2.	F	9.	F	16.	T	23.	F
3.	F	10.	F	17.	T	24.	T
4.	T	11.	F	18.	T		
5.	T	12.	T	19.	F		
6.	F	13.	T	20.	T		
7.	F	14.	F	21.	T		

Completion Statements

1.	employee	allocation	
2.	journal		
3.	requisition		
4.	dates	dates	timely

5.	existence		
6.	large	analytical	
7.	zero	balance	omitted
8.	existence		
9.	existing	included	
10.	cutoff	observed	
11.	origin	date	
12.	inventory	payments	
13.	omitted		

Multiple-choice Questions

1. B
2. D
3. B
4. C

CHAPTER 18

True-false Statements

1.	T	8.	F	15.	F	22.	T
2.	T	9.	T	16.	T	23.	T
3.	F	10.	T	17.	T	24.	T
4.	F	11.	F	18.	F	25.	T
5.	T	12.	T	19.	T	26.	F
6.	T	13.	F	20.	F	27.	T
7.	F	14.	T	21.	T	28.	T

Completion Statements

1.	adherence	consistency		
2.	expense	asset		
3.	balance	operations		
4.	transactions	few	material	several
5.	gross	depreciation		
6.	invoices	receiving		
7.	reasonableness			
8.	footing			
9.	completeness	more		
10.	existing	recorded		
11.	unrecorded	disposals		
12.	recomputing	consistently		
13.	independent	adequacy		

Multiple-choice Questions

1.	D	5.	B
2.	B	6.	D
3.	C		
4.	A		

CHAPTER 19

True-false Statements

1.	T	8.	T	15.	T	22.	T
2.	F	9.	F	16.	T	23.	F
3.	T	10.	F	17.	F	24.	T
4.	F	11.	T	18.	T	25.	T
5.	F	12.	T	19.	F	26.	F
6.	T	13.	F	20.	F	27.	T
7.	F	14.	F	21.	T	28.	F

Completion Statements

1.	listing	tags	
2.	tags	listing	
3.	sufficient	quantity	
4.	extension	foot	
5.	tags	test	counts
6.	inquiry	owned	
7.	obsolete		
8.	invalid		
9.	examine	tagged	
10.	shipping	excluded	
11.	receiving	included	
12.	McKesson & Robbins Company		

Multiple-choice Questions

1.	D	5.	D	9.	C
2.	C	6.	A		
3.	A	7.	B		
4.	C	8.	D		

CHAPTER 20

True-false Statements

1.	F	8.	F	15.	F	22.	T
2.	T	9.	T	16.	T	23.	F
3.	F	10.	F	17.	F	24.	T
4.	T	11.	F	18.	F		
5.	T	12.	T	19.	F		
6.	T	13.	T	20.	T		
7.	F	14.	T	21.	T		

Completion Statements

1.	single	material
2.	legal	obligation

3.	independent		
4.	notes	accrued	interest
5.	bank	reconciliation	
6.	duplicate	authorization	
7.	completeness		
8.	minimal	annual	declaration
9.	recording	internal	verification
10.	imprest	dividend	
11.	existing	accurately	disclosed
12.	APB	FASB	
13.	restriction	dividends	
14.	confirmed	transfer	

Multiple-choice Questions

1.	D	4.	D	7.	C
2.	B	5.	D		
3.	A	6.	C		

CHAPTER 21

True-false Statements

1.	F	8.	T	15.	T	22.	T
2.	F	9.	F	16.	T	23.	T
3.	T	10.	T	17.	T	24.	T
4.	T	11.	F	18.	F	25.	F
5.	F	12.	T	19.	T		
6.	F	13.	T	20.	T		
7.	T	14.	F	21.	F		

Completion Statements

1.	receipt	disbursement	
2.	imprest	approved	
3.	into	out	
4.	would not		
5.	would		
6.	affected	most	desirable
7.	last	tracing	cutoff
8.	outstanding	cutoff	
9.	existence	accuracy	completeness
10.	received	directly	
11.	verify	reconciling	inaccessible
12.	bank	service	
13.	transactions	balances	
14.	imprest	independent	

Multiple-choice Questions

1.	B	5.	D	9.	D

2.	C	6.	D
3.	D	7.	B
4.	C	8.	D

CHAPTER 22

True-false Statements

1.	T	8.	F	15.	F	22.	T
2.	F	9.	T	16.	T	23.	T
3.	T	10.	F	17.	F	24.	F
4.	T	11.	T	18.	T	25.	T
5.	F	12.	T	19.	F		
6.	F	13.	T	20.	F		
7.	T	14.	F	21.	F		

Completion Statements

1.	relations	suggest
2.	recalled	existed
3.	responsibility	regardless
4.	nature	opinion
5.	review	initial
6.	analyze	legal
7.	post	balance
8.	would	did
9.	direct	required
10.	representation	
11.	expand	restrict

Multiple-choice Questions

1.	A	5.	C
2.	C	6.	C
3.	B	7.	B
4.	C		

CHAPTER 23

True-false Statements

1.	F	8.	F	15.	F
2.	T	9.	F	16.	F
3.	F	10.	T	17.	T
4.	F	11.	T	18.	F
5.	T	12.	T		
6.	T	13.	T		
7.	F	14.	F		

Completion Statements

1.	criteria		
2.	positive		
3.	agreed-upon	procedures	
4.	comprehensive	GAAP	
5.	high	level	no
6.	compilation	representation	assurance
7.	can		
8.	inquiry	analytical	
9.	limited		
10.	does not		
11.	cannot		
12.	procedures	evidence	

Multiple-choice Questions

1.	B	5.	C
2.	A	6.	D
3.	C	7.	A
4.	A		

CHAPTER 24

True-false Statements

1.	T	8.	F	15.	F
2.	F	9.	T	16.	T
3.	T	10.	F	17.	T
4.	F	11.	T	18.	F
5.	T	12.	T	19.	F
6.	T	13.	F	20.	F
7.	F	14.	T	21.	T

Completion Statements

1.	management	performance	
2.	purpose	distribution	nonfinancial
3.	efficiency	effectiveness	
4.	objectives	resources	
5.	purpose	scope	
6.	organizational	special	assignments
7.	board	president	
8.	Institute	Internal	Auditors
9.	independence	competence	
10.	historical	comparable	agreement
11.	planning	evaluation	follow-up
12.	management	consulting	
13.	two-year		
14.	program		
15.	accordance	government	

Multiple-choice Questions

1.	A	5.	D
2.	B	6.	C
3.	B	7.	C
4.	C	8.	C